I0821557

THE CITY OF IMAGINATION

VALERIO MORABITO

Novato, CA

This book is dedicated to my son Dario.

ORO Editions
Publishers of Architecture, Art, and Design
Gordon Goff: Publisher

www.oroeditions.com
info@oroeditions.com

Published by ORO Editions

Copyright © 2020 Valerio Morabito.

All rights reserved. No part of this book may be reproduced, stored in a retrieval system, or transmitted in any form or by any means, including electronic, mechanical, photocopying of microfilming, recording, or otherwise (except that copying permitted by Sections 107 and 108 of the U.S. Copyright Law and except by reviewers for the public press) without written permission from the publisher.

You must not circulate this book in any other binding or cover and you must impose this same condition on any acquirer.

Authored by Valerio Morabito
Edited by Valerio Morabito
Foreword by James Corner
Afterword by David Leatherbarrow
Book Design by Alessia Latella and Valerio Morabito
Managing Editor: Jake Anderson

10 9 8 7 6 5 4 3 2 1 First Edition

ISBN: 978-1-951541-17-0

Color Separations and Printing: ORO Group Ltd.
Printed in China.

ORO Editions makes a continuous effort to minimize the overall carbon footprint of its publications. As part of this goal, ORO Editions, in association with Global ReLeaf, arranges to plant trees to replace those used in the manufacturing of the paper produced for its books. Global ReLeaf is an international campaign run by American Forests, one of the world's oldest nonprofit conservation organizations. Global ReLeaf is American Forests' education and action program that helps individuals, organizations, agencies, and corporations improve the local and global environment by planting and caring for trees.

CONTENTS

First of all, I would like to thank Richard Weller for the fascinating discussions that have characterized our personal and academic friendship: arguments from food to landscape architecture, from architecture to painting, and from drawing to literature have been continuously present in our ideas. Different points of view have never created problems, but were opportunities to reflect and understand more.

During one of these conversations, he suggested that I collect, in a book, some drawings I made over a ten year period. Reflecting on this long process, this volume has been shaped into a narrative with form and logic that closely resembles what Richard suggested to me during our conversations.

Special thanks goes to James Corner, who invited me for the first time to teach at Penn many years ago. I want to thank him for the beautiful words he wrote for this book. I could easily spend many pages thanking him for the many opportunities he has provided to me throughout my life, but will simply state here, thank you my friend.

I thank David Leatherbarrow for writing a beautiful page of this book, which confirms mutual esteem that makes me proud.

I would like to thank the Stuart Weizmann School of Design, University of Pennsylvania, and Dean Fritz Steiner for his support of this book. Thanks to my colleagues and friends at Penn, who have made me feel a part of the vital community of the University of Pennsylvania. To Anuradha Mathur and Dilip Da Chuna for the excellent and intensive discussions about representation, visualization, imagination, and creativity. To Karen M'Closkey and Keith VanDerSys for the friendship, support, and elegance in our discussions and conversations. To Christofer Marcinkoski, who suggested the idea of collecting cities, which comes from the title of his book The City That Never Was (title should be italicized). He could write several books with this title and all of them would be as extraordinary and exciting as the first. To Sonja Duempelmann for her advice. I hope that one day the passion for trees we share will become a joint project. To David Gouverner who was fundamental colleague and friend during my time at Penn. To Lucinda Sanders who has been a wonderful guide and friend during my teaching experience and time at Penn.

Thanks to John Dixon Hunt. I am very proud to share a strong friendship and mutual esteem with you.

I hope that who will read this book, some day, can visit me in Reggio Calabria, a small interesting city in Italy, and can visit the Università degli Studi Mediterranea di Reggio Calabria where I studied and now teach, and which allowed me to the extraordinary experience of teaching at Penn. Thanks to Giampiero Donin who appreciated my drawings, paintings, and design from the very beginning of my studies. He was been like a father throughout my academic whose wisdom and guidance I greatly value. Thanks to Daniela Colafranceschi who I invited to Penn to share my experience there.

Alessia Latella was essential in the process of writing the book, suggesting updates, and editing. Without her this book would not have been possible. Thank you to Krista Reiner, for reading the initial text, and for helping me to improve my English throughout the process.

Above all, a special thanks goes to my wife Stefania Condurso who was able to tell me in a clear, intuitive, precise, and unquestionable way if my drawings were beautiful or not, without who I could not have complied the selections for this book. She is the soul of this book.

ACKNOWLEDGMENTS

Morabito's lines extend and enfold in myriad ways. His lines are like journeys, drawn out and across the page, mapping, remembering, mistaking, and eventually concluding, although not always with any finality. More typically, his journeys are incomplete, unfinished, fragmentary, and fleeting. As his hand moves the pencil to mark and stake out an otherwise blank surface, there is literally an unfolding of space, time, and memory, a making-in-process. These are imaginary places, memory traces, errant scribbles that both survey and project worlds of possibility. Rather than representational likeness, Morabito's emphasis upon the process of drawing as discovered making is critical to understanding and appreciating the images collected in this book. For Morabito's art is not simply a recording of cities, landscapes, and places that have left inspirational impressions and feelings in his mind, but more fundamentally an imagining of new possibilities and effects, the body of which resides not so much in some other place or reference, but upon the paper itself, as an autonomous artifact, the residual debris that might very well lay the foundations for the *City of the Imagination*.

At the same time, these drawings are not simply artistic abstractions. When seen in the context of Morabito's thoughtful text and body of references–Italo Calvino most prominently–the work as a whole points to a fundamental concern of cities, architecture, and landscape: a concern with perception, experience, and memory. This is phenomenological, subtle, and bound very much into time and circumstance. And yet, given the prevalence of image and media today, one might think that designers simply foreground form and immediate presence over the subtleties and vagaries of time, and perhaps many do. But as Walter Benjamin and others have pointed out, cities and landscapes are never viewed as perceptible objects; they are more "absorbed" over time through use, movement, event, stories, recollection, forgetfulness, and cultural code.

The city is often experienced in a state of distraction, with people not really paying attention but unwittingly picking up fragments, remnants, bits-and-pieces, all accruing over many different journeys of time. It is never a complete image, more a set of traces, partial recognitions, as well as yet-unrealized horizons. Here, we can perhaps begin to see the real value of Morabito's work, not only as artistic production (drawing) but as research into how physical places in the world accrue meaning, memory, effect, and potential.

Places are not only geographically locational but also lodged in the psyche of those who use and occupy these spaces, and the very nature of that understanding is never as complete as a single image or object. Being able to place a place is instead an always accruing palimpseste of perceptions, influences, memories, and errors, and as such will always escapes full capture–photography and even virtual reality experiences notwithstanding! Only through the process of work, the work of remembering and projecting, tracing and tracking, might one both recall certain aspects of a place while at the same time laying down the foundations for an as-yet unrealized other place. Like good maps, these tracings array a field of orientation and organization while also pointing to alternative journeys. And, like precise architectural drawings, Morabito's emphasis upon plan and section points less to the sensual impressions of a place but moreso to the measures, the arrangements, and dispositions that create the physical settings of everyday life.

Hence the drawings point to an instrumental utility in design and planning, delineating the structures of non-object type place–the place of topography, loci, in between, and beyond.

FOREWORD
MORABITO'S LINE

James Corner

THE IMAGINARY COASTLINE CITY

This map is a collection of many sketches made over a long period. They are traces of different experiences, places, cities, and landscapes. Here, they are combined in a sophisticated extended city, developed along an imaginary coastline. "Mapping is a fantastic cultural project," James Corner says in starting his famous essay "The Agency of Mapping." Empires, countries, armies, explorers, navigators, pirates, and collectors have created their projects using and manipulating maps over time. During everyday life, people make maps to explain where they are, where someone lives, and to draw addresses. It is possible to see old maps that were used to explore new lands and unknown places; they are combinations between real direct experiences made by cartographers and stories collected from explorers, travelers, and merchants. Everybody tries to map precise information to inform someone else about something, even if this information is not real, or is distorted and manipulated. For these reasons, maps change their targets: adding, simplifying, modifying, and inventing lines, shapes, images, patterns, and data to be more exact to the scope they were conceived. Therefore, maps are expressions of what we believe and know, and they open windows onto what we do not know and understand; they are a cultural imagination of where we are and where we would like to be.

CYCLE

It is in the *wilderness* of cities rather than in nature that the imagination of these drawings comes to life. Without any heroic emphasis, these drawings result from the observation of traces, evident or discreet, in the urban landscape, and the process to collect and memorize traces is the way to consider memory as a primary medium for creativity.

This text and the drawings try to explain how to recognize traces in cities, ways to display them on a map of memories, and how to draw them out from the map for their use in improving our imagination, ideas, and design.

The selected collection of over 150 drawings, thought and imagined over many years, delineates a personal city experience.

No single drawing in this book is a representation of cities in-situ; all of them are interpretations, translations, and combinations of traces collected and selected while teaching, working, experiencing cultures, and eating food in many different cities around the world. They represent cities that could have been and have never been[1].

In line with the latest discoveries or *imagined* ideas concerning the imperfection of the universe, and recent theories of the imperfect evolution of species, the drawings of this book are a journey through the imperfection of imagination and the exactitude of representation.

The text and drawings are also a tribute to Italo Calvino, who is a source of ideas I refer to many times when it is necessary to explain and clarify some critical passages of the imagination. Calvino had and still has an essential role in writing and imagining cities; his most well-known book, *Invisible Cities*, is an extraordinary example of how words might create images and many times how these images made by words might be translated into drawings. His work is a fundamental reference to suggest what students can read to improve their imaginations; *Six Memos fro the Millennium* is a contemporary guide to aim for lightness, consistency, and beauty in creativity and design, even if beauty is not a word that Calvino talks about.

THE CITY OF IMAGINATION

Valerio Morabito

LINES OF IMPERFECTION

I have always thought that imperfection plays a pivotal role in imagination, but in design fields such as urban planning, architecture, landscape architecture, and regional planning, "imperfection" is a word to avoid or, better, something to correct in order to reach perfection. It might be accurate, but the idea of imperfection is not related to design errors to be corrected; it is related to the imagination, which avoids any concept of perfection to be free to evolve and create. Two books I read recently help me to explain better what imperfection is in the process of imagination.

The first book is *La Nascita Imperfetta delle Cose,*[2] which roughly translates to "The imperfect birth of things." It speaks about the beginning of our universe[3] and describes its primordial state: a quantum accumulation of particles staying together in perfect symmetry in the absence of shape and matter. Suddenly, without any apparent meaning, there was a minimum asymmetry made by inflation due to a small particle. In that moment and for an unclear reason, the matter survived to the antimatter, and the universe was borne, imperfect and asymmetric in shapes and forces. A little imperfection caused the incredible evolution of our universe that is a combination of contingencies and causalities, just as Epicurus swerve theory of atoms predicted.

The second book is *Imperfezione: Una storia naturale,*[4] which roughly translates to, *Imperfection: A Natural History/Story.* It is significant to note that the book title is ambiguous as storia in Italian is used for both "history" and "story."

According to Darwin's theory of evolution, a method based on laws and causalities,[5] the book explains how life evolved without any predestined vision; the evolution of a particular species could have taken place as it did or in many other ways; by chance, it happened as we know it today. Evolutionary processes are unpredictable because the previous stages of systems are necessary but not sufficient to predict future steps in advance. Future states of the system are randomly dependent on former states. The consequence is that the production of processes is contingent and related to critical points. Thus, evolution is made and provoked by the imperfection of many different combinations.[6]

Therefore, imperfection produces more ideas and evolutions than perfection, and cities, like many other things humans have created, are imperfect inventions. Spiro Kostof said that "the tendency" of many different theories "often is to see urban form as a finite thing, a closed thing, a complicated object. A city, however perfect its initial shape, is never complete, never at rest."[7] Kenneth Lynch wrote: "cities are too complicated, too far beyond our control, and affect too many people, who are subject to too many cultural variations, to permit any rational answer."[8]

This text does not explain what the imperfection of cities means but tries to explain how imperfections imprint traces on the surfaces of cities. Working from these traces, the drawings of this book are based on the unpredictable contingencies of the imperfect city "never at rest."

[1] The phrase is borrowed and transformed from the title of the book *The City That Never Was*. The book is about a series of cities that have never been finished. Using examples from different countries, the book narrates the economic crisis as one of the main cause of the interrupted development of these contemporary new cities. In the drawings of this book, however, the idea of unfinished cities is used to imagine and create unexpressed or uncommon narrations of cities.

Marcinkoski C., *The City That Never Was,* New York, USA: Princeton Architectural Press, 2015.

[2] Tonelli G., *La Nascita Imperfetta Delle Cose,* Milano, Italy: BUR Rizzoli, 2018.

[3] Ibid.

[4] Pievani T., Imperfezione: Una storia naturale, Milano, Italy: Raffaello Cortina Editore, 2019.

[5] Pievani T., *Anatomia di una Rivoluzione. La logica della Scoperta Scientifica di Darwin*, Milano-Udine, Italy: Mimesis, 2013.

THE SURFACE OF CITIES AS SOURCES OF TRACES

Kristof and Lynch's quotations are found at the beginning of their respective books, The City Shaped and Good City Form, like superficial traces introducing the deep meaning and significance of cities. By taking into consideration the sociological, cultural, and geometric superficial traces of cities, imperfect relations of imagination are established. They design intuitive relationships with different cultures that do not require an immediate explanation of them; they copy and reinterpret spaces that do not need any description of their origins; they accept social contradictions that do not require any rationalization. Therefore, the drawings of this book are intuitive evolutions of traces found on the surfaces of cities: sometimes they are proposals, and sometimes they are interpretations. My interest in cities' surfaces is not tied to the usual negative connotations of the superficial. Calvino wrote, "only after knowing the surface of things, you can push yourself to look for what is below. But the surface of things is inexhaustible."[9]

In The Blue Flowers, speaking of the Duke of Auge, Ramond Queneau wrote,[10] "On September 25th, one hundred and sixty-four, on the day of the day," it is possible to climb "to the higher terrace of the tower of his castle to consider, for a little moment, the historical situation. He found it unclear. Remains of the past were still dragged here and there. On the banks of the nearby river, a Hum or two were camped; not far away from a Gallic, perhaps Edueno, dazzled his feet in the fresh stream. On the horizon, the collapsed silhouettes of some Roman law, great Saracen, old Franco, unknown Vandals were drawn. Normans drunk calvadòs." It is one of the most convincing explanations of what the surface of cities can contain in only a superficial glance.

Toward the end of the 1990s and in the early 2000s, a series of books such as *The Earth from Above*[11] showed photos of landscapes, both natural and human-made, taken from the sky. These photos revealed the beauty of found landscapes[12] around the world. Among these books, *Taking Measures Across the American Landscape* holds a preeminent position in the research of superficial traces to be collected in the map of memories from which my imagination can be built.

It is possible to collect and select traces looking at the surface of cities from above, which is an interesting technique to use and exercise to do. By selecting and collecting traces, it is possible to design a map in which the accumulation of tiny fragments creates a new ground, a surface of imagination, upon which the hidden and evident "traces of a living context" operate.

READING AND SELECTING TRACES

To read, recognize, and choose specific typologies of traces on the surfaces of cities, it is necessary to talk about the revolutionary idea that Marc Bloch[13] introduced at the beginning of the twentieth century for the interpretation of history. He argued that the importance of elements from everyday life is that they are preparatory sketches for causing historical events, opening new readings of history. It can be read through many

[6] Pievani T., *Imperfezione: Una storia naturale*, Milano, Italy: Raffaello Cortina Editore, 2019.

[7] Kostof S., *The City Shaped,* London, England: Thames & Hudson, 1991.

[8] Lynch K., *Good City Form*, Cambridge, USA: The MIT Press, 1981.

[9] Calvino I., *Mr. Palomar*, San Diego, New York, London: Harcourt Brace Jovanovich, publisher, 1985. It is a collection of short stories which all begin from small traces of daily life.

[10] Queneau R., *I fiori Blu*, Milano, Italia: Einaudi, second edition 2014. Italo Calvino translation.

[11] Bertrand Y. A., *Earth from Above*, New York, USA: Harry N. Abrams, 2002.

[12] Morabito V., *Paesaggio Astratto*, Reggio Calabria, Italy: Biblioteca del Cenide Editore, 2002.

[13] Bloch M., *Apologia della Storia o Mestiere di storico*, Milano, Italy: Einaudi, 2009.

diverse fields such as economy, agriculture, and sociology, among others, by proving that events are combinations of unexpected contingencies. As well, Bloch understood that small tools, for example, those used for agriculture, had a direct impact on the development of history; consequently, he called these kinds of elements "traces of history."

Cities have many traces to read, starting from the most evident and tangible traces concerning cities' shapes, forms, and spaces, passing through the intangible traces related to rituals, economies, and cultures. To select some of them, the methodology used in *Complexity and Contradiction in Architecture*[14] works because it breaks and divides "architecture into elements." It is a technique that is the opposite "of the integration, which is the final goal of the art." However, counterintuitive this may seem, "such disintegration is a process present in all creation, and it is essential to understand. Self-consciousness is necessarily a part of creation and criticism."[15] In a similar vein, Cosgrove writes that each selection of traces "from the whole of creation to its tiniest fragments" are "moments in coming to knowledge of the world," bringing one "to further cognitive engagements."[16] A self-conscious or unconscious fragmentation of the whole is an exercise that can be done using different methodologies and tools. Cities can be fragmented by technical and theoretical speculations based, for instance, on ecological processes, resilient necessities, urban functions, agricultural relationships, and architectural events, or it is possible to fragment cities using methodologies borrowed from literature, philosophy, and art.

The method of selecting traces used to make the drawings in this book is informed by artistic movements such as abstract art, dada, surrealism, and precisionism. Artists like Paul Klee with his rational poetic vision of reality, Ivey Tanguy with his irrational precise landscapes made by formal and informal objects, and Charles Demuth, who meticulously fragments cities, are just a few examples to point out, but the list could be much longer. Paul Klee's work exemplifies how an entire landscape composition may be made by punctuating evident organizational traces rendered in simple forms with the traces of imperfections. His paintings and drawings from his trip to Tunisia[17] are a crucial milestone in developing this approach. Among the landscapes made of scrolls, grids, and curved-edge polygons, the traces of imperfections are open to many different interpretations. Tanguy helps us to pay attention to small or big elements which, though they appear integrated into the landscape, have, in reality, distinct meanings and particular languages. Charles Demuth shows us how to use precision to represent city fragments and how to transform such fragments into intimate domestic parts of our cities.

Literature plays a fundamental role in reading and recognizing *superficial* traces of cities as well. Walter Benjamin wrote: ""Not to find one's way around a city does not mean much. But to lose one's way in a city, as one loses one's way in a forest, requires some schooling. Street names must speak to the urban wanderer like the snapping of dry twigs, and little streets in the heart of the city must reflect the times of day, for him,

[14] Venturi R., *Complexity and Cotradiction in Architecture*, New York, USA: The Museum Of Modern Art, 1992.

[15] Ibid.

[16] Cosgrove D., *Mappings,* London, England: Reaktion Books L.td, 1999.

[17] Baumgartner M., *The journey to Tunisia 1914*, Berlin, Germany: Hatje Verlag Gmbh & Co, 2014.

as clearly as a mountain valley. This art I acquired rather late in life; it fulfilled a dream, of which the first traces were labyrinths on the blotting papers in my school notebooks."[18] When "the snapping of dry twigs" is listened to in the city, it means that it is possible to memorize a trace to a map. In the *Trilogy of New York*,[19] a man wandered around New York City collecting unused objects to give them new names. If an object no longer works concerning its primary function, we need to change its name. A pen that doesn't write is no longer a pen. For this man, it was necessary to invent a new vocabulary.

When Marcel Duchamp decided to compete anonymously for an art competition[20], he wandered around New York City, seeking an object able to represent his idea of art without artists. When he saw a fountain in a fountain shop window, he understood it was the fitting object to be used for representing his innovative idea of art; later known as the ready-made artistic theory. Duchamp found an object embodying in itself both the surface to paint and the scene to be painted. Simultaneously, changing the orientation of the object from its previous function, he altered the meaning of the object and mapped a new perception of the landscape around it. Adding a signature, he opened the understanding of the object to many different interpretations. For students (and not just for them) in landscape architecture, urban design, and architecture, Duchamp's method of finding objects (traces) in the city to be transformed into something else is an essential activity. Alongside a scientific approach to better understand sites through precise data and information, recognizing ready-made landscape traces is a creative method of complementary poetic and artistic analysis. Going back and forth between scientific and poetic study, it is possible to create an imperfect balance between the certainty of science and the unpredictability of intuition, between the accuracy of data and the poetics of imperfections, between the beauty of measures and the aesthetic of beauty.

It is possible to select five different typologies of superficial traces:

1. The true traces; they are real objects and elements that are part of the landscape scene.
2. The false traces; they are traces that they are not.
3. The ephemeral traces; they are traces without any shape, form, and matter. They are from poems, novels, rituals, and so on.
4. The insignificant traces, which are elements without any apparent quality or meaning. They are like stem cells, capable of taking on many other definitions and qualities;
5. the absent traces which are traces that it is not possible to recognize. In this case, it is necessary to bring traces from other places, cities, landscapes, novels, poems, and so on - that can be part of the context.

There is no strict boundary among these traces, and they can be interchanged, overlapped, and related. In a place, it is possible to find one or more, and sometimes it is possible to see them all.

[18] Benjamin W., *Immagini di Città*, Milano, Italy: Einaudi, 2007.

[19] P. Auster, *The New York Trilogy*, London, England: Faber and Faber Limited, 1988.

[20] It is important to remember here that there are discussions about the true origin of the Duchamp fountain. By now it is common thought to indicate the Baroness Elsa von Freytag-Loringhoven as the true author or close collaborator of Duchamp in the elaboration of this ready-made.

TRACES ON THE MAP OF MEMORIES

An essential aspect of collecting/selecting traces is how to design the map and where to imprint memorized traces. The way to develop the map is a significant moment since memory, one of the most personal characteristics of our imagination, by its very nature, generates imperfection. As Mark Bloch argued, historians have their subjectivity, and therefore the same traces can be different depending on who observes them. Aristotle stated that senses receive the form of things without their substance. Using a metaphor, he explained that the soul is like a wax tablet upon which objects imprint their shapes. Even when the objects are no longer present, their forms remain.

The "wax tablet," which begins each drawing in this book, is a map of memorized traces. Such a map is based on the interplay between reality and imagination. Two relevant examples come from literature: one is *Correspondences* by Charles Baudelaire, and the other is *L'Infinito (The Infinity)* by Giacomo Leopardi. In "Correspondences," Baudelaire writes that Nature is a forest of pillars through which man passes "in a deep and tenebrous unity,/Vast as the dark of night and as the light of day," because, "There are perfumes as/Sweet as oboes, green as meadows...With the power to expand things into infinity." In the poem *L'Infinito*, Leopardi uses a hedge as a metaphor for the wall that divides the measurable of the real from the immeasurable of the infinite, a real perception from an intimate, imaginative experience: "This lonely hill was/always dear to me,/ and this hedgerow,/which cuts off the view/of so much of the last horizon./But sitting here and gazing, I can see/beyond,/unending spaces,/and superhuman silences,/and depthless calm." Both Baudelaire and Leopardi talk about passing between two states. One state is more physical—the forest of pillars and the lonely hill—while the other is more imaginative—"infinity" and the "unending spaces." Making a map of traces is a similar act of passage. A map of traces is not a static map divided into its real and imaginary parts, but rather a dynamic and ambiguous tool for moving between reality and imagination.

Calvino's short story *Dall'Opaco (From the Opaque)* help to understand the ambiguous dynamic nature of a map of traces. He describes a landscape divided into two zones: the opaque one and the light one. He puts himself in between these two zones with his back to the opaque one. Moving back and forth, he increases the zone of opaqueness when he moves toward the light, and vice versa.

Traces move on the map without any predictable, precise, geometrical, or measurable organization. The absence of organization and the precariousness of positions leave traces to be transformed according to purposes and contingencies; in a dynamic exchange of meanings and roles, a singular trace collected in China might be used to imagine a city in Italy or vice versa. It does not mean that a Chinese ornament, for example, can be used in Italy with its shape, form, and significance, but the idea of that ornament, because of a particular contingency, might be used to imagine a new design idea in a different place.

It is possible to say that the traces of memories work like the *clinamen* of Lucrezio[21]: due to contingencies and opportunities, they disturb the normal flow of our thoughts just as the clinamen disrupt the linear

[21] Lucrezio, *De Rerum Natura*, Milano, Italy: Einaudi, 2003.

[22] Telmo Pievani 2019.

[23] Corner J. Hirsch A. B., *The Landscape Imagination*, New York, USA: Princeton Architectural Press, 2014.

[24] Hood W., *Color Fields*, in, *Representing Landscape Architecture*, edited by Treib M., London, England: Taylor & Francis, 2008.

[25] Wittgenstein L., *Culture and Value*, Chicago, USA: University of Chicago Press, reprint edition, 1984.

vertical flow of atoms.[22] A map of traces is a dynamic instrument made by the accumulation of experiences, information, poems, and scientific data. Like a genome map, it is imperfect, with information continually reset, deleted, replaced, relocated, and accumulated even if it is not immediately useful. In constant operation, this map is the primary source for imagining cities.

FROM THE MAP OF TRACES TO LINES

Contingencies caused by *clinamen* produce reactions into the map of memories; these reactions select and translate traces into notes, which are first analog lines in the process of imagination; later, these lines become sources for designing the cities of imagination.

Some many different media and tools can be used to translate traces into notes: digital drawings, videos, and essays[23] are just few of them. The use of the hand to make sketches is one of the most potent methods. Sketches are the very first moments when intuitions make ideas. Klee's famous phrase, "a drawing is a simple line going for a walk," could be rephrased as a sketch is the starting point from which traces become lines that produce contingent walks within the imagination.

Sketching on a napkin, newspaper, or notebook is the first act "of creation, articulated even in the most simple terms." It is "a momentous occasion in a designer's practice."[24] I have proved, teaching a representation class at Penn, that even if students have what in Italy is called "una mano poco felice," literally, "a little happy hand"—an expression reserved for people who cannot draw well - they can create intelligent lines. The impossibility of drawing correctly forces us to follow imperfection as a fundamental element of the narrative process, by which it is possible to perceive the world differently. Even today, after years of practice, my hand always decides to do imperfect things that differ from what my mind desires.

The mind and the hand are what Calvino calls "difficult loves." They are like lovers with complicated relationships to define, evolve, maintain, and discover over time. Ludwig Wittgenstein said: "I really do think with my pen because my head often knows nothing about what my hand is writing".[25] Probably, Wittgenstein knew what Giordano Bruno[26] wrote about the relationship between the hands and the intellect. Bruno thought that humans are different from animals only because they use hands, underlining that animals have the same intelligence without the possibility to manifest it because they do not have hands. He wrote, "The gods had given the man the intellect and hands. It consists of being able to operate according to nature and beyond the laws of nature itself. Providence has given action to the hands, and contemplation to the intellect. In this way, there is no contemplation without action and action without intellect." [27]

A few years before Bruno wrote this, Michelangelo painted the fresco for the *Sistine Chapel* in Rome, where he represented the passage of life between God and humans. In his fresco, God does not use the mind to transmit life, but establishes a contact with the human by hands; hands are the medium for creating life. Michelangelo traced an imaginary lifeline from God's head to the man's head, passing along God's arm, and

[26] Filippo Bruno, known as Giordano Bruno, was an Italian Dominican philosopher and writer, who lived during the 16th century. His thought, framed in Renaissance naturalism, blended the most diverse philosophical ancient materialism, Averroism, Copernicanism, Lullism, Scotishism, Neoplatonism, Hermeticism, mnemonics, Jewish and Kabbalistic influences—but revolved around a single idea: the infinite, understood as the infinite universe that comes from an infinite God, made of infinite worlds, to be loved infinitely. https://it.wikipedia.org/wiki/Giordano_Bruno.

[27] Bruno G., *Spaccio della bestia trionfante*, 1584.

through his hand, this line enters into the hand of the man and, through his arm, it arrives at his mind, which acquires life and energy. Importantly, the imaginary line seems to be interrupted by a space between the two hands; they do not touch each other.

It is in this space that Michelangelo opens unexpected possibilities and clinamen for humans to build their own identity. This tiny gap is the space where humans can operate "outside the laws of nature," from which our imagination takes courage, and governs duality; the small can be significant, the finite can be endless, the beautiful can be ugly, and the real can be unreal.

It is necessary to define better what "outside the laws of nature" means nowadays. It is not to operate against nature, merely a way to imagine differently, and thinking with hands might help to do this.

MEMORY, TRACES, LINES, AND DRAWINGS

There are different ways in which memory can operate together with imagination in reaction to traces.
I will delineate five, but there are more:

1. The waiting memory;
2. The immediate memory;
3. The transforming memory;
4. The adding memory;
5. The imaginary memory.

These ways operate in combination—interconnectivity, and interchangeability. It is possible to mix, cut, and display the categories of memories in many different ways.

The waiting memory is a reaction toward a real object, element, or system of things after allowing a significant gap in space or time. In this gap, the memory starts its process of selection, and only when it has abstracted the reality enough does it imprint a memorized trace on the map. A delay might similarly occur when it is necessary to convert the traces of a map into notes. A long-time might pass before the hand reacts to the typology of traces. For example, the translation from the traces of New York and its abstraction took more than two years before any drawings of New York were made from the traces. The drawings of Matmata or the Ksour came to life over a similar timeline.

The process of imagination and abstraction, which culminates in a critical moment by a reaction of the hand, is well explained by a short Chinese story told by Calvino in his essay "Quickness:"[28] "Among Chuang-tzu's many skills, he was an expert draftsman. The king asked him to draw a crab. Chuang-tzu replied that he needed five years, a country house, and twelve servants. Five years later, the drawing was still not begun. 'I need another five years,' said Chuang-tzu. The king granted them. At the end of these ten years, Chuang-tzu took up his brush and, in an instant, with a single stroke, he drew the most perfect crab ever seen."

[28] I. Calvino, *Exactitude, in Six Memos for the next Millennium,* Cambridge, USA: Harvard University Press, 1988.

In immediate memory, the memory fixes its traces very quickly, and the hand reacts almost immediately to them. The drawings of Prague are indicative of this process. Traces were drawn the first day after visiting the city. The first sketch of the map of Prague was made on the second day. Then, over one year, it was redrawn many times until it found its best shape. The same process was used in creating the industrial city of Duisburg. When I crossed the German motorway to Oldenburg, industrial buildings escaped from the trees of the forest next to the highway. From that moment, my hand started drawing lines making real the false trace; the false trace is an ambiguous intellectual construction outside of any precise logic. From the lines drawn at that moment, many imaginary industrial cities emerged among the forests, raised on the rocks, perched on the sea, and dug into abandoned industrial buildings.

In transforming memory, the memory fixes its traces almost immediately, but they are not yet useful for any drawings. These traces stay in the map over a long period, waiting for a contingency and an opportunity to operate on them. They expect to be transformed. The hand tries to extract these traces on many occasions, leaving abstract notes and lines on notebooks and paper. When an intuition or idea starts a drawing, these abstract notes can be used and transformed in precise purposes and specific drawings. The drawings about Venice are emblematic: they do not represent Venice, but they were made from the traces left on the map of memories by the city of Venice.

The adding memory occurs when a city does not release any traces. It can happen many times. In these instances, the memory takes some traces from poems, paintings, stories, and so on to relate and add to those specific cities. To these adding memories, the hand can react immediately, after waiting, or, in many cases, it does not react at all. But the traces are there on the map even if they are not useful. Examples of this are the drawings of Wonderland Cities that were a result of a visit to a Tim Burton exhibition at MOMA.

The last memory is the imaginary memory. It is when drawings come before visiting cities. The memory needs to have memory, and it is possible to say, from the future, anticipating what it can perceive. The memory borrows traces from other places, from literature, poetry, painting, sculpture, music, or anything else, which helps to build an imaginary context. The hand reacts immediately to these traces, extracting them and using them to draw a city. This happened for some drawings of Shanghai and some drawings of Newcastle, for example. Sometimes the imaginary memory does not have any real cities to relate to, and it builds its city with unreal traces and spaces.

FROM IMPERFECTION TO EXACTITUDE

When lines take shapes and forms from the memory of traces to be developed into cities, like the ones in this book, or to design spaces for projects and competitions, imperfection requires precision. I have now mentioned many times how imperfection is an essential aspect of imagination, from which anything can happen. When, however, something then does happen, the question arises: How is it possible to pass from the imperfection of imagination to the exactitude of representation? What is the relationship between imperfection and precision?

Again, Calvino explains it very well, this time in the essay, "Exactitude."[29] At the beginning of the essay, he writes about the qualities that exactitude has to have in his opinion:

1. A well-defined and well-calculated plan for the work in question.
2. An evocative of clear, incisive, memorable visual images.
3. A language as precise as possible both in the choice of words and in the expression of the subtleties of thought and imagination.

There is a contradiction between the idea of imperfection and the concept of exactitude, but Calvino himself finds the solution to this duality. He does it using an example of literature that is, seemingly, the opposite of exactitude. He uses the vague and imprecise language of Giacomo Leopardi: "The light of the sun or the moon, seen in a place from which they are invisible, and one cannot discern the source of the light; a place only partly illuminated by such light; the reflection of such light, and the various material effects derived from it; the penetration of such light into places where it becomes uncertain and obstructed, and is not easily made out, as through a cane brake, in a wood, through half-closed shutters, etc., etc.; the same light in a place, object, etc., where it does not enter and strike directly, reflected and diffused by some other place or object, etc., where it does strike; in a passageway seen from inside or outside, and similarly in a loggia, etc., places where the light mingles, etc., etc., with the shadows, as under a portico, in a high, overhanging loggia, among rocks and gullies, in a valley, on hills seen from the shady side so that their crests are gilded, the reflection produced, for example, by a colored pane of glass on those objects on which the rays passing through that glass are reflected; all those objects, in a word, that by means of various materials and minimal circumstances come to our sight, hearing, etc., in a way that is uncertain, indistinct, imperfect, incomplete, or out of the ordinary."[30]

Calvino says that Leopardi, to define the vague and indefinite, uses a "highly exact and meticulous attention to the composition of each image, to the minute definition of details, to the choice of objects, to the lighting and the atmosphere, all to attain the desired degree of vagueness."[31]

Another example that proves imperfection and exactitude are two sides of the same coin is the famous drawing made by Joseph Turner, under commission from John Ruskin,[32] to represent the Pass at Faido. Despite the accurate scale of the pass, Turner compressed the verticality of the view by both lowering the viewpoint and removing the sky. Turner wanted to represent his personal, monumental, evocative, and sublime perception of the pass, without having any intention to be precise about the real morphology of the site. Looking at the watercolor drawing, we feel inside the torrent. The drawing was, moreover, not only a precise representation of being in the pass but was an exact representation of the idea of passing through the chain of Alps, which are symbolically crucial as a geographical division between two parts of Europe.

[29] Ibid.

[30] Leopardi G., *Zibaldone*, L'Aquila, Italy: REA edizioni, 2011.

[31] Calvino I., *"Exactitude"*, in, *Six Memos for the next Millennium*, Cambridge, USA: Harvard University Press, 1988.

[32] https://www.themorgan.org/collection/drawings-and-prints/247364

[33] Eco U., *Open Work*, Milano, Italy: Bompiani Editore, 1968.

It is possible to say that imperfection is concerned with the process of ideas. It helps to open,[33] improve, evolve, connect, and relate concepts to many different possible contingencies, causalities, and opportunities. Nevertheless, when ideas encounter the "turning points" of their evolution, for example, when they become the basis of design for a public space, a building, or a park—or of precise drawings like the cities in this book, they must reach an exactitude concerning the function and role for which they were conceived.

CONSISTENCY FOR IMAGINING THE DESIGN

The relationship between imperfection and exactitude depends on consistency, which is the last word of Calvino's Six Memos, which he wanted to write but could not. This word is full of significance because he did not fill it with any thoughts, and I like to think that consistency is related to the idea of time. To prove it, I use what Anaximander wrote about time:

> Whence things have their origin,
> Thence also their destruction happens,
> As is the order of things;
> For they execute the sentence upon one another—The condemnation for the crime—
> In conformity with the ordinance of Time. [34]

Replacing Anaximander's word "ordinance," which seems too authoritarian, with the word "consistency," I draw and design my imagination: from the imperfect collection and selection of traces made by memory, through the abstract interpretation of them realized by hand sketches, to the exactitude of representing ideas with precise techniques of representation. The drawings of this book are exercises to improve my capacity to create consistency between imperfection and exactitude, to give a specific meaning to the lines of imagination.

These drawings are a different form of communication than the beautiful renderings produced in endless numbers. They are "verbal drawings"[35] with a precise grammar and syntax recognizable from the qualities of lines that are the words and alpha bet of the drawings. The shape of lines, their quality, their particular connection to each other, their coherence, their hierarchy of positions, and their placements traced on a surface are fundamental elements for writing drawings. The limited use of colors, the repetition of gestures, and the combination of imperfections with precise relationships are a few rules to follow when writing with lines.

As verbal drawings, they try to write stories rather than represent sites. They do not attempt to photograph a precise moment in time, but to select and arrange elements according to a movable and active narrative. This is related to Umberto Eco's idea of "open works" in the realm of music. However, musical performances and verbal drawings have two different aims and aesthetic significance. Taking at least the idea of the road sign from Eco, it might be said that contemporary verbal drawings are between artworks and road signs. A verbal drawing can be transformed after academic discussions, clients' desires, and citizens' critiques with-

[34] *Anaximander* (Anaximandros; c. 610—c. 546 BC), was a pre-Socratic Greek philosopher. Anaximander was an early proponent of science and tried to observe and explain different aspects of the universe, with a particular interest in its origins, claiming that nature is ruled by laws, just like human societies, and anything that disturbs the balance of nature does not last long. Like many thinkers of his time, Anaximander's philosophy included contributions to many disciplines. In astronomy, he attempted to describe the mechanics of celestial bodies in relation to the Earth.

[35] Morabito V., *Verbal Drawings: mapping landscape ides*, Pechino, Cina: LAF, Landscape Arrchitecture Frontier, n. 41 "Observation and representation," 2019.

out invalidating its original significance; it is possible to assert that, like the frame of a building, its aesthetic extends[36] through the addition of technical and poetic requirements, rather than changes meaning. Contemporary verbal drawings might, therefore, be described as "open frameworks" rather than "open works." As frameworks, they are tools to imagine and create innovative ideas of contemporary cities.

The drawings in this book are not the statute of consistency between memories, traces, lines, and ideas. For me, they are simply exercises in which to operate imagination together with memory. To work imprecision into the strict, narrow space of exactitude. They are a prelude of design. In the end, my drawings help me to design an idea of the city that I can then use each time I have to give a correct response to a particular project and site.

COMPETITIVE TREES

This part of the text talks about trees. It is not an accurate explanation about trees made by an expert scholar on them but is instead dedicated to the particular attitude that trees have in conquering critical scenes in the spaces of cities.

There are many different typologies of combinations between trees and the spaces of cities. Trees can stay along main streets, very well maintained to show power, organization, and efficiency, designed and organized through specific desire and will.[37] They can live along narrow streets participating in domestic life by being an integral part of the community; they can wait in parks enjoying the presence of someone; they can take care of people in public spaces, having moments of peace away from the chaotic rhythm of busy cities; or they can be part of the quite, silent life of small villages. In cities, trees testify about the richness of neighborhoods and communities; in some others, their absence is the proof of abandonment and poverty. In certain cities, often characterized by informal settlements, trees are so close to buildings that they seem to be part of them, growing and surviving in critically uncomfortable spaces, spaces that are often small and crowded with activities and people.

In these critical circumstances, trees show their intelligence, which I am interested in.

The relationship between trees and architecture is not a new one. Starting from the Babylonia Gardens, it continues to develop today as an inextricable combination in contemporary landscape and architectural projects. Nevertheless, it is in the *Vedute di Roma*, especially in the *Veduta dell'Appia Antica*[38] made by Piranesi that it is possible to discover the unique attitude of trees in competition with architecture. It is not a simple well-organized relationship, but a dramatic, dynamic, and sublime competition between trees and architecture. It is a competition for having more landscape, more ecology, more nature in the city: in a word, more beauty.

Following Piranesi's utopian idea that trees can invade cities, I have collected many traces related to the competition of trees for conquering or sharing spaces on the surface of cities.

[36] Morabito V., *The extended representation of landscape*, Spain: Paysea, 2004.

[37] Dümpelmann S., *Seeing Trees: A History of Street Trees in New York City and Berlin*, USA, Yale University Press, 2019.

[38] Marino G., *Le vedute di Roma di Giambattista Piranesi. Dalla collezione del duca di Wellington*, Mantova, Italy: Johan & Levi, 2005.

In the small village of Nantou in Shenzhen, the trees are in contact with every surface of the urban structure, both vertical and horizontal. The majestic olive tree in the city of Chefchaouen emerges from a ridiculously small space and marks the city as a monument. Along the colonial streets of the old city of Guangzhou, the trees enter into the buildings, push the pillars of the porches, invade the balconies and terraces indifferent to any difficulty, magnificent and noble. In the courtyards of Riads in Marrakech or Fes, trees rise toward the light. It is easy to fall in love with orange or olive trees that stretch upward—slender and light as abstract ornaments. The massive canopy of the horse chestnut tree in one of the small squares of Montpelier occupies all the space available and weaves its relations with delicate touches to the roofs of the surrounding buildings. The fig trees in the courtyards of Matmata, in the south of Tunisia, represent the poetry of life enclosed within a protected place, invented to survive the desert tyranny. The incredible shapes that trees take on in traditional Chinese gardens are proof of their attitude to beauty, to the emotion that comes from beauty in its ideal form. The enormous trees of Rittenhouse Square in Philadelphia are like superheroes of the landscape[39], protecting anyone who walks around them, sits under them, or watches them. The giant ficus magnolia along the Reggio Calabria seafront seek their space, invading the concrete pavement, wrapping themselves around the benches, and exchanging relations between the city and the sea. Examples are endless.

All these relationships between trees and the surfaces of cities have left traces of memories transformed into lines, sketches, and doodles; later, they have been developed in many different cities of imagination. Sometimes these cities are trees, the dancing town of Shenzhen is an example, or trees cover the whole city with their vast, surreal, and unreal canopies. Sometimes trees are part of ornaments of the city, other times, they design cities by controlling every centimeter of their spaces. When trees create the cities of imagination, these cities are the expression of a utopian idea of cities that it is challenging to realize but easy to imagine.

APPENDIX: INSTRUCTION TO USE THE BOOK AND ITS CITIES

Although the drawings of cities are grouped according to themes, many cities could be moved from one section to another: they are interchangeable.

The order of the chapters does not follow any rule, and they have no hierarchical sequence. Only the last section, regarding the idea of time related to cities, influenced by many recent physical theories that hypothesize the non-existence of time[40], is deliberately placed in the end.

All of these drawings have been manipulated, finished, or created using an iPad: because of this, it is possible to say that they are digital hand drawings. In any case, whatever the technique was, the hand remains the main actor in making ideas and drawings.

These visions of cities, as previously stated, are exercises of imagination and creativity. During design competitions or projects, shapes and forms of these exercises might find real places to support intuitions, ideas,

[39] Morabito V., *SuperHero Landscape*, London, England: Taylor & Francis, Journal: Studies in the History of Gardens & Designed Landscape, 2011.
[40] ROVELLI, C., *L'ordine del tempo,* Milano, Italy: Adelphi, 2017.

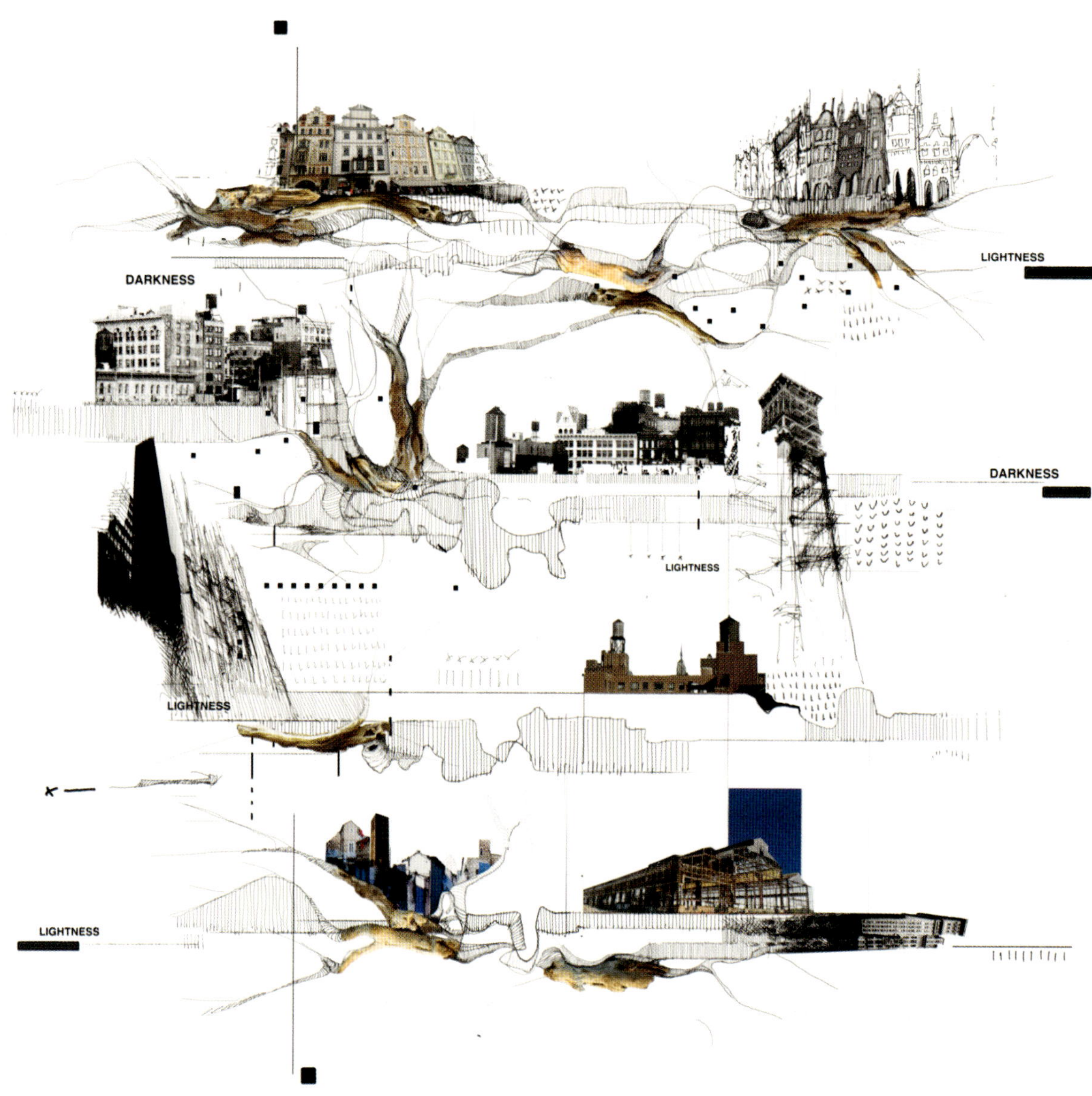

ABOUT FORMAL AND INFORMAL: AN IDEA OF BEAUTY

Collisions, combinations, and relationships between order and disorder, formal and informal, are sources of beauty. With more accuracy, beauty nestles inside those particular resilient spaces produced when the formal and informal touch and intersect each other. In touching and crossing, they shape spaces where approximations and imperfections can perceive unconventional rhythms. Without having a positive or negative approach toward either, we can pass many times between formal and informal, and vice versa, to design resilient spaces of beauty.

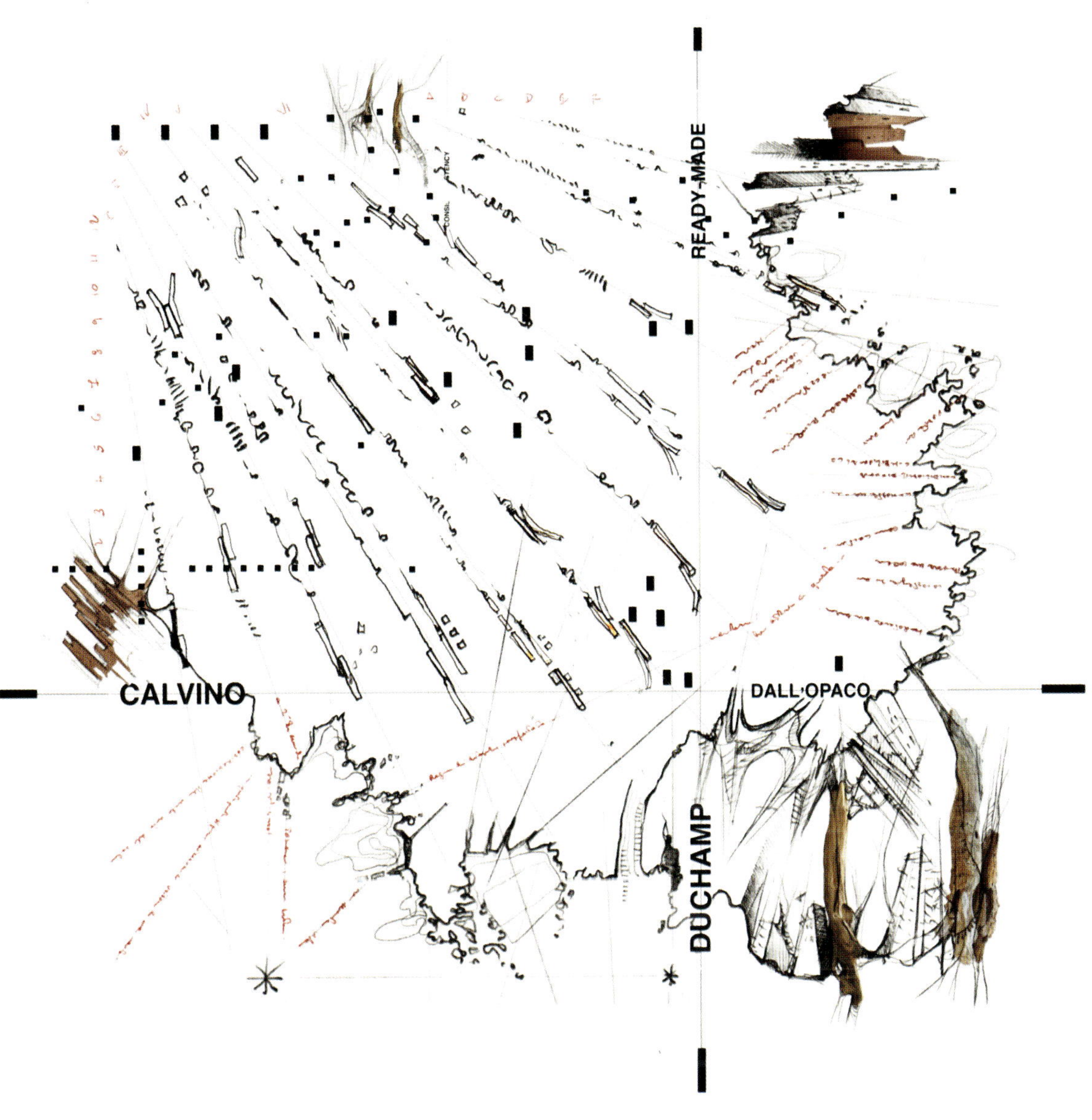

FROM "OPAQUE"

This imaginary map is a free interpretation of the bay Italo Calvino described in his short story "Dall'Opaco," or "From Opaque" in English. Calvino believes a light zone exists in front of us, and an opaque one exists to our back. Each area is contracted or expanded in relation to our movement. From above, he gives us the perception of the bay in its totality; while walking among vernacular landscape objects, he provides us with the knowledge of diversity. This drawing contains a series of added lines; dots, squares, rectangles, and free shapes coming from the sea to reach the bay; they are Duchamp's ready-made objects.

CITY OF GROUND

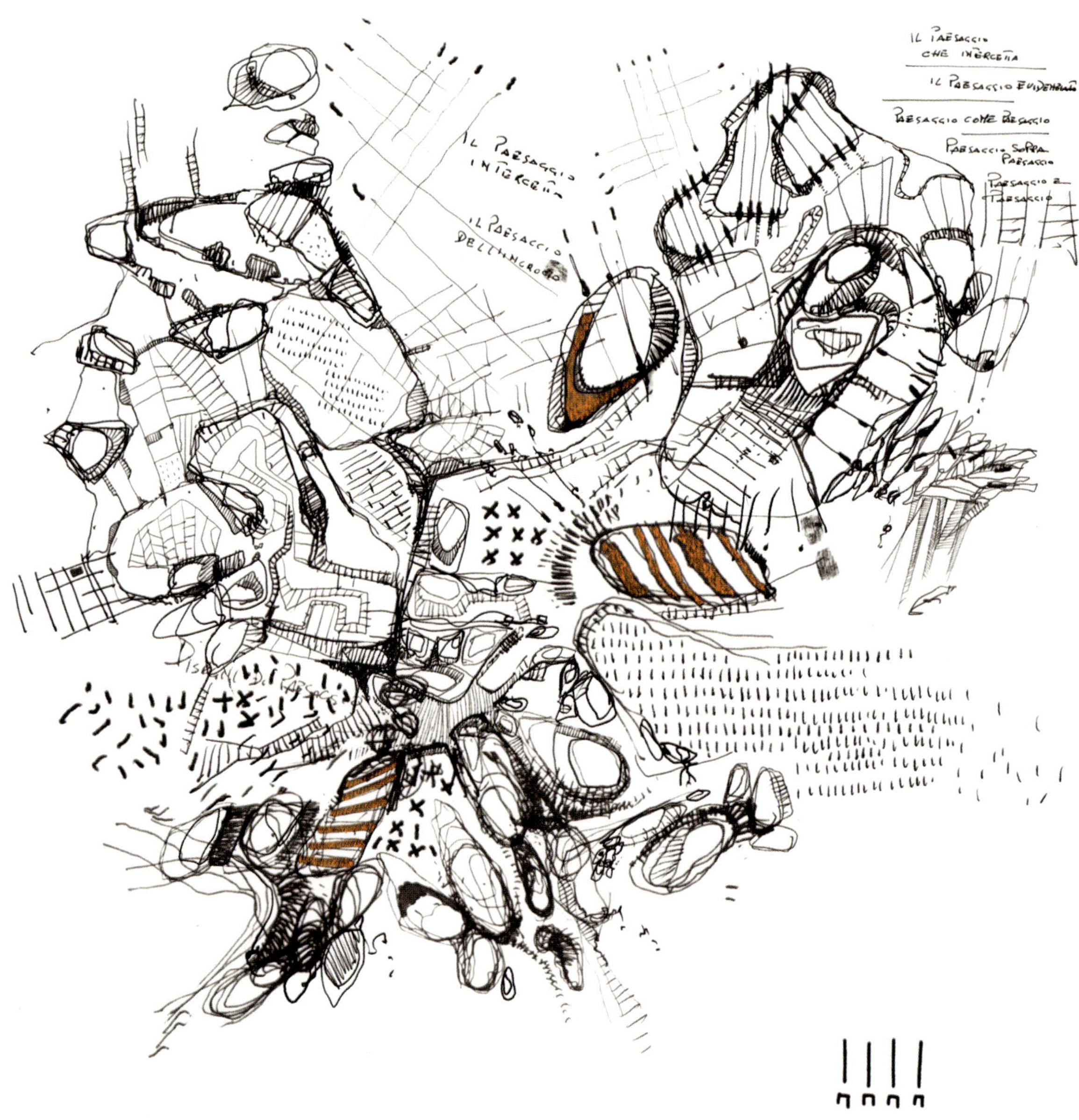

MAPPING EXERCISES FOR IMAGINARY LANDSCAPES

Sometimes it is necessary to train the hand to decipher the rhythm of ideas. In doing this, the hand usually draws a first elementary line or shape, without any apparent reason and any explicit significance. Later, these elements produce other ones, and then others. In creating these maps for no reason, the hand becomes accustomed to collecting every impulse coming from unordered memories and capable of putting them together in precise combinations, rhythms, and compositions. After a few exercises, the hand thinks by itself, capable of tracing thought maps. Ludwig Josef Johann Wittgenstein said, "I really do think with my pen, because my head often knows nothing about what my hand is writing."

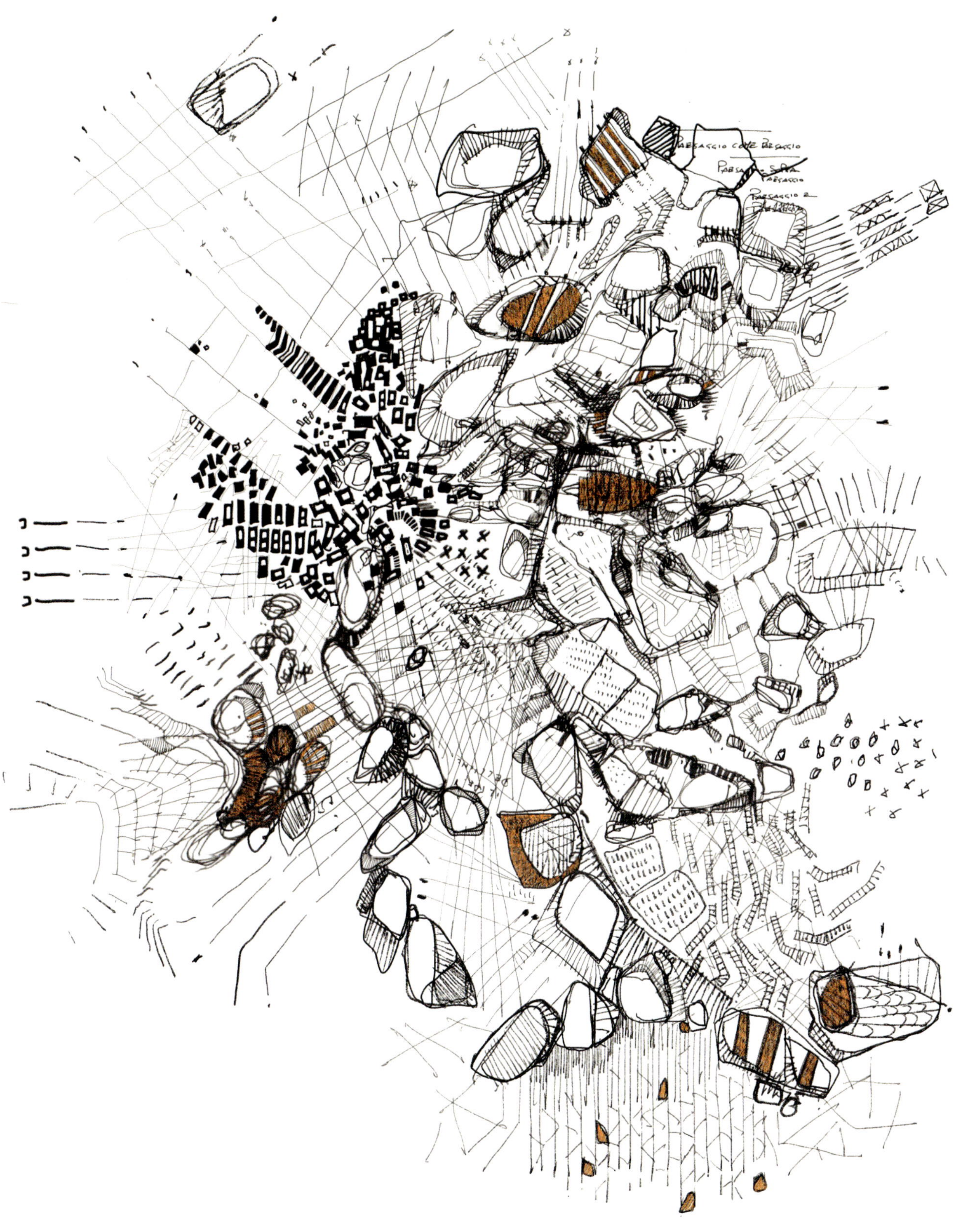
PAESAGGIO COME PAESAGGIO
PAESAGGIO
PAESAGGIO 2

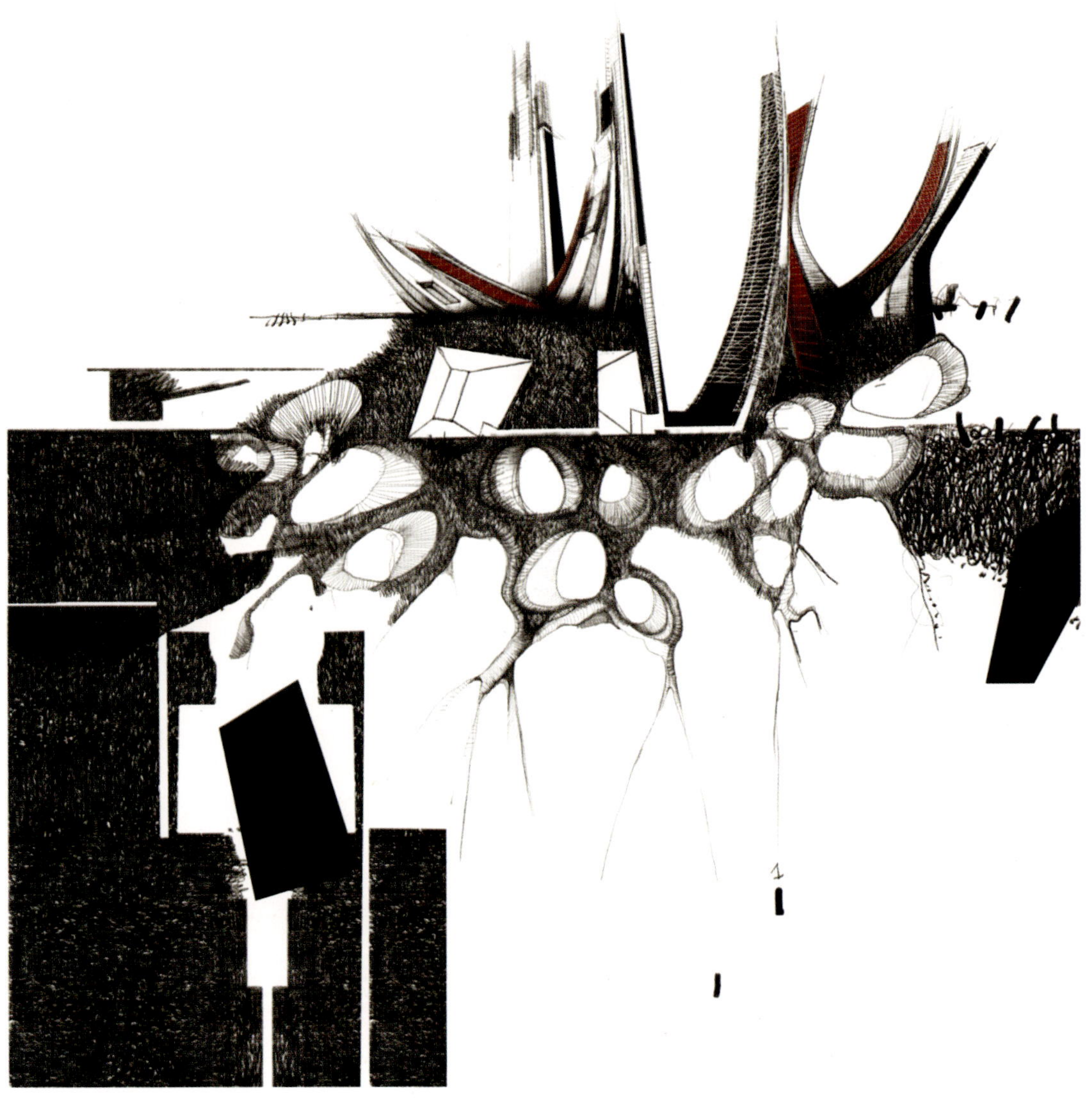

UNDERGROUND CITY

The idea of drawing ground cities came from Naples. It is a twin city: its underground city is the negative (or positive) representation of the city above. Visiting its underground, shaped by Greek and Roman tunnels, rooms, water containers, vaults, domes, chimneys, ramps, and stairs, is to experience a different city's landscape. Here we lose our collective perception of space, and we must improve our capacity to map. Straying quickly in this place, we have to collect every small insignificant detail to orient ourselves; we are Benjamin walking in a forest.

EDINBURGH UNDERGROUND

This drawing came to light after visiting Edinburgh. At that time, it was impossible to experience the underground city. Its inaccessibility created the urgency to imagine it. This long city in the form of a section represents a journey into Edinburgh's ground. It was easy to imagine a landscape made by roots, tunnels, vaults, secret spaces, and buildings going deep into the ground and coming up with unexpected shapes.

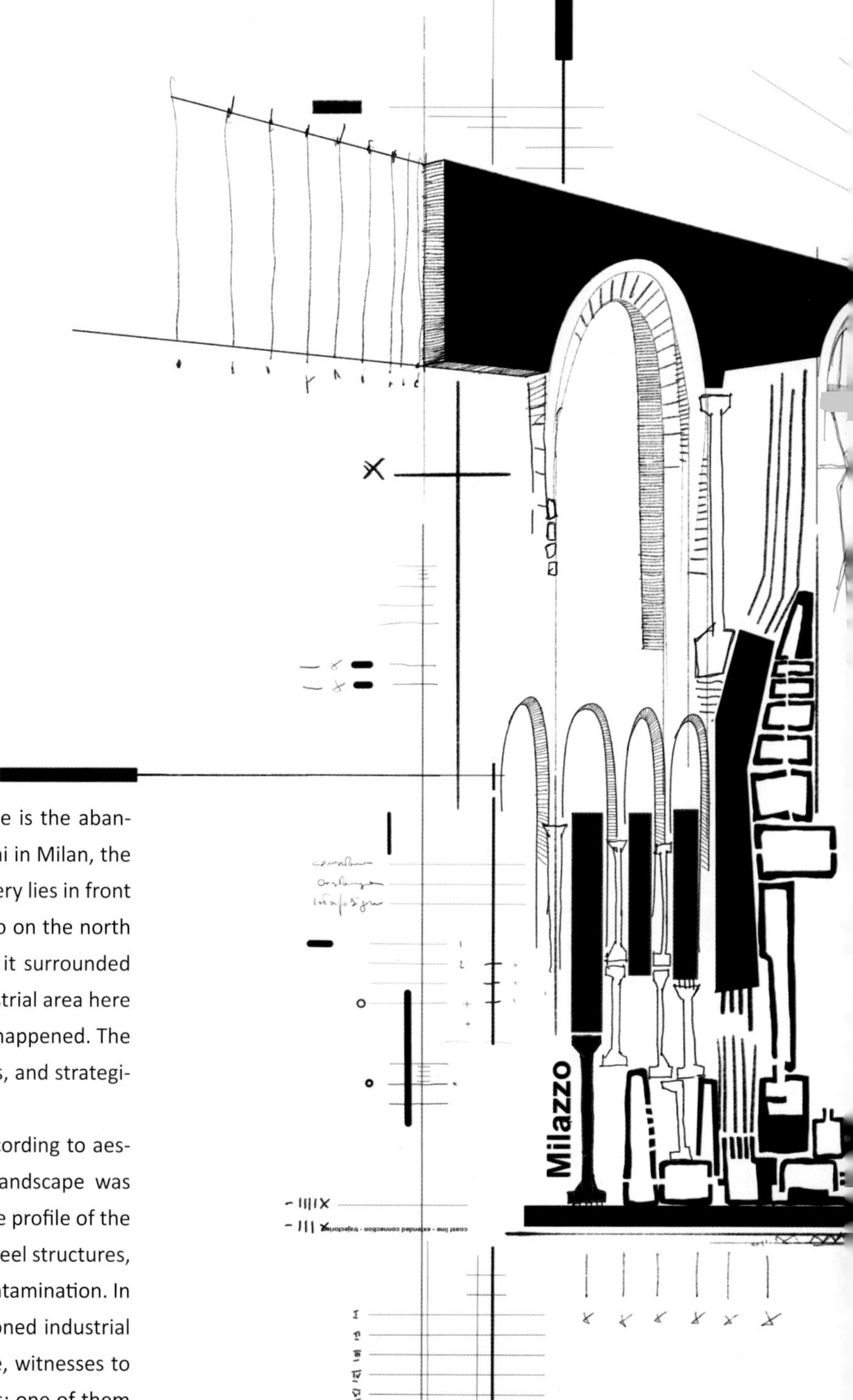

INDUSTRIAL UNDERGROUND

This drawing is a combination of two industrial sites: one is the abandoned site of the former Falck Areas in Sesto San Giovanni in Milan, the other is the Milazzo refinery in Sicily. The Milazzo oil refinery lies in front of the Mediterranean Sea, close to the Eolian Archipelago on the north Sicilian coast. Amazement and fascination rise in seeing it surrounded by beautiful Mediterranean landscapes. Planning an industrial area here was a mistake, but it is possible to understand because it happened. The refinery is in a bay, protected by lousy weather conditions, and strategically connected with the long east-Italian coast.

On the one hand, we have a landscape perceived according to aesthetic and ecological values. On the other hand, the landscape was evaluated by engineering and economical approaches. The profile of the refinery extends a pier into the sea. Its pipes, chimneys, steel structures, and containers root into the ground, drawing a map of contamination. In Sesto San Giovanni, near Milan, Falck Areas is an abandoned industrial landscape. A few important industrial relics are still there, witnesses to the past of this place. They are significant steel structures; one of them is called T3, another one T5. The entire area will be developed with new urban structures and a new park. It is easy to imagine that the soil was profoundly polluted and modified by the industrial activities, and a series of abandoned basements testify to an underground made by tunnels, rooms, and vaults. Without any particular interest in the elevated steel structures, this drawing pretends to invent a new massive landscape that goes deep under the existing buildings. It creates a combination of the depth of the sea of the Milazzo refinery and the extent of the industrial soil of the former Falck Areas.

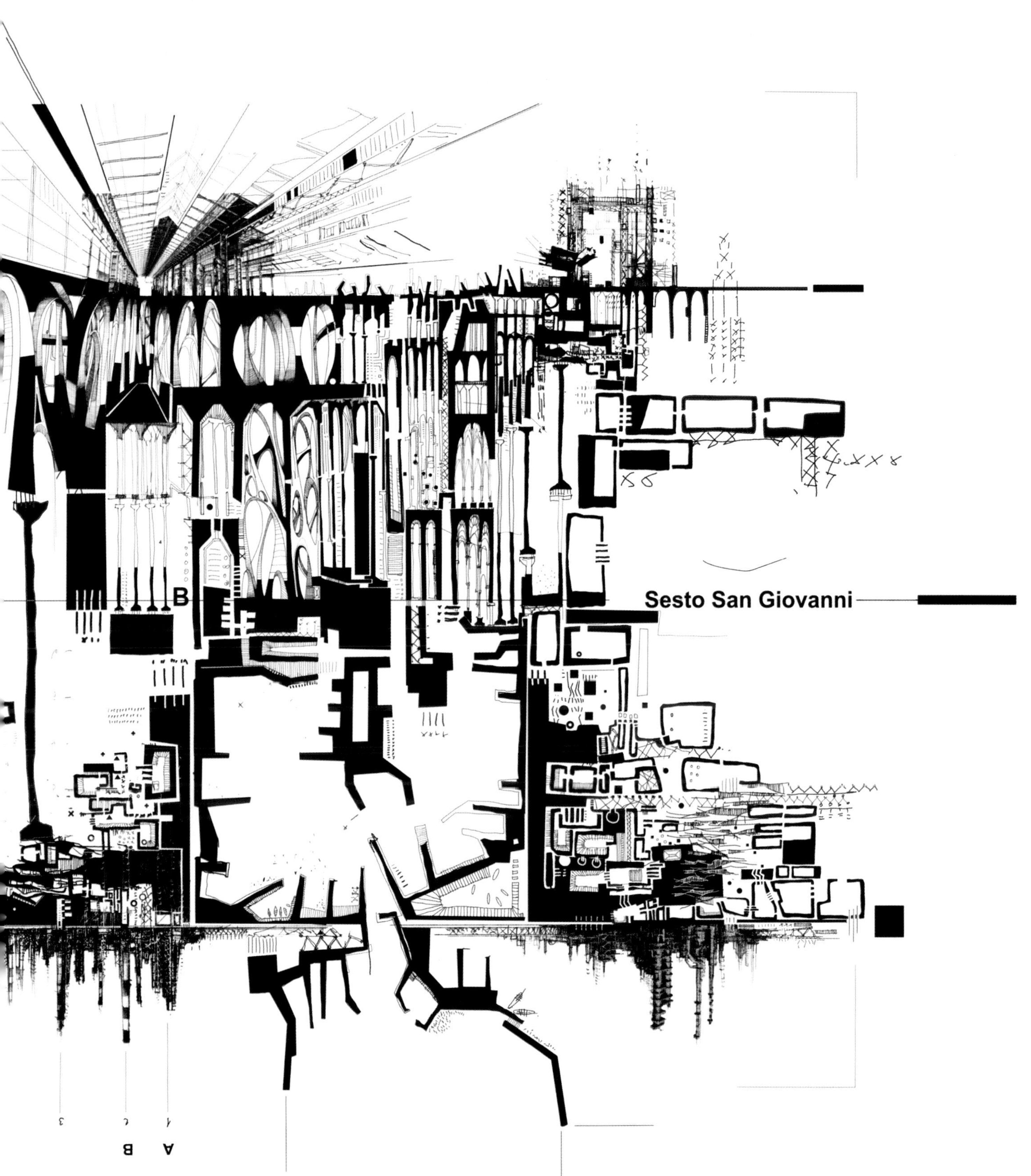

B
Sesto San Giovanni

DUISBURG NORTH, CITY OF INDUSTRY

To reach the city of Oldenburg from an unknown airport, we drove along a German Highway, passing through a dense forest near Duisburg. It was possible to see many industrial buildings emerging from the thick compact volume of the forest's red canopy. The memory created this illusion in my mind.

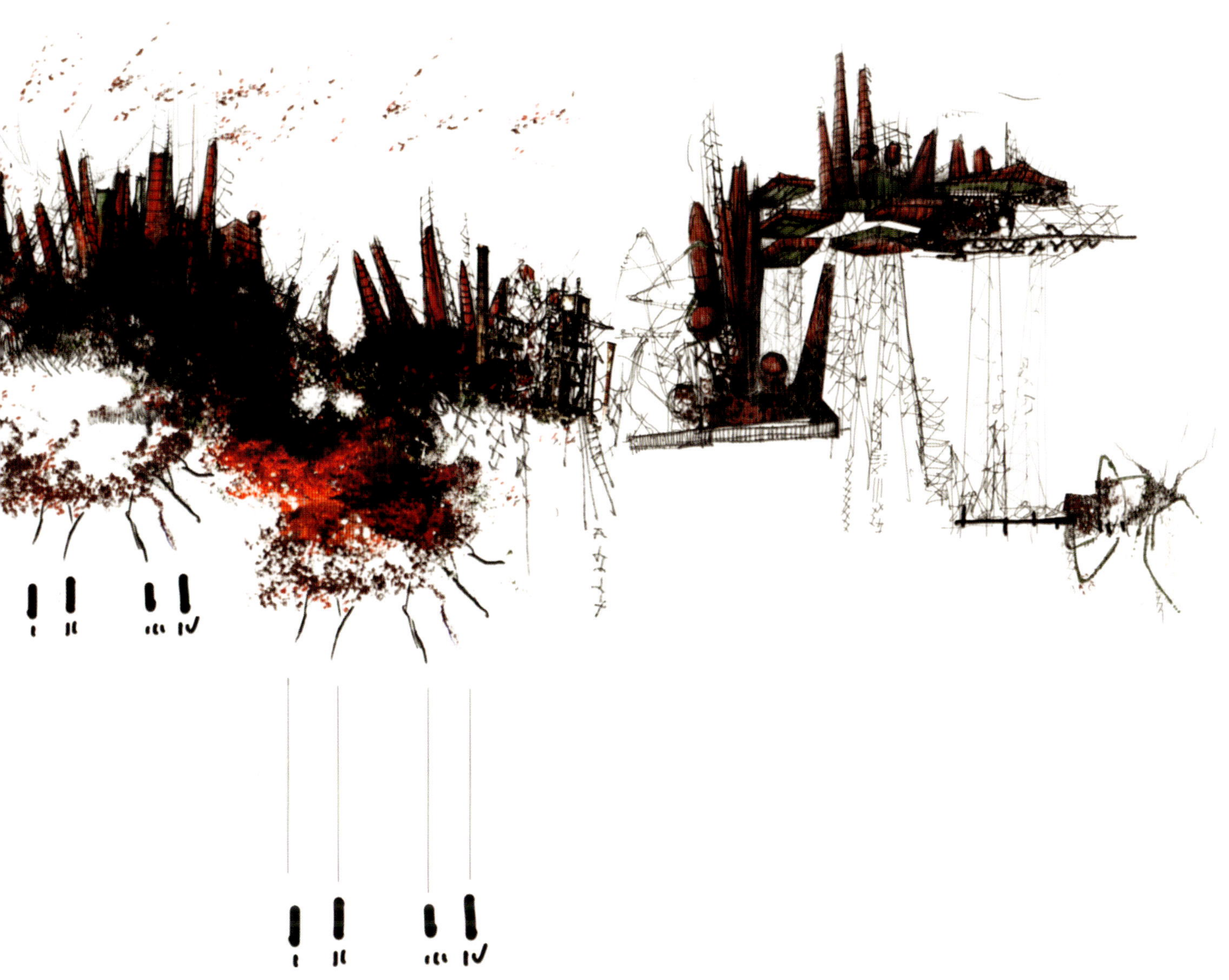
i ii iii iv
i ii iii iv

COLLECTION OF ROCKS

Meteora is a rock formation in central Greece, hosting one of the largest and most complex Eastern Orthodox monasteries, second in importance only to Mount Athos. This drawing explores the idea to build imaginary monasteries settled over a collection of different rocks coming from Morocco, Corsica, Spain, and Italy. The selection of rock photos, along with their juxtaposition, manipulation, and overlap, has been modified, cut, implemented, and reduced many times to find the best landscape possible for the monastery; it is still seeking change.

CITY OF SEIGE

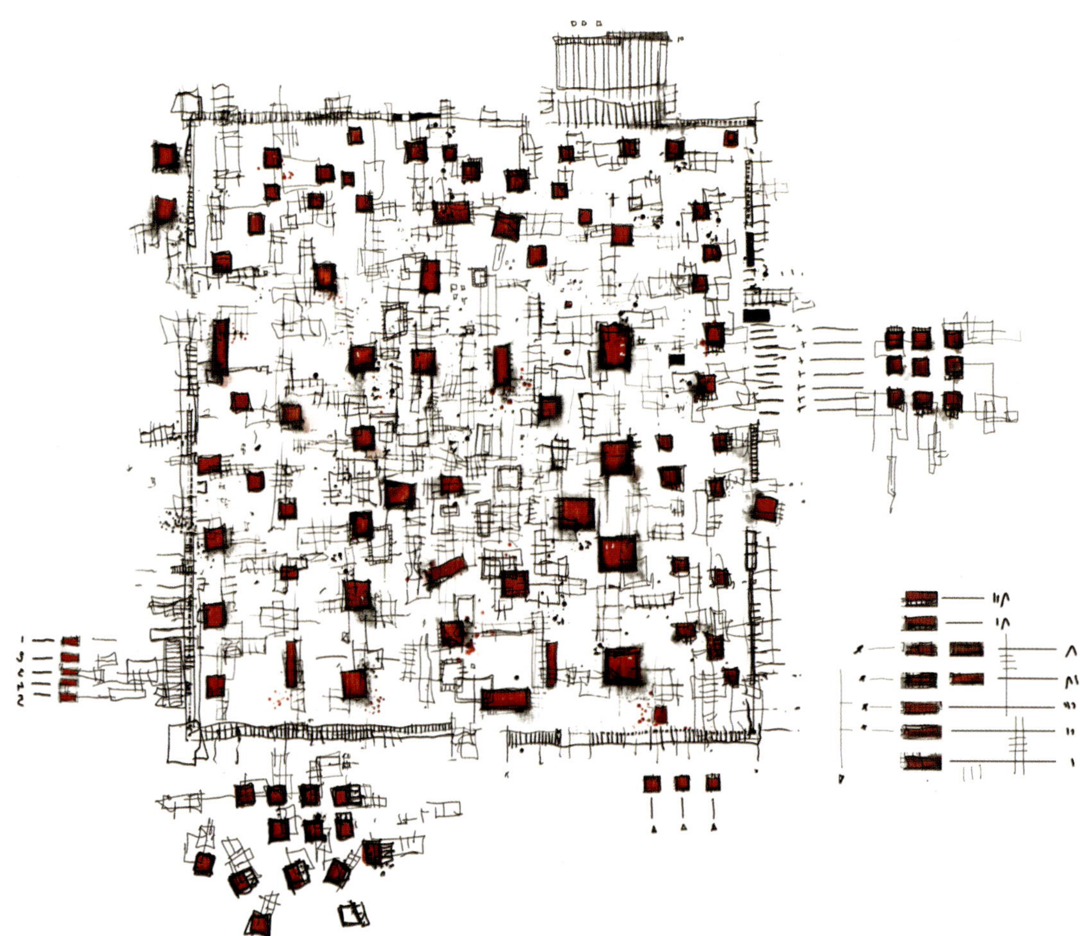

SIEGE OF LUCCA

If someone visits Lucca, they will be impressed by its ancient Renaissance walls. Many drawings, old and new, represent the wall's monumentality, now surmounted by big trees. This first drawing about "siege" wants to avoid a real representation of the walls. Staying on the walls and looking down at the landscape, the drawing is a map of an enemy's camp. An abstract organization of red tents describes the physical camp structure. The camp is surrounded by a perimeter that gives the entire area a precise organization. A series of lines mark the whole camp; they are enemies' movements and secret strategies created for invading the city. Not one of the Lucca walls is in this drawing, because it is an unreal idea of a generic siege landscape. The second drawing pretends to be more realistic; in front of Lucca's walls, enemies devise strategies to conquer the city.

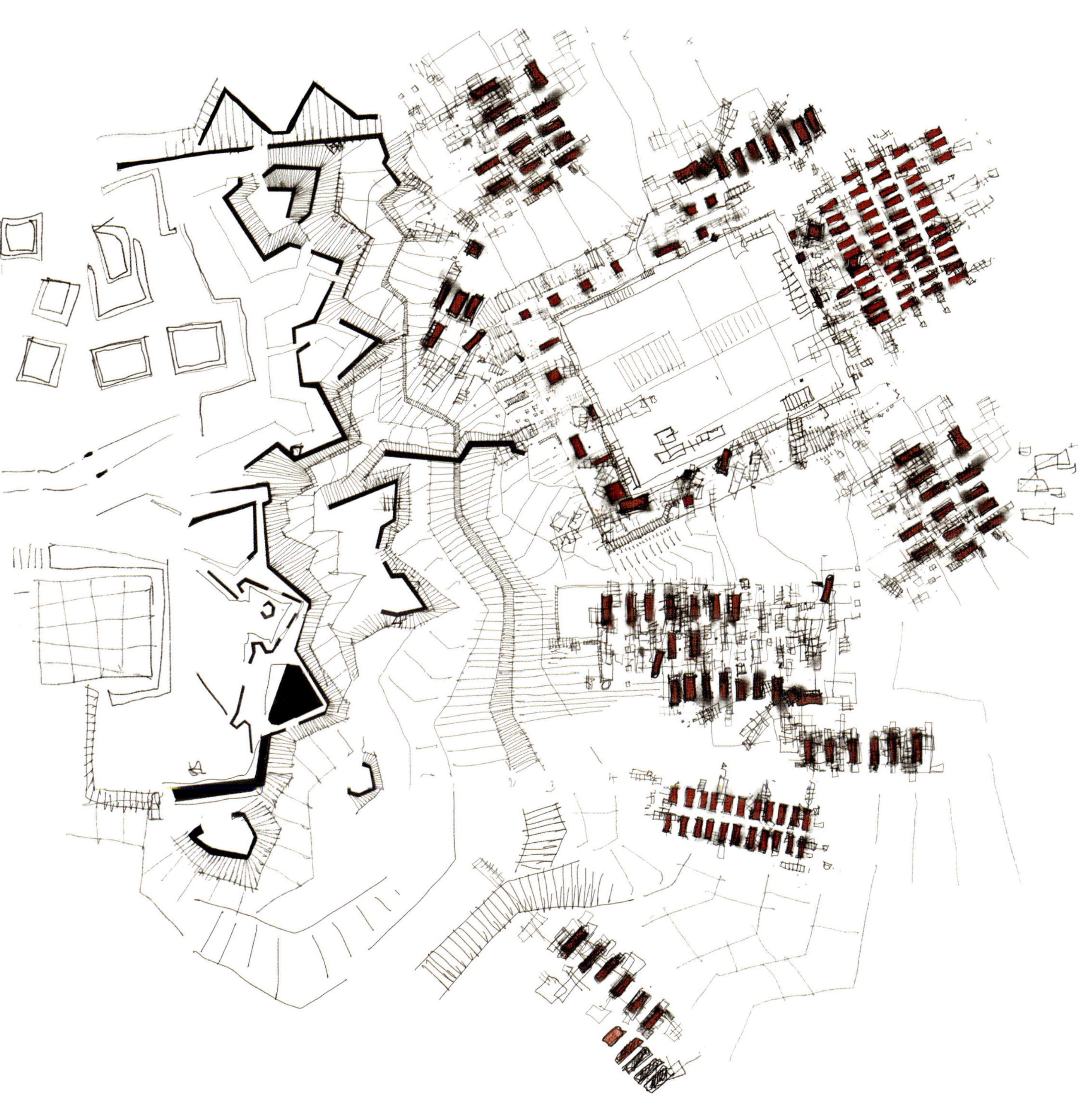

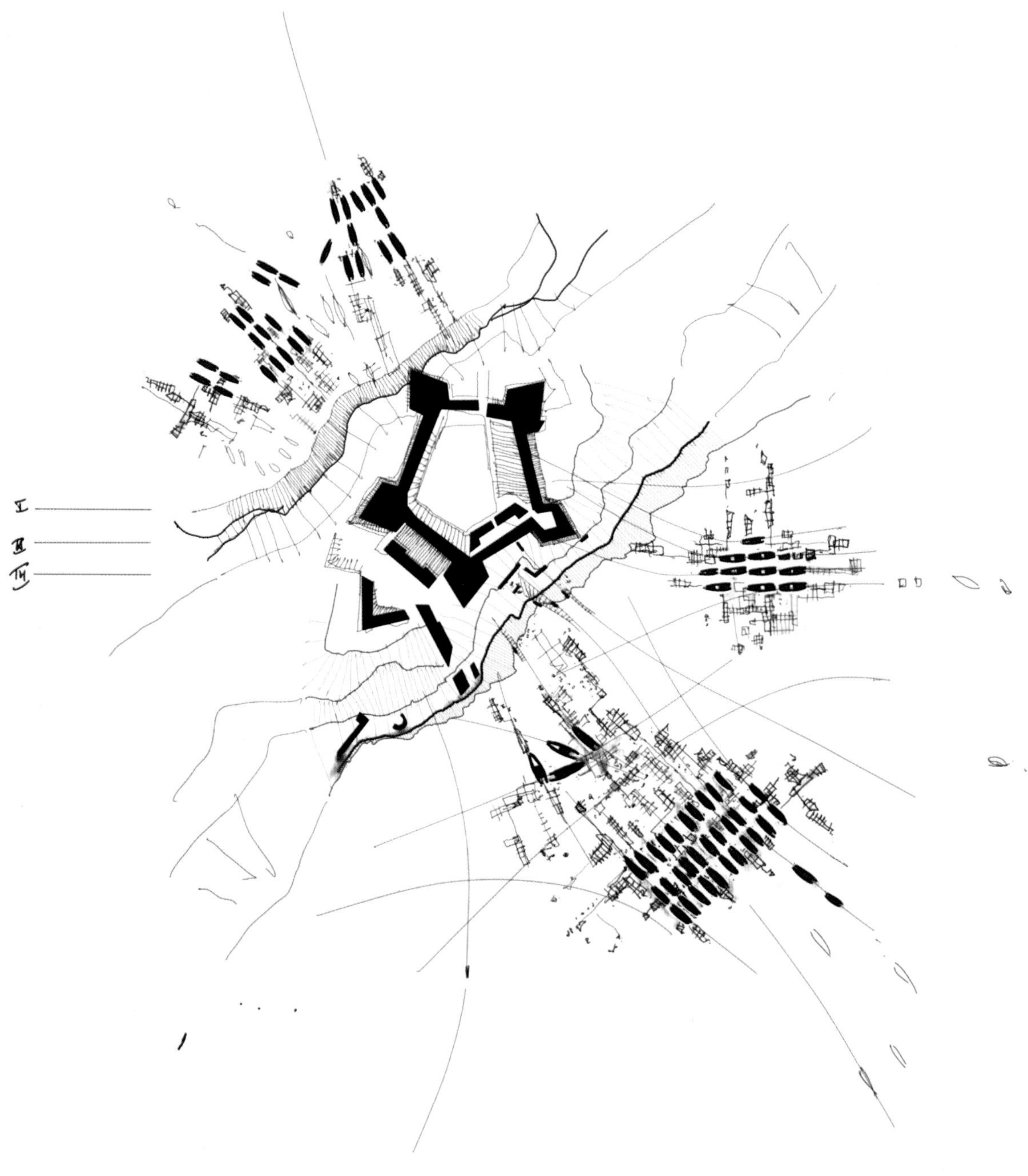

SIEGE OF MESSINA

The Spanish built the fortress at Messina after having conquered Sicily. They made this fortress in a particular morphological formation, called "area Falcata," which means "a land looking like a sickle." The large building had two functions: the official one was to protect the city of Messina from enemies; the second one was to protect the Spanish from the city of Messina itself. This drawing shows both scenarios. It is an exercise in imagining towns through the lens of siege.

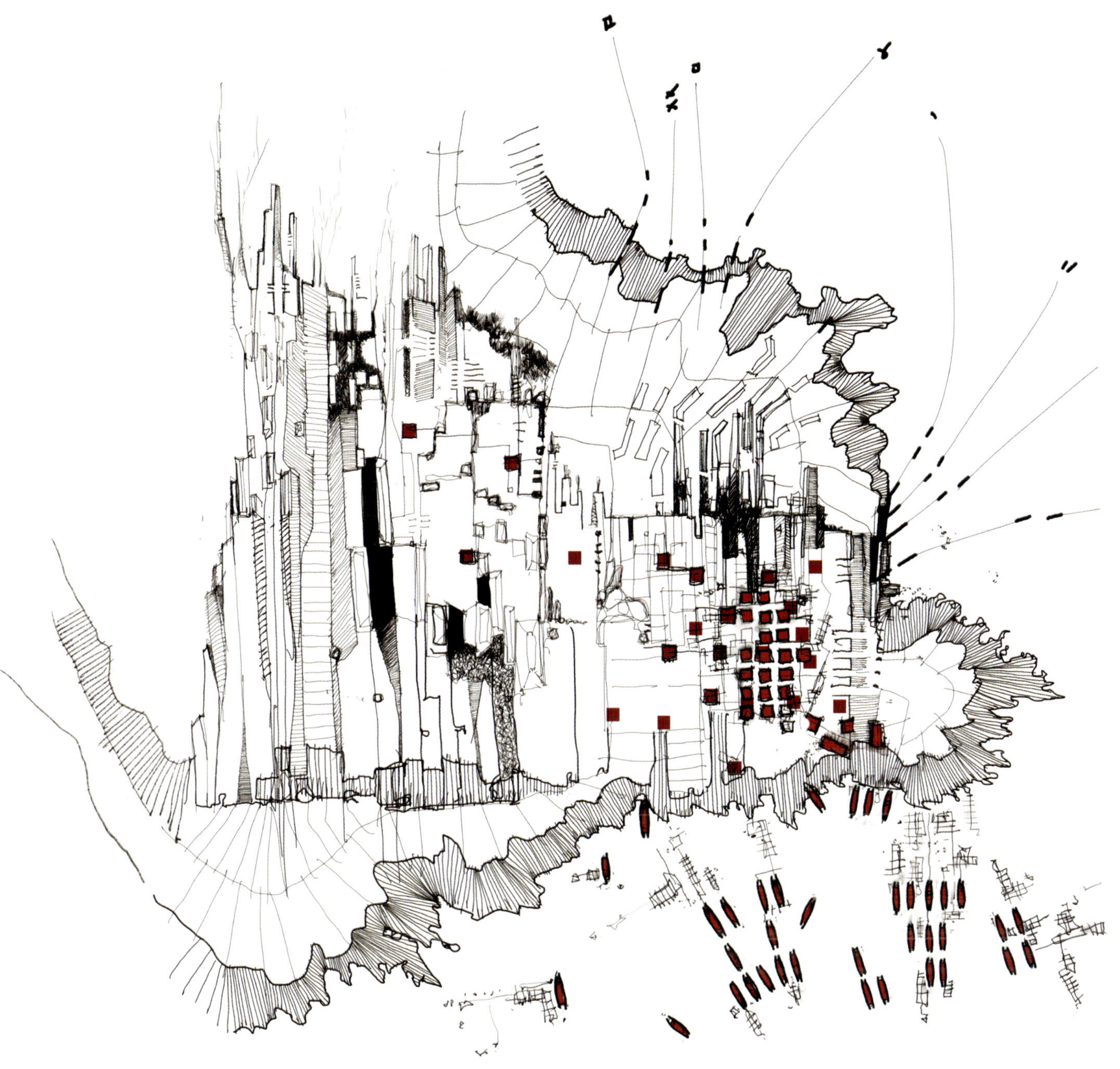

SIEGE OF MILAZZO

The Castle of Milazzo is one of the biggest fortresses along the in the Mediterranean Sea. It has a long history, starting with Arab domination and then passing to Spanish control until the unification of Italy. The Spanish added the last ring of massive walls, which are the actual perimeter of the fortress. It seems that the castle was conquered numerous times by enemies.

NEW YORK MAPS

If I had to look for colors to represent the city of NY, I couldn't find any, except for the black ink of my pen and the white of my paper. So, NYC's drawings have a dark atmosphere. This darkness is not meant to resemble darkness in the city; on the contrary, the city's atmosphere is full of vitality, community, movement, innovation, and research; it is a city full of colors. Using black and white evokes and reveals the city's contradiction and uniqueness; tracing its spaces continuously is to dissolve and recompose the city's compactness many times; every building, street, park, and public space can be employed to imagine the real and unreal city at the same time. These two drawings, and the following ones, are acts of mapping the ephemeral imaginary darkness of NYC.

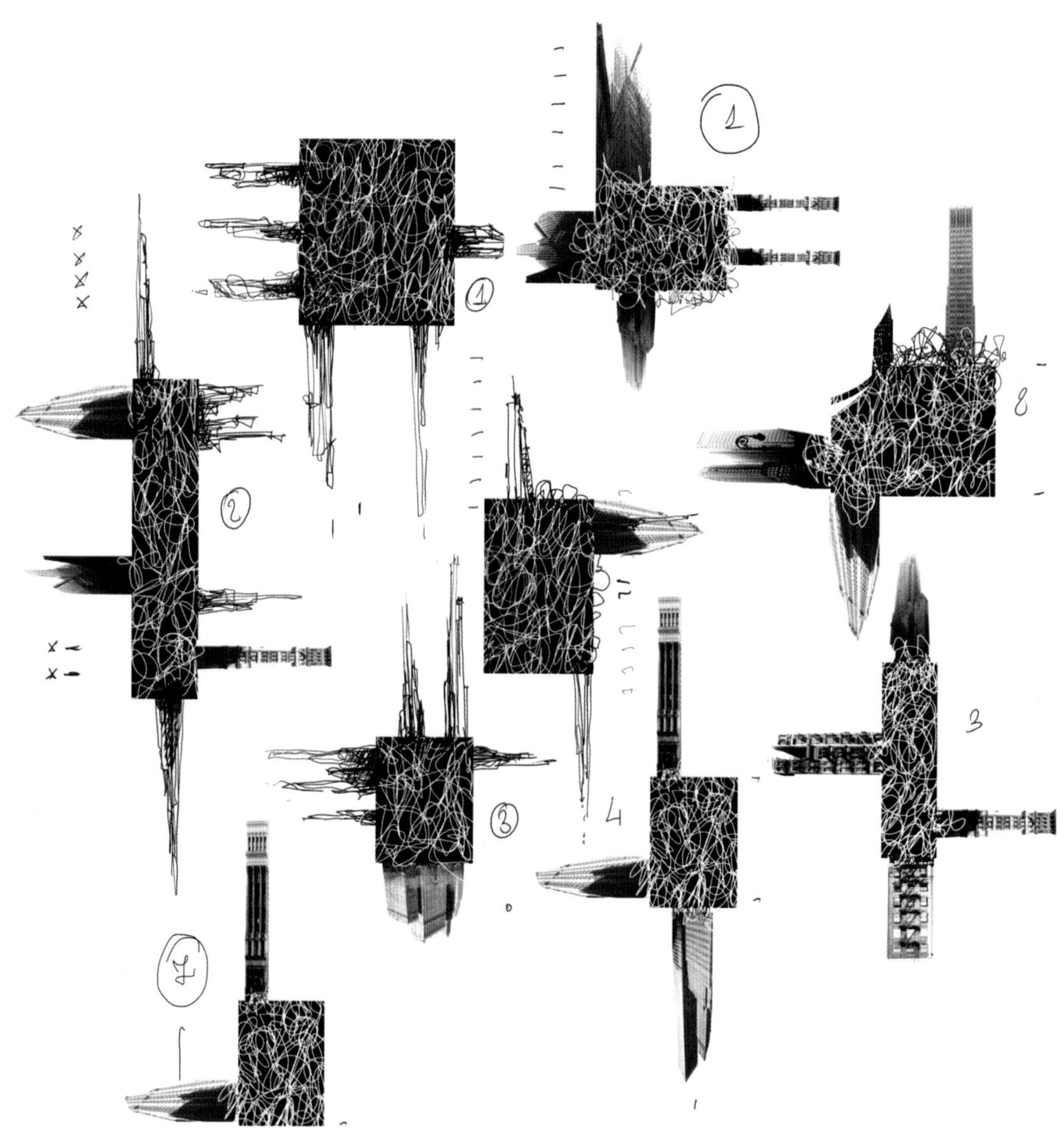

NEW YORK PUBLIC SPACES

There are many public spaces in NYC. A few are large parks, others are small gardens, and many are squares. Central Park is an icon of the city, a space par excellence in the creation of the city's idea. After taking photos of many buildings – straying in the city like a shy flaneur – the images were transformed to redraw the buildings' shapes, colors, and consistency. A new vocabulary of NYC's buildings was ready to be organized following new imaginary public spaces and parks. The first drawing dislocates the buildings around a series of public spaces made by blackboards engraved with white lines. Although it appears to be based on a free scheme, the drawing is a precise combination of scale, measures, and distances among all the elements.

NEW YORK CENTRAL PARK

The second drawing is shaped starting from Central Park's vegetation: a big mass of continuous lines intertwined with each other. The buildings were settled along the perimeter of this abstract park, which is the main actor in the urban scenario. The park welcomes and distributes places where buildings can settle, according to its desires and needs.

CENTRAL PARK'S SECTIONS

Every time I visit Central Park I imagine its sections as imprecise points in order that I might envision them differently. I enjoy thinking about how the trees push the buildings back, how they contain them in a different space, and how their strength competes with the strength of the architecture.

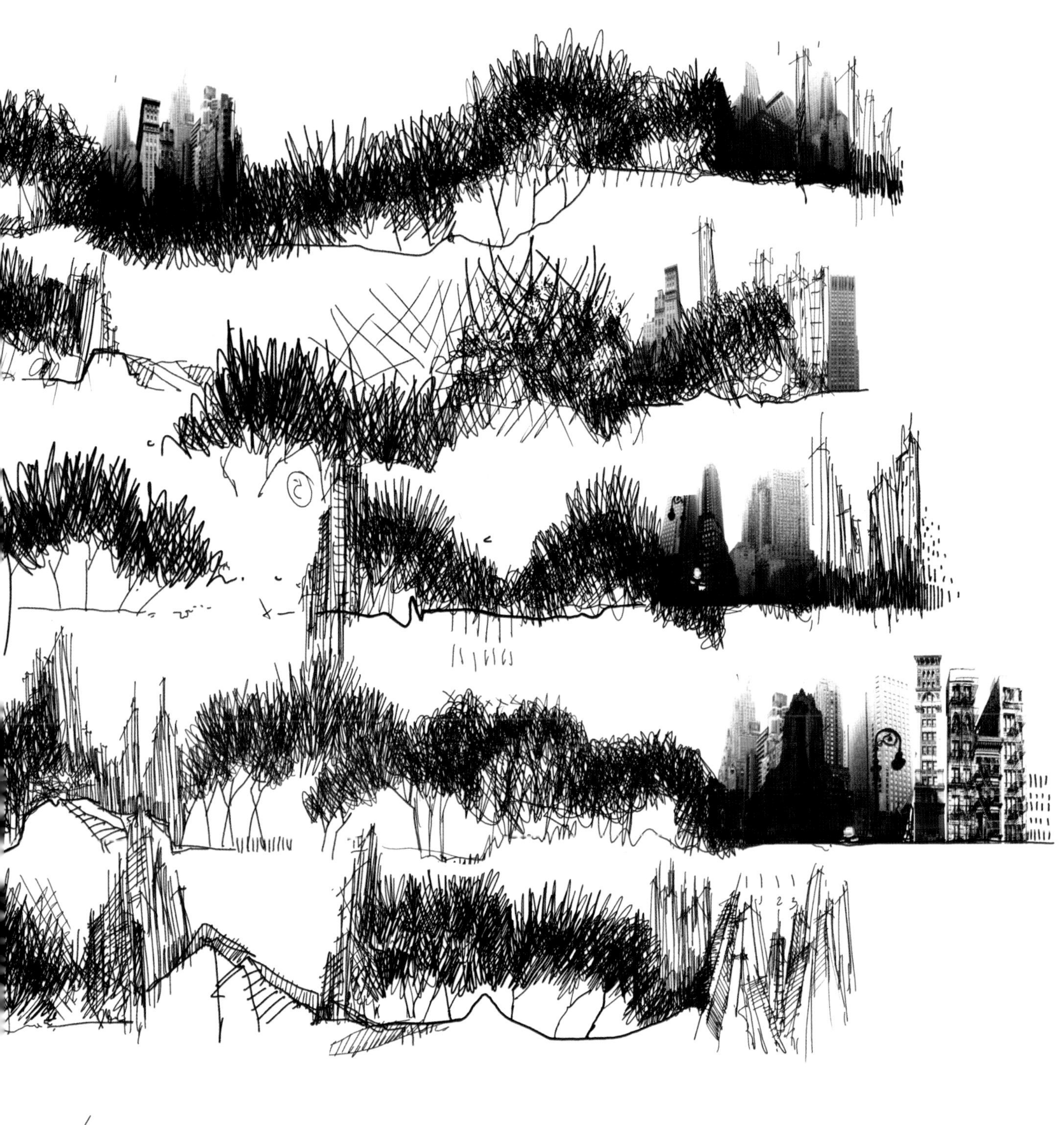

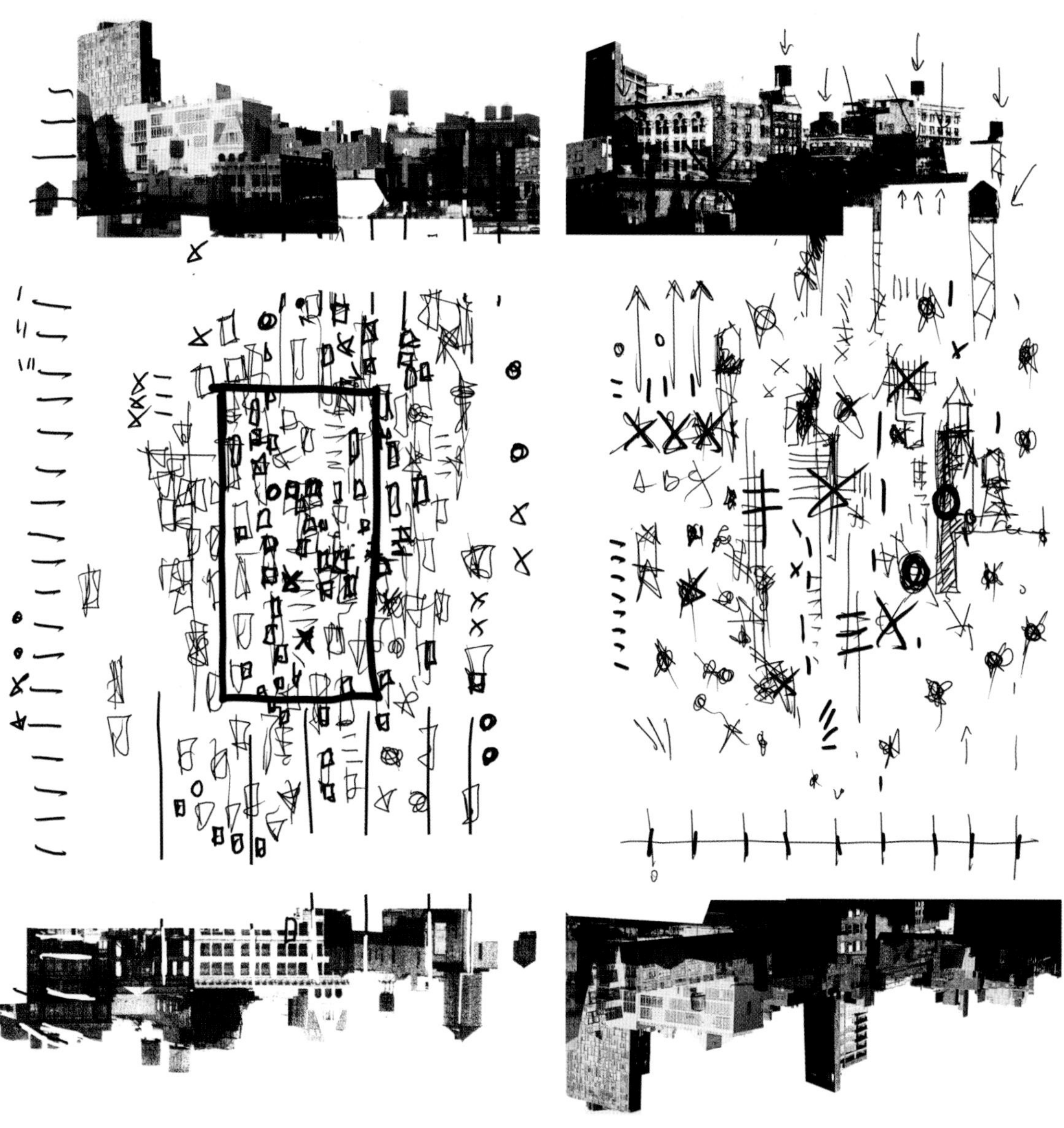

NEW YORK STREETS SEEN FROM ABOVE

NYC has two perspectives: one looks from the bottom up, the second looks from the top down. Representing evocative spaces using the first perspective is simple; buildings climb up and stretch toward the sky, emphasizing the perspective's deepness. However, when we look down from above, the city is crushed and flattened. For this reason, the two drawings avoid a perspectival representation. Using photos depicting the upper part

of Soho, they create a middle space where to collect abstract signs, notes, doodles, and scribbles. They talk about codes devised to interpret the vitality of NYC streets. Some of the codes are reminiscent of Jean-Michel Basquiat's ancestral vocabulary of symbols, coming in particular from the oil painting *Pegasus*, which is the real trace from which these drawings belong to.

HIGH LINE CITIES

"After forty years of writing fiction, after exploring various roads and making diverse experiments, the time has come for me to look for an overall definition of my work. I would suggest this: my working method has more often than not involved the subtraction of weight. I have tried to remove weight, sometimes from people, sometimes from heavenly bodies, sometimes from cities; above all, I have tried to remove weight from the structure of stories and from language. Whenever humanity seems condemned to heaviness, I think I should fly

like Perseus into a different space. I don't mean escaping into dreams or into the irrational. I mean that I have to change my approach, look at the world from another perspective, with a different logic, and with fresh methods of cognition and verification. The images of lightness that I seek should not fade away like dreams dis-solved by the realities of present and future." I like to use these ideas of Calvino's on "lightness" to describe these two drawings, which speak about changing approaches to looking at cities.

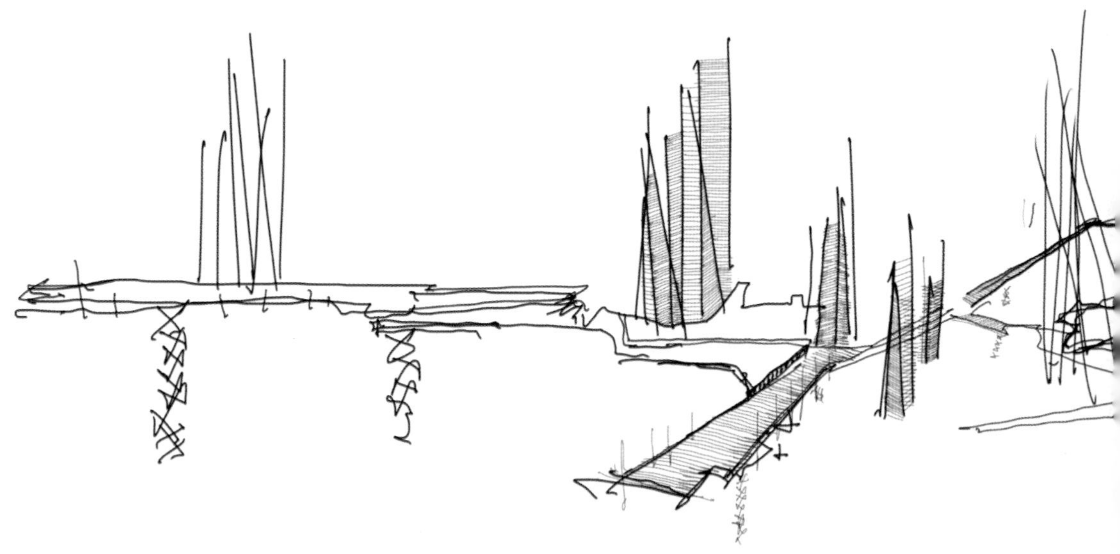

INTESTINE NEW YORK

The High Line ingests, swallows, and pushes its visitors toward a higher city level. It is a slow approach that makes us feel part of a unique process of urban digestion. The complex simplicity of the High Line reveals the intention to introduce visitors to an unreal experience as if it were an augmented and virtual reality. Passing through it, the visitors' perception is modified and altered until they are ready to explore an unexpected place, the unknown land of an intestine. Taking photos to protect the memory from being overloaded with impressions, a multitude of complicated spaces appear and disappear along the intestinal tract. Touching the vegetation plays an essential role in the digestion process, soothing souls, improving dreams, and expanding the imagination.

Italo Calvino believed that his imagination and creativity were a process of digestion, with knowledge as the food and literature the expulsion. The High Line ingests us, the incredible multitude, changing and returning us—perhaps improved—to the "normal" life of New York City.

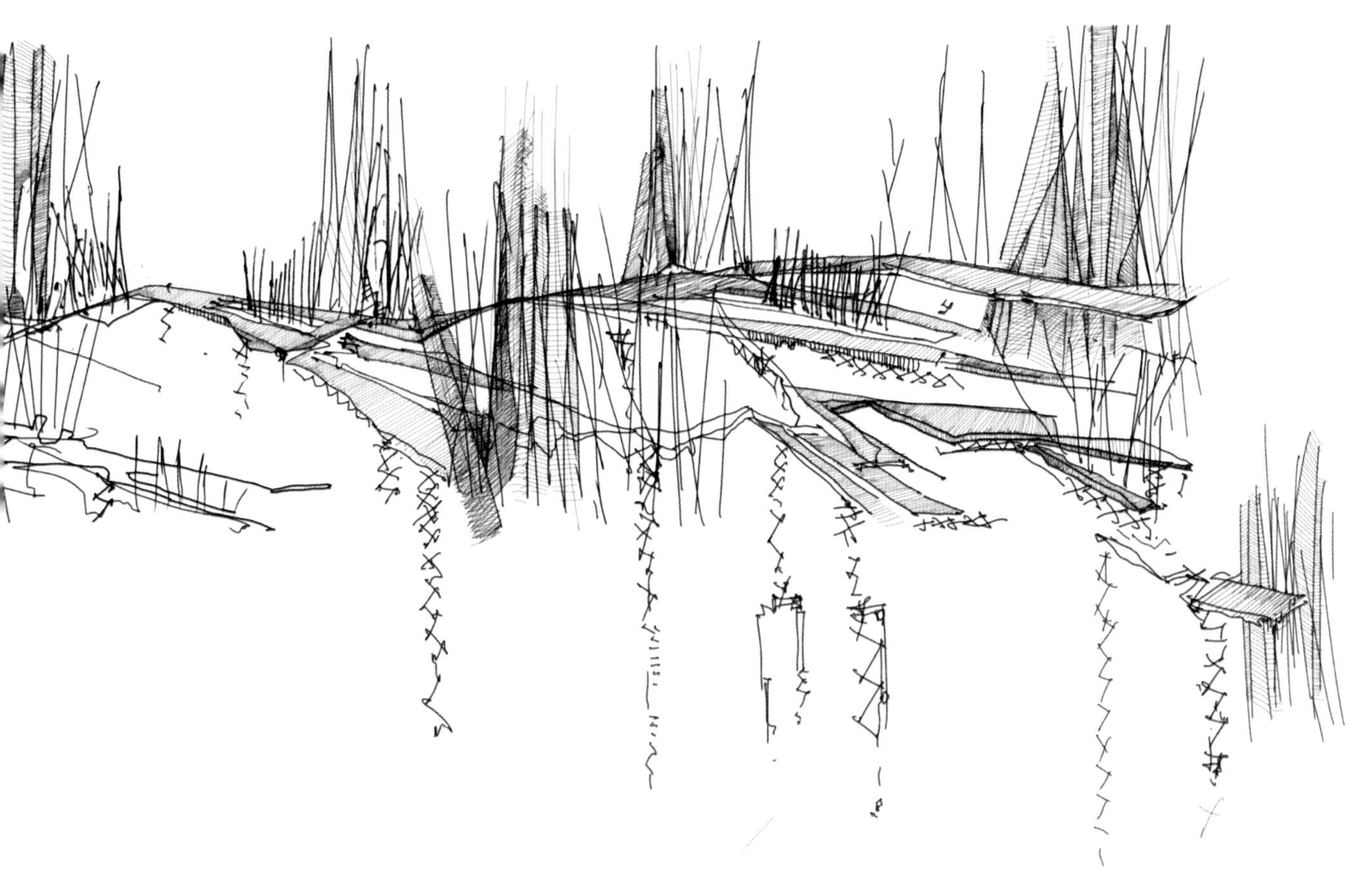

CITY OF EARTH

TANNERIES IN FES

The tanneries in Fes are ancient examples of industrial landscapes, strictly connected with the urban fabric. The city's buildings, made basically by rectangular or square shapes, generate a strong compact volume characterized by an end-less sequence of collisions, overlaps, and penetrations. Suddenly, into this compact space, an industrial landscape based on small circular and square containers opens a big void: it is the space of the tanneries. Their structures are lower than the urban fabric, and for this reason, they collide and try to conquer space from buildings that surround them. In doing this, the tanneries create interesting moments of discontinuity. The explosion of colors, people jumping from one little container to the other one, the smell, and the animal skins hanging on the walls all around gives an image of space without time.

IMAGINING THE MEDINA OF FES

Fes is an ancient medina in Morocco founded between the eighth and the ninth centuries. After visiting the city many times, it is possible to understand the meaning of its democratic urban space; it is based on the absence of any geometrical hierarchies among the different spaces and buildings that shape the medina. The drawing is a free interpretation of this space, made by adding building after building in a long process of urban tectonics. Walls and doors, surrounding and protecting the inner space of the city, make a fascinating and dynamic relationship between inside and outside. The final result is an endless, interconnected, intricate succession of city traces. The city becomes a whole entity seamlessly, where every element, object, and space in the city is built according to an intuitive holistic vision.

FOUNTAINS IN FES

Walking through the streets of Fes, as in every other city in Morocco, you will come across magnificent monumental fountains. Their presence enlightens the urban space and makes it almost impalpable. They change the normal flow of space in the city, giving a new and emotional perception. These two drawings are a free interpretation of the relationship between water, fountains, and traditional ornaments of Arab cultures. Sometimes, in small squares, there is the presence of marginalized trees, usually plane trees; but in these drawings (like in many others) trees become protagonists in designing and organizing the new space of the city.

COURTYARD IN FES

The courtyards of the riad, typical Moroccan houses structured around an empty interior space, are inventions of beauty. If the streets, squares, and public spaces of Fes follow an informal urban structure, the inner courtyards of the riads are geometrically organized according to precise square or rectangular figures made by well-defined proportions. Sometimes, the columns and beams of the portico of two or more floors that surround these spaces are finely worked wood with small abstract geometric patterns. The surface of the courtyard is often decorated with magnificent mosaics in brilliant colors. Inside these spaces, there are sometimes olive, orange, or fig trees. Free from the need to protect themselves from the wind, they grow upwards in an unusual way. They become light in search of the sun.

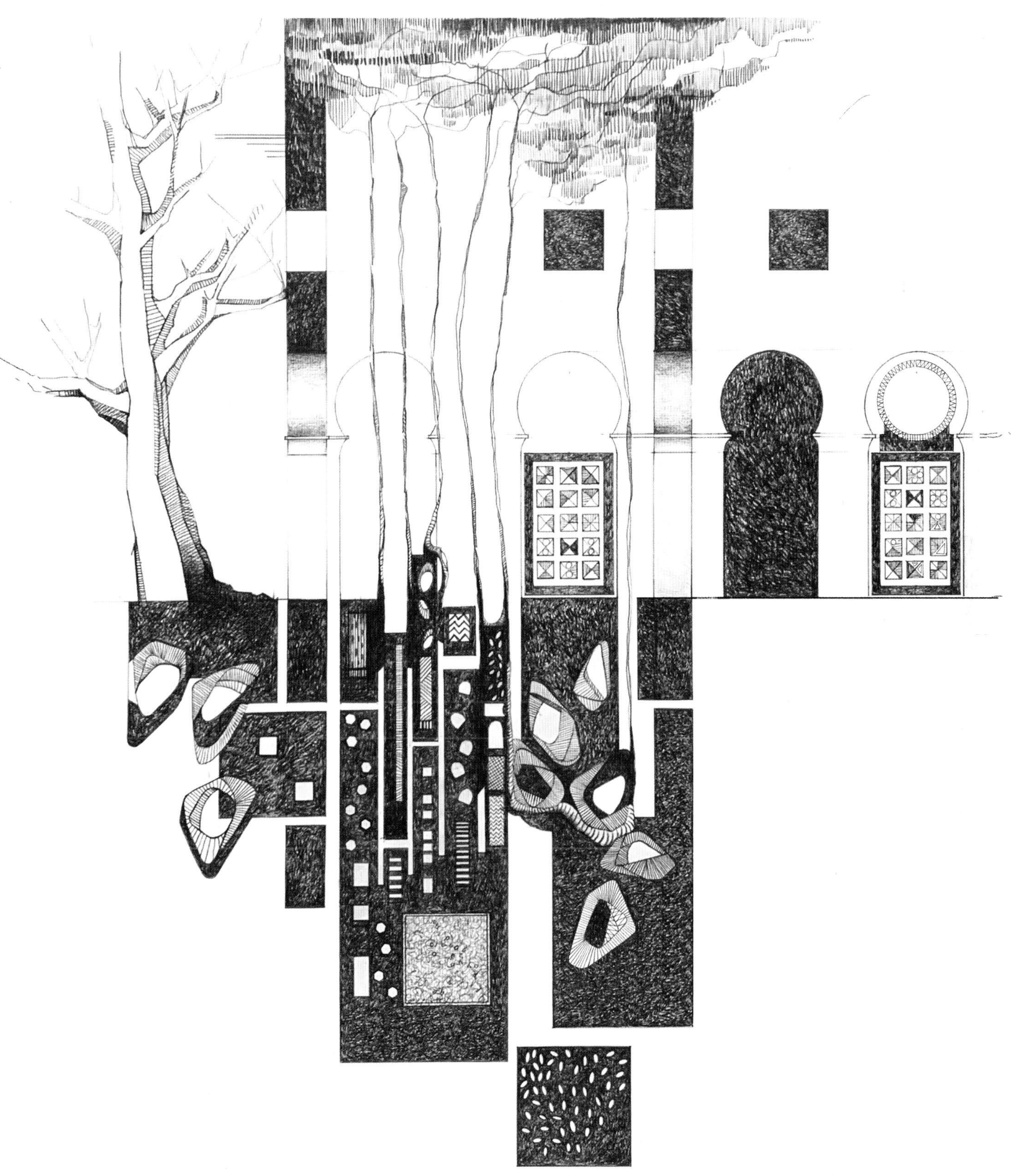

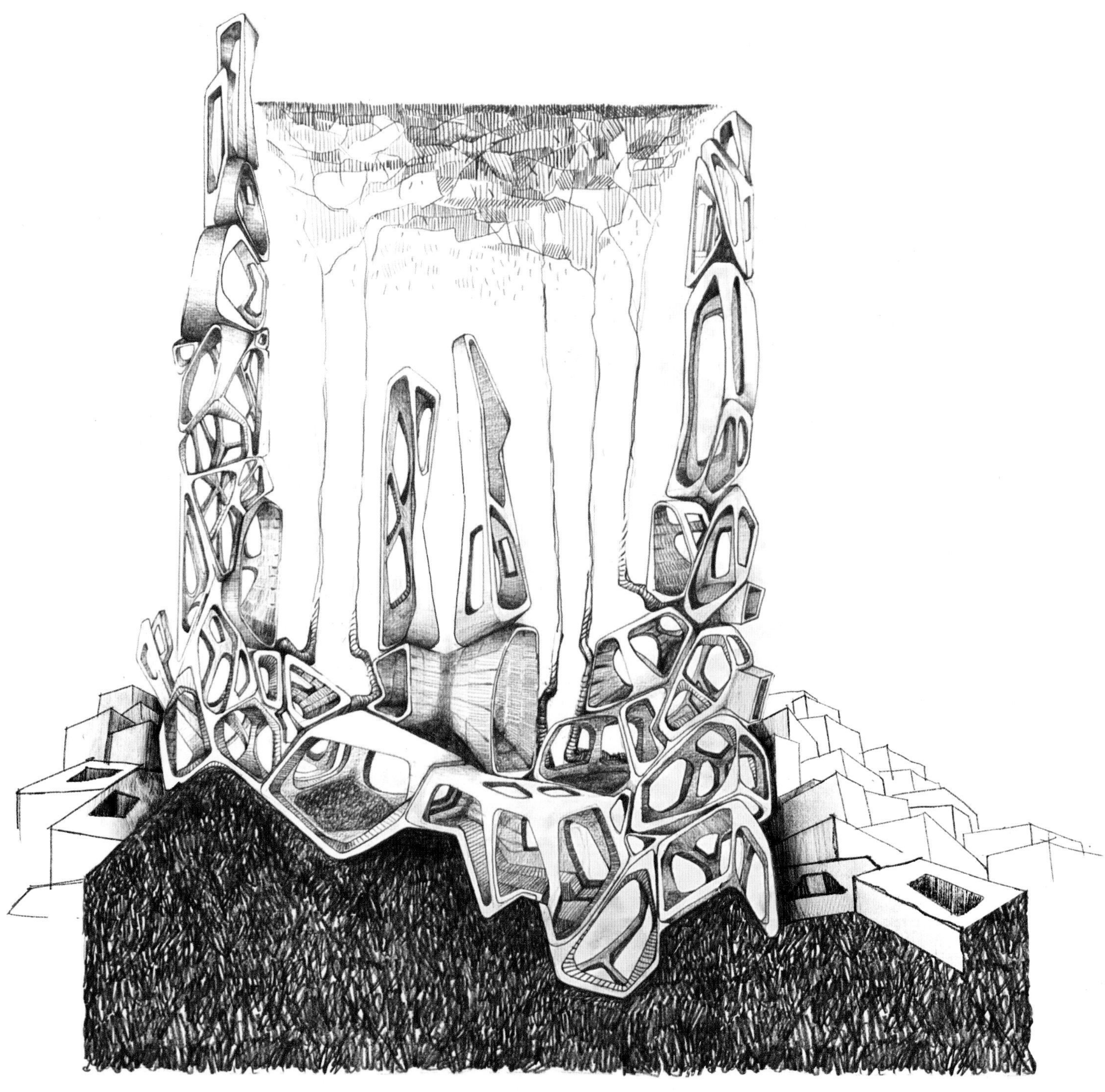

TOWERS IN FES

The horizontality of the medina of Fes, like many other Arab cities, is emphasized by the towers of the minarets. Beyond their religious value and the understanding of the Arabic words, the sound that rhythmically comes from them is an integral part of the space of the city. The design of the towers of Fes is not a modern interpretation of the classical minarets, but simply the voices of the city. They rise from the compact volume of the urban space to be materialized according to a language of forms and sizes that is a synthesis between the immaterial sounds of the city and the materiality of its buildings.

STREETS IN FES

Someone like me who has no sense of direction in cities might think that Fes is an impossible city to explore. But after some time, if you look carefully at the various traces of its urban system, the doors, the colors, and the activities along the urban corridors of Fes can help you learn how to orient yourself by building a personal map of the city. Sections make the design of this map: the city is divided according to precise memories, and at the bottom of each urban corridor you can see a particular structure; a tower, a tree or other element that allows us to stray in the city without fear.

THE MAP OF MATMATA

Matmata is a small Berber town in southern Tunisia. Some of the local Berber residents live in traditional underground "troglodyte" structures. The structures, typical for the village, are created by digging a large pit in the ground. Rooms are drilled around the perimeter of this artificial cave. Some of these homes are connected by tunnels that form passageways. This drawing is a simple map of what this landscape fixed in my memory.

THE SURFACE OF MATMATA

THE GROUND OF MATMATA

Visiting Matmata is like visiting a city without a city. The surface of the desert is the city itself, a negative that is added. Unfortunately, some contemporary buildings, built on the surface of the hills, have disfigured the pure surface of Matmata made by holes. It is not nostalgia for an absolute past, but there is a sense of poverty every time we encounter one of these new buildings. When the surface is pure and engraved by the hole houses, we perceive the simple idea that a different civilization has belonged to the earth and its ground.

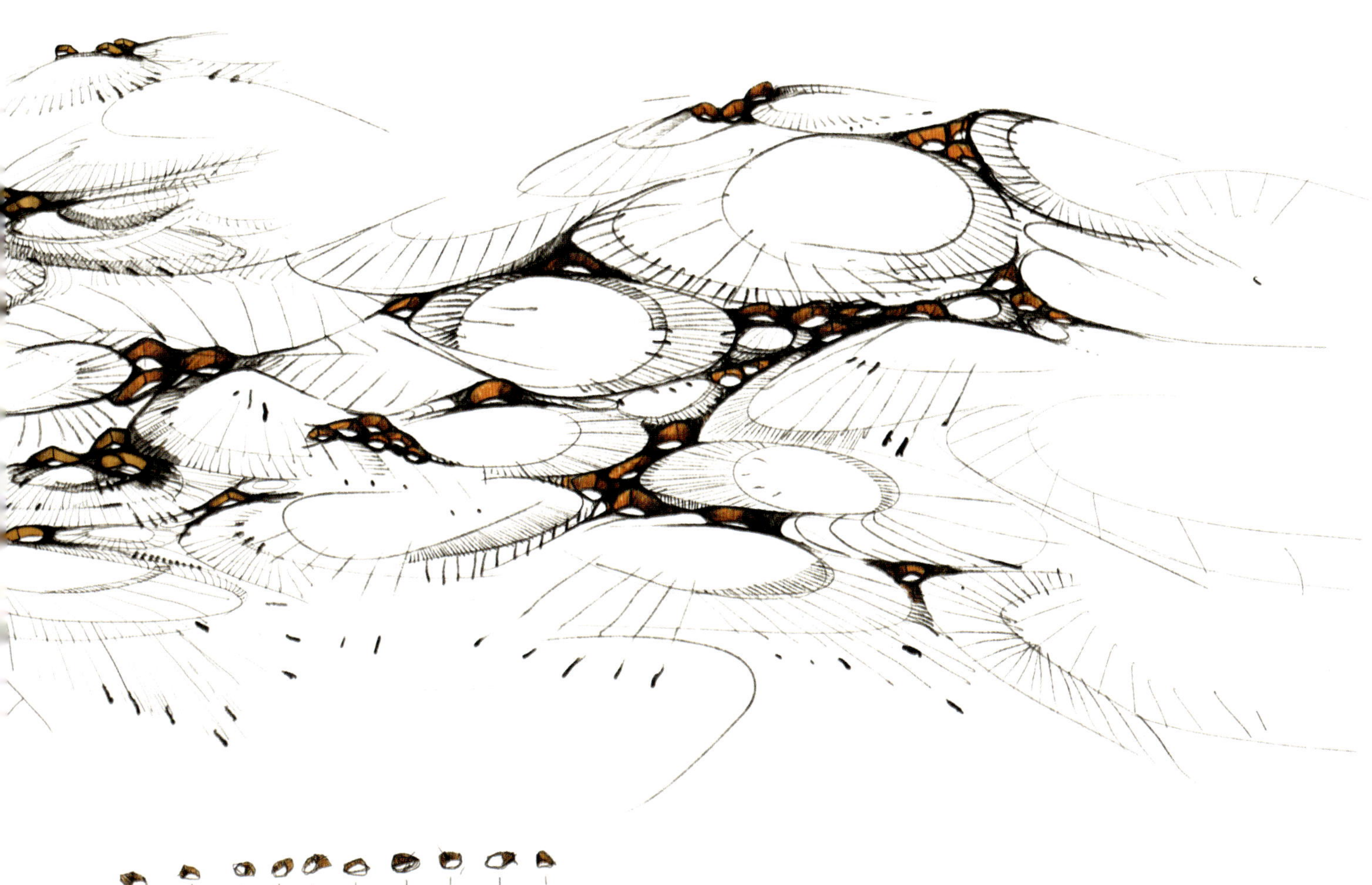

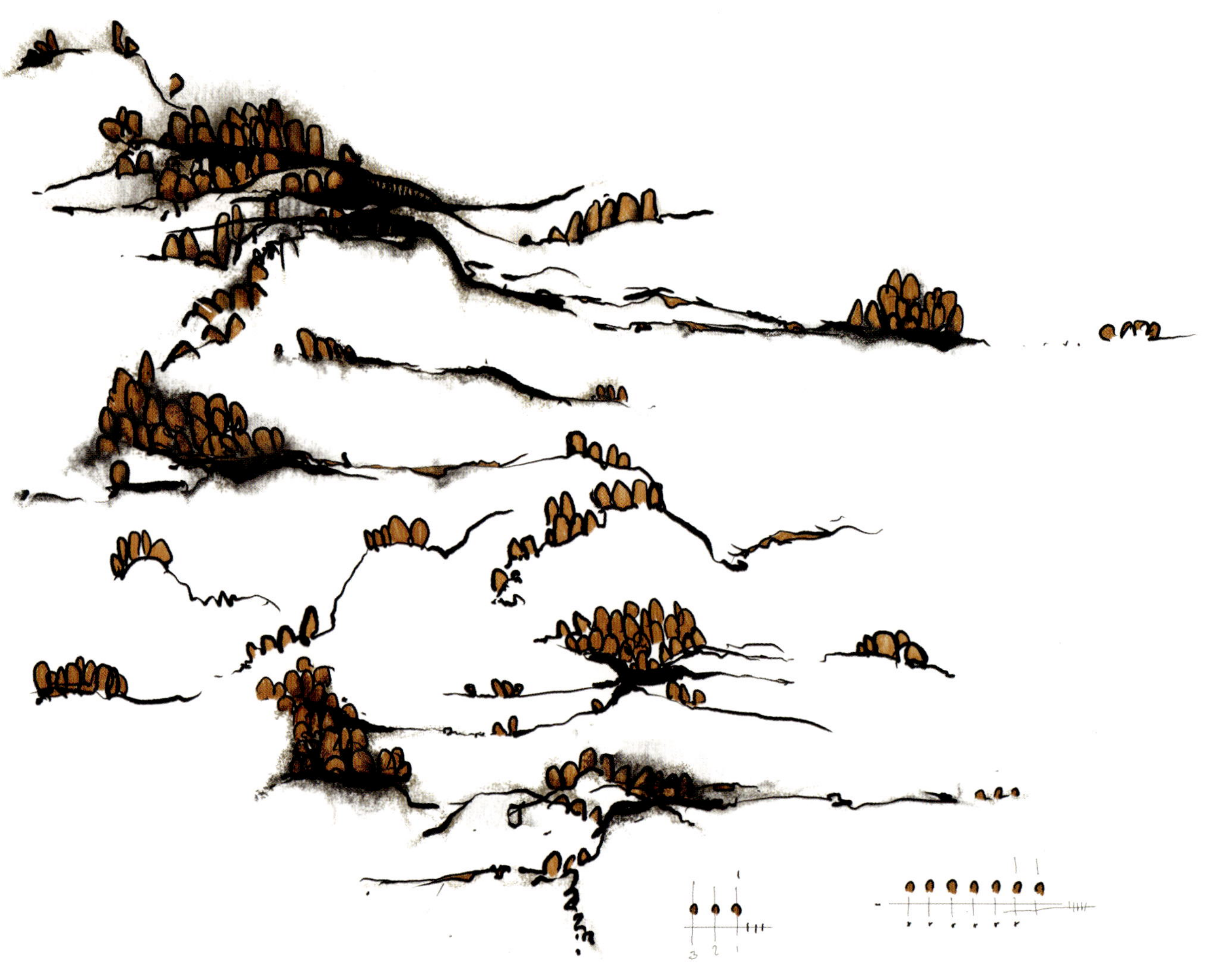

KSOUR OF MOUNTAINS

In the Tunisian desert, we can visit fortified granaries, typical of Berber nomads of the Atlas Mountains. Their shapes are based on rectangular plans, resulting from a group of buildings with two or more floors. The external walls form fortifications. One or more monumental doors communicate with the outside while inside courtyards are multiuse spaces. The technique used to build them was simple; a vault made by the same measure, construction process, and materials–sand and stone–is repeated many times, everywhere. Traveling along the desert of Tunisia, we can see, on top of small hills, these beautiful fortifications. They are simple, familiar monuments talking about an idea of movement. The food was stored in these granaries, and people were free to move around the desert exploring an endless notion of space. These drawings are memories from a touristic version of nomadic movement through the desert. Having tea under tents or pergolas, the pouring technique that moves the teapot away from the glass until it forms a long tea line evokes invisible desert trajectories.

DOUIRET

In Tunisia, there is a city called Douiret. Today, it is a ruined Berber village in the Tataouine district in the southern Tunisian desert. Like Chenini, it was a fortified granary on top of a hill, called *ksar* (plural *ksour*.) The desert hills are characterized by particular geology made by an alternation of rock platforms and sand layers. Douiret and Chenini were first established by digging buildings between two rock platforms, which usually served as roofs and floors. Later, new outdoor spaces were added. Looking at these two cities, it evident that the desert of Tunisia is a landscape of horizontal lines.

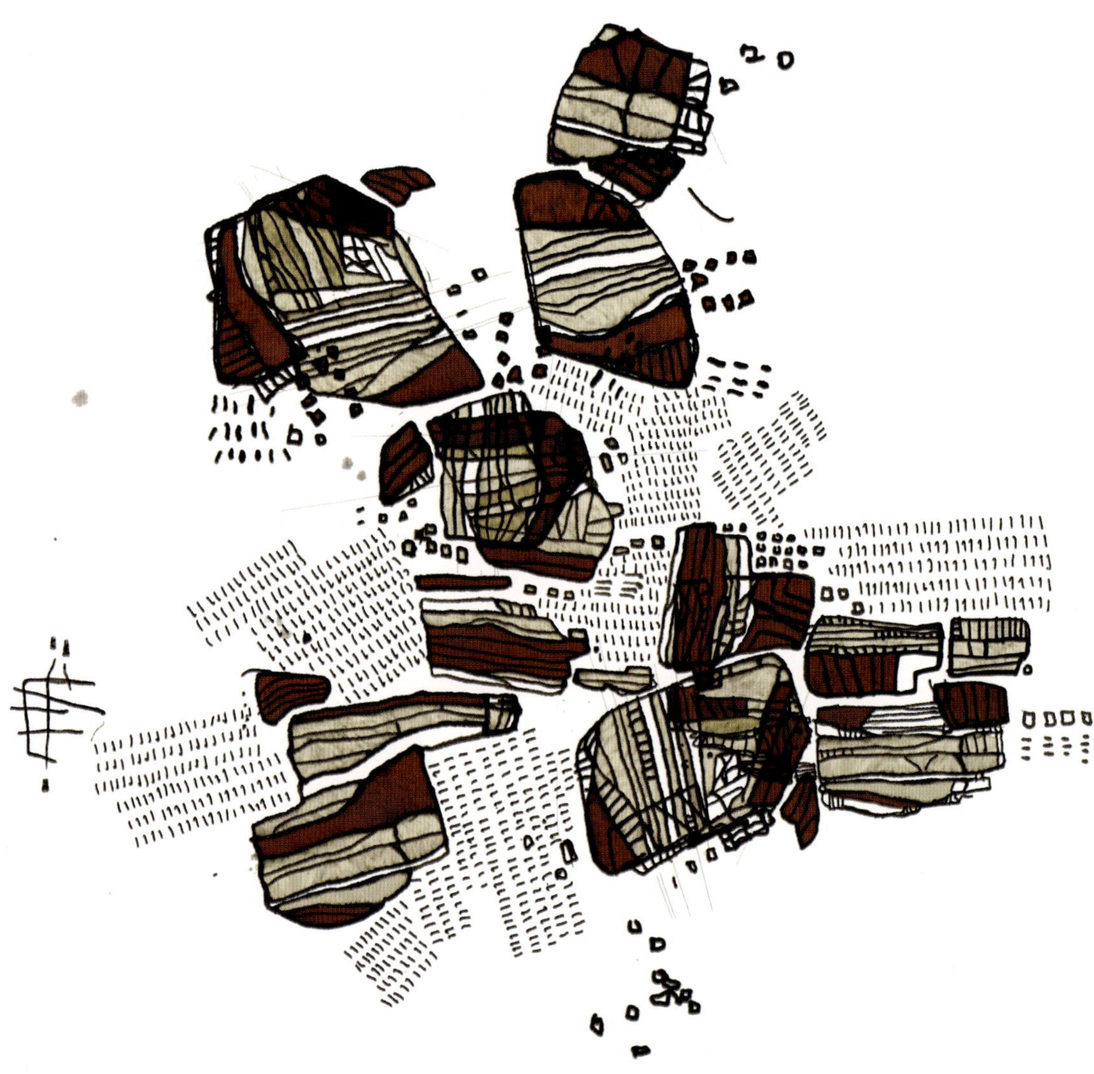

LANDING TO CASABLANCA

If we land by plane in Casablanca during the summer, one can see an incredible agricultural landscape made by shades of brown. The shapes of the agricultural fields are geometrical plots divided by linear lines, forming an intricate endless network. These drawings try to design new agricultural fields no longer based on a continuous system of linear lines, but somewhat discrete pieces contained by curvilinear edges. They articulate a complex

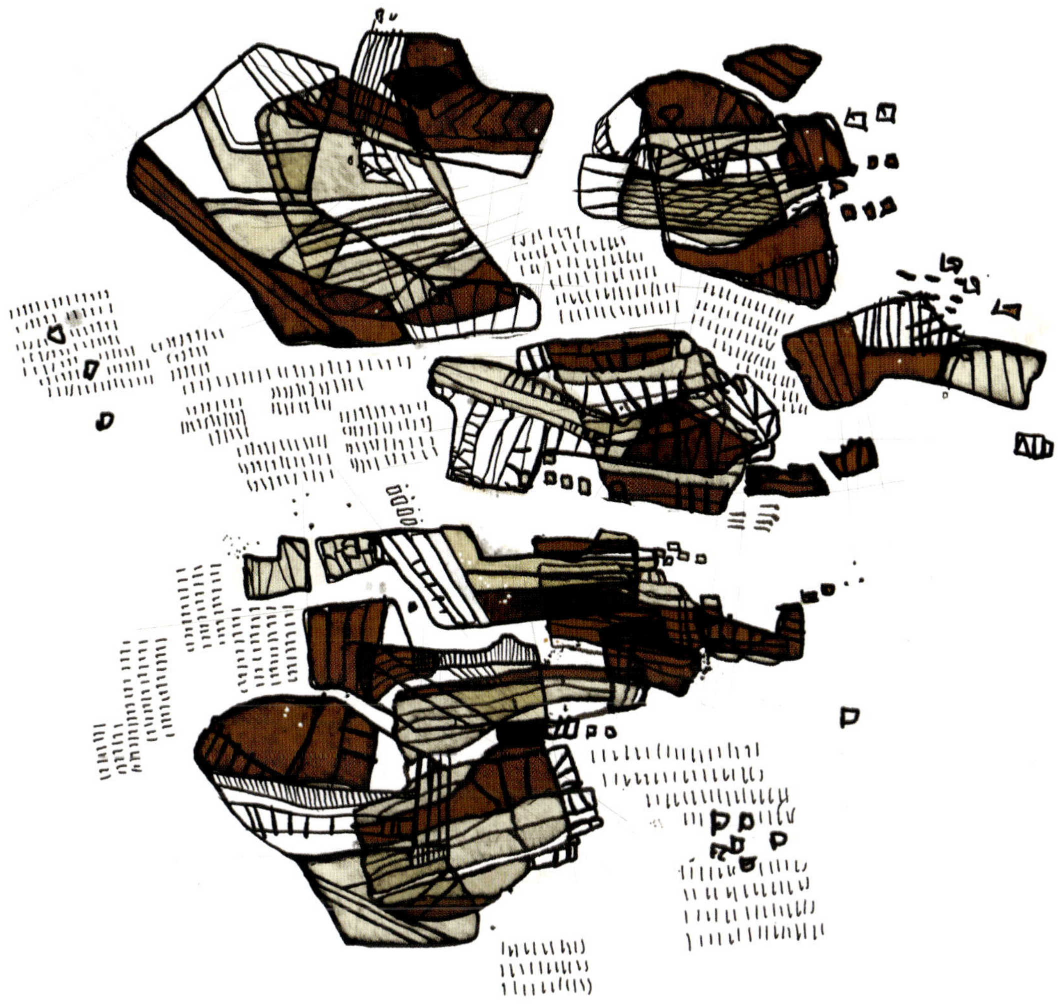

grammar in which the relationships among the agricultural fields are made by approaches and withdrawals, overlaps, and detachments. It is no longer the landscape observed from the air, nor an agricultural landscape on a plain morphology. It has become an exercise in imagining fields broken by the presence of cities and complicated morphologies. Agriculture remains as fragmented memories.

CITY OF BRIDGES

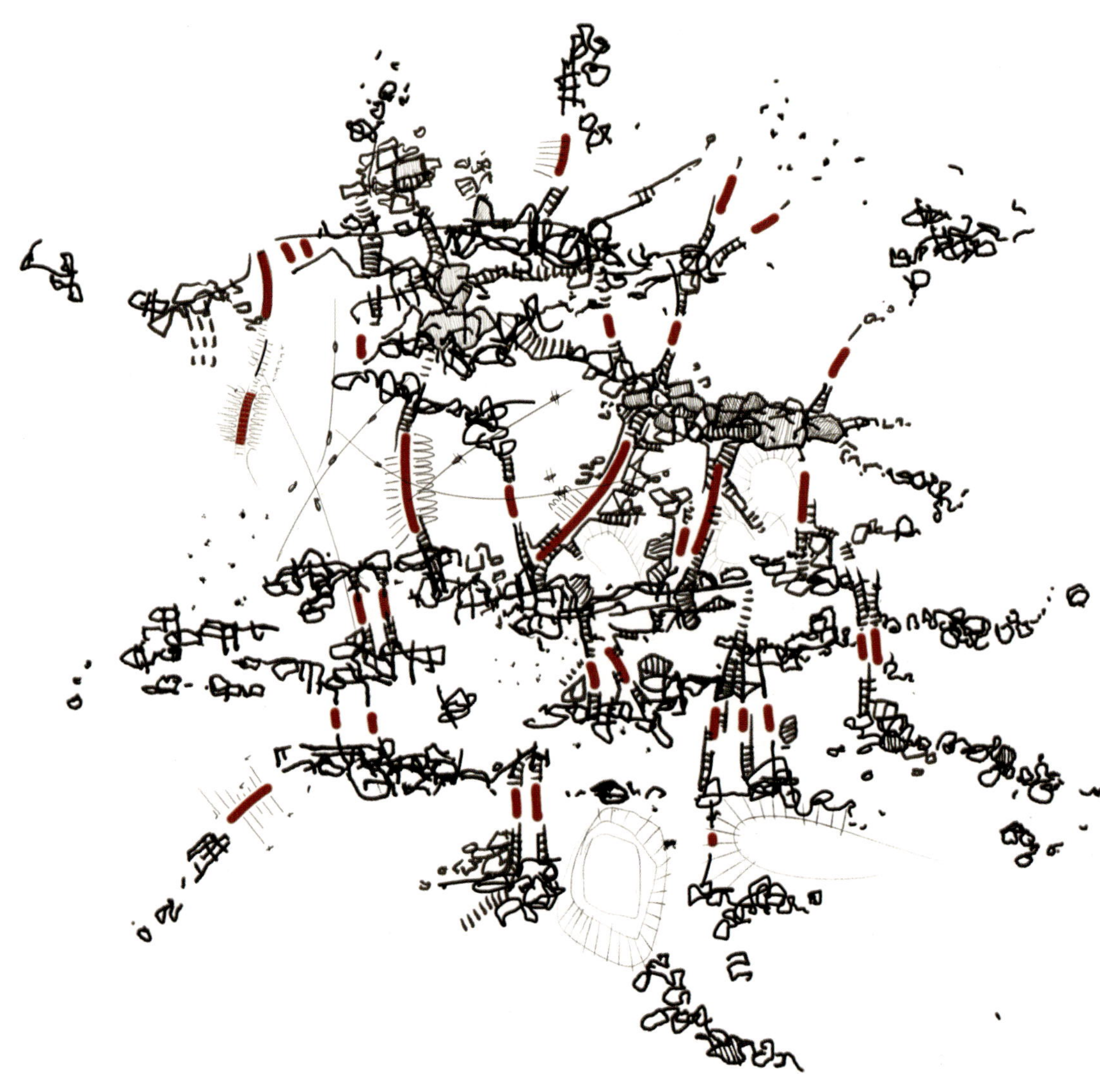

LANDING IN FINLAND

Landing in Helsinki, an infinite number of small islands come into appearance, comprising a landscape of disconnected points. In representing this landscape, there was the necessity and desire to connect some of these points. These two drawings are maps of an elaborate labyrinthine landscape, in which we try to decipher the best route to enter the city or to escape it.

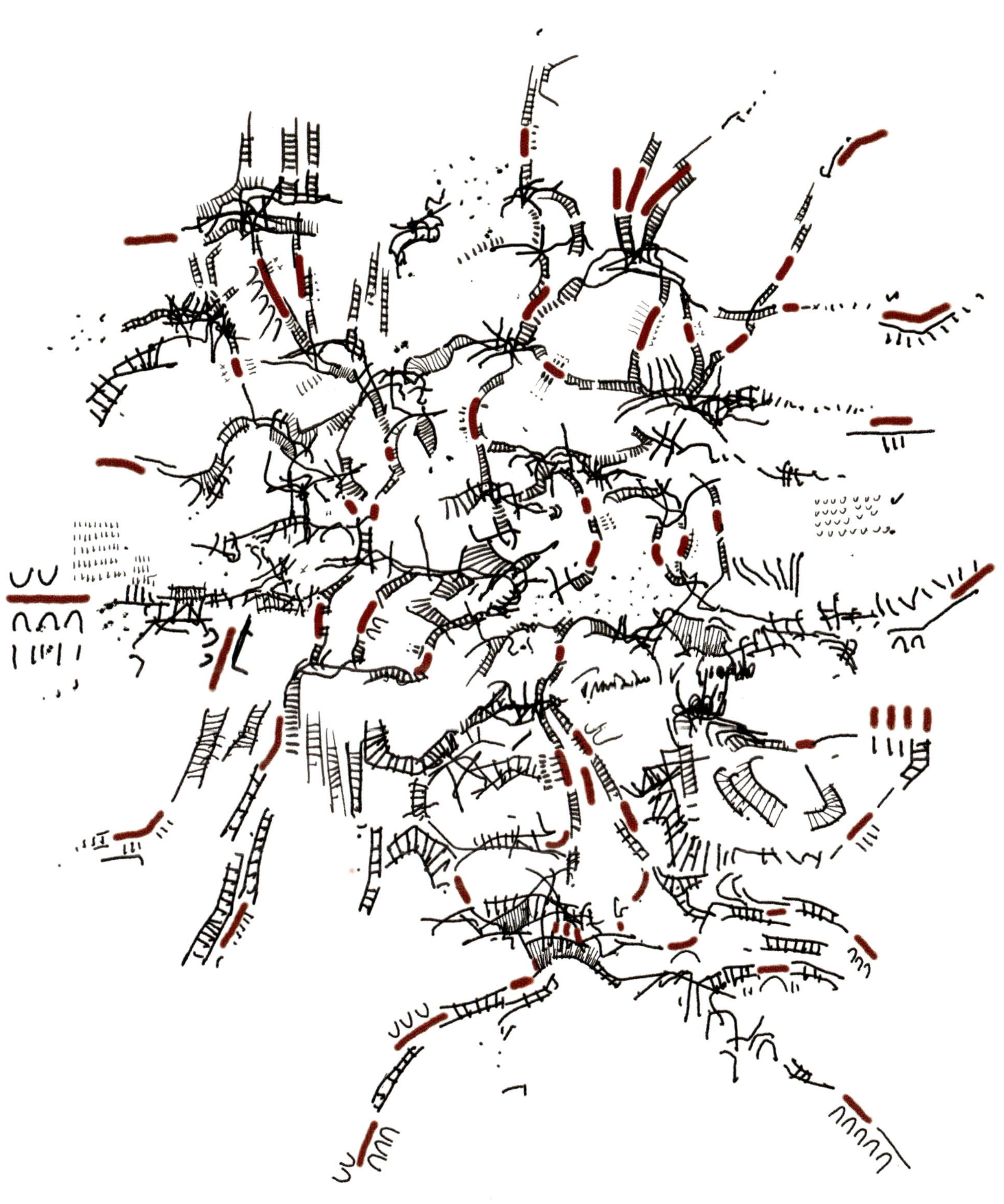

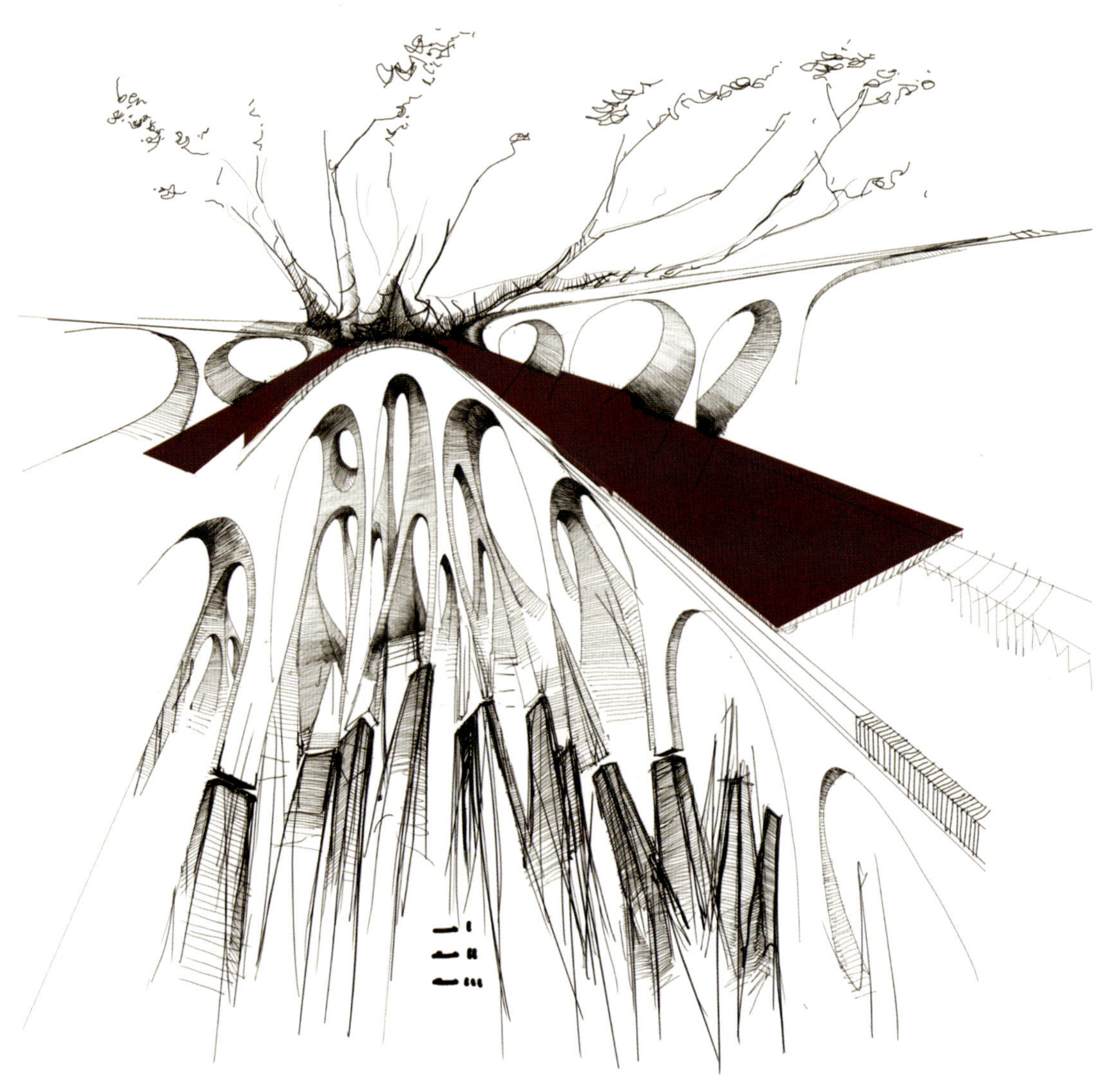

CHINESE BRIDGES

Sometimes it is complicated to understand from where a drawing comes, which traces and clues are hidden inside sketches and notes. Sometimes memories originating from paintings, stories, and drawings become confused and mixed with others based on real experiences. When it happens, it is much more difficult to relate them to a specific drawing. Therefore, it is difficult to place these two drawings in a precise moment or coming from accurate traces. I like to think that the one called "old traditional Chinese bridge" came from studying and seeing many traditional Chinese landscape paintings. To look at these paintings is an exercise in perceiving space escaping from the perspective of a Renaissance lord. Different points of view play a game of landscape in

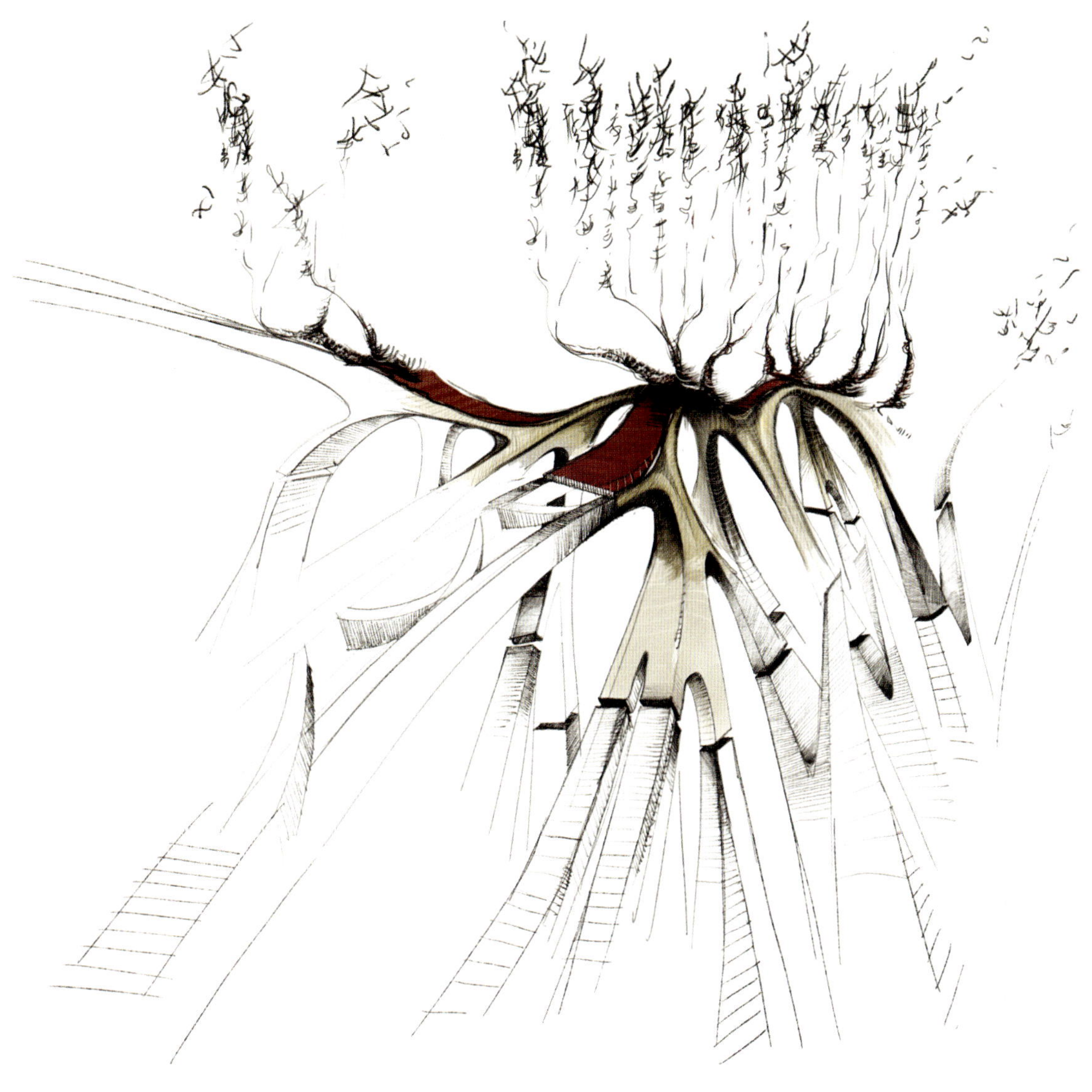

which numeric scale is not essential. The absence, produced by white void spaces, is the leading guide of the entire scene. The representation of monumental and common trees emphasizes the nature of rock, water, and sky. The presence of small artificial elements, pavilions, pergolas, and bridges establish important landmarks like points on a map. Starting from these elements, these two drawings decide to use "traditional" Chinese bridges. They approach an idea of landscape in which bridges shape a city's spaces and let vegetation cross over them.

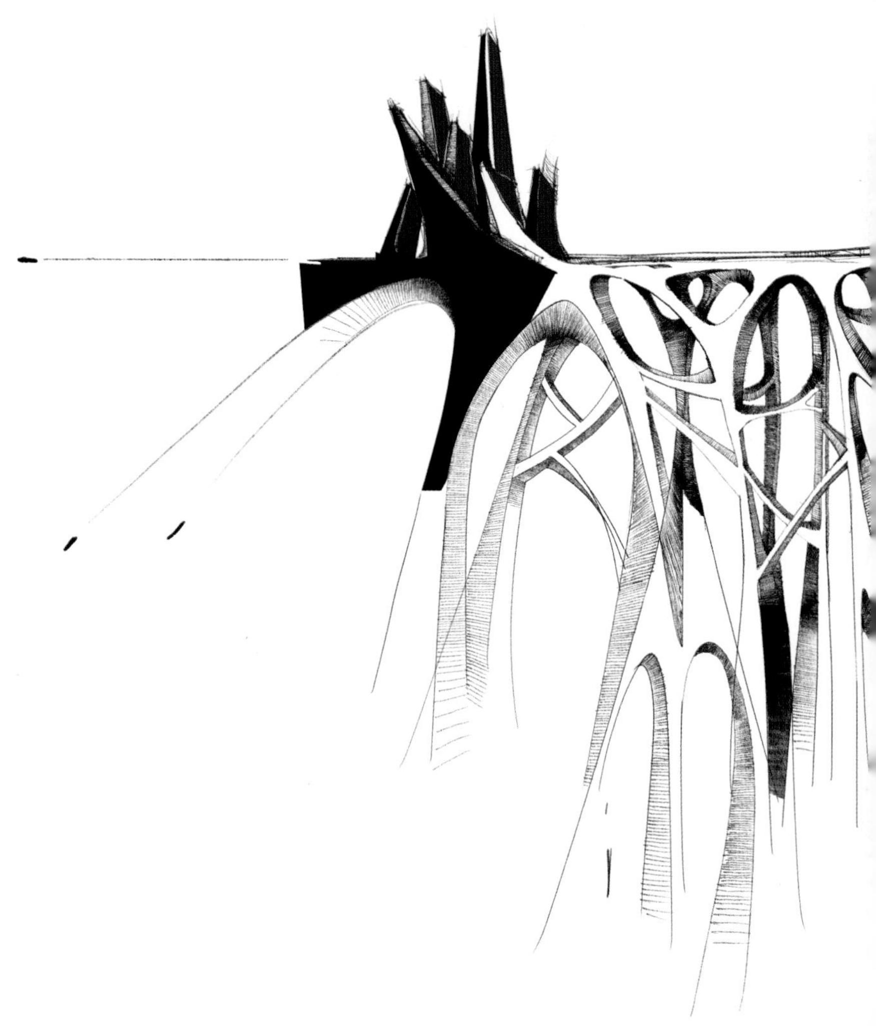

BRIDGES OF NEWCASTLE

These drawings were made before a lecture at the Newcastle University School of Architecture, Planning, and Landscape. Sometimes it happens that drawings come before visiting a city, and they are visualizations of unreal memories about these places. Knowing Newcastle as a city of bridges, the drawings imagined a city in which the bridges were more significant than the urban structure. Buildings appear small and marginalized by the shape of bridges. The drawings were further developed after visiting the City of Ljubljana, where Jože Plečnik built a typical example of landscape bridges. He divided one big bridge into three different lines. On one side of the river, the lines are connected and form a unique space, and on the other side, the three lines touch the riverside at distinct points and shape three different spaces. Aquatic vegetation has entered the voids between these three lines becoming an integral part of the bridge.

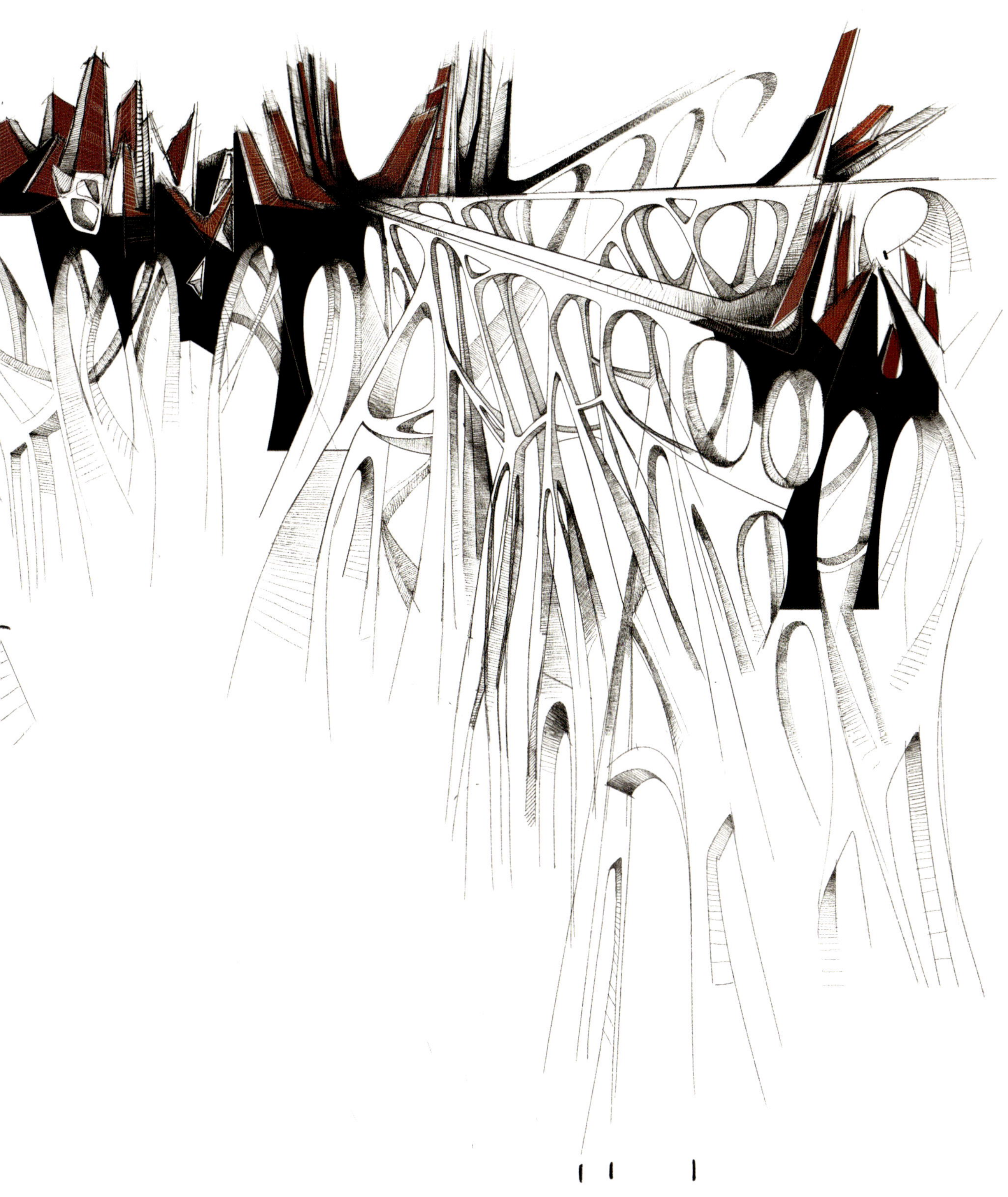

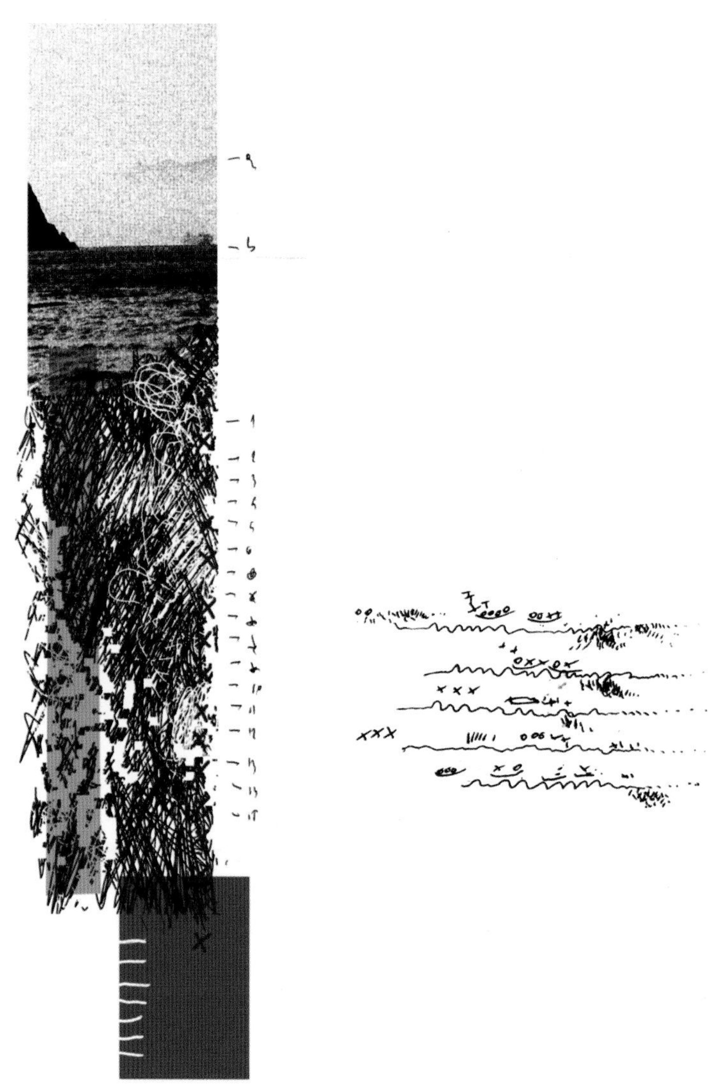

BETWEEN REGGIO CALABRIA AND MESSINA

This is a place of many legends. From here, Homer passed and challenged the ire of Scylla and Charybdis, the two monsters defending this strait. In reality, this place is the conjunction of two seas, the Tyrrhenian Sea and the Ionian Sea. Having different temperatures and levels, when they touch each other, they create currents

and vortices. In the past, these turbulent waters made navigation difficult. Nowadays, this place is painted by a multitude of boats and ships tracing ephemeral lines and trajectories on the surface of the sea. From them, we can trace maps in hopes of reaching faraway and unknown places.

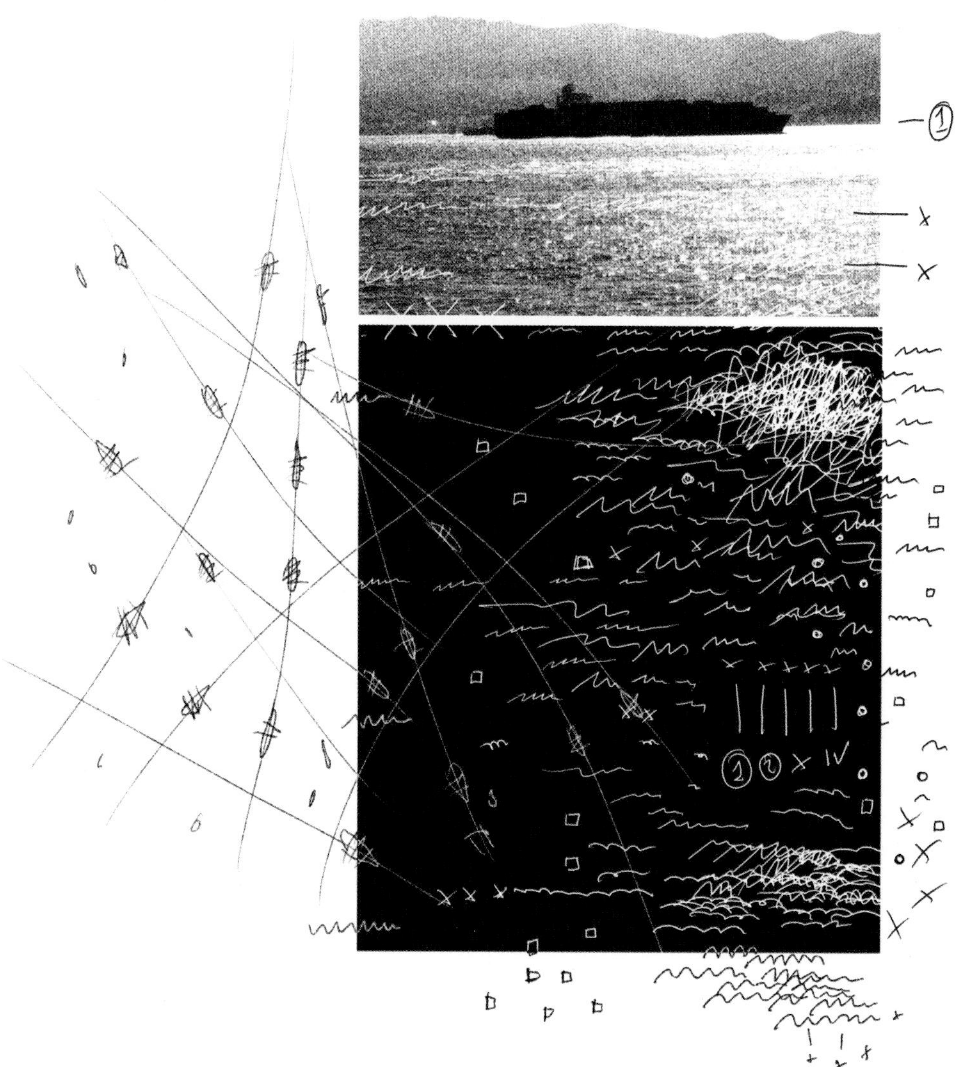

THE DEEP-SEA BETWEEN REGGIO CALABRIA AND MESSINA

Among the many stories regarding this place, there is the "Fata Morgana legend." Fata Morgana is the Italian name for "Morgan the Fairy," sister of the legendary King Arthur. She had, among other talents, the ability to create complex mirages. One of them was about the Strait of Messina. According to the legend, Fata Morgana produced a mirage in which Messina appeared very close to Calabria. In the past, the optical illusion induced many people to try and swim from Messina to Calabria; as a consequence, they died. This drawing attempts to

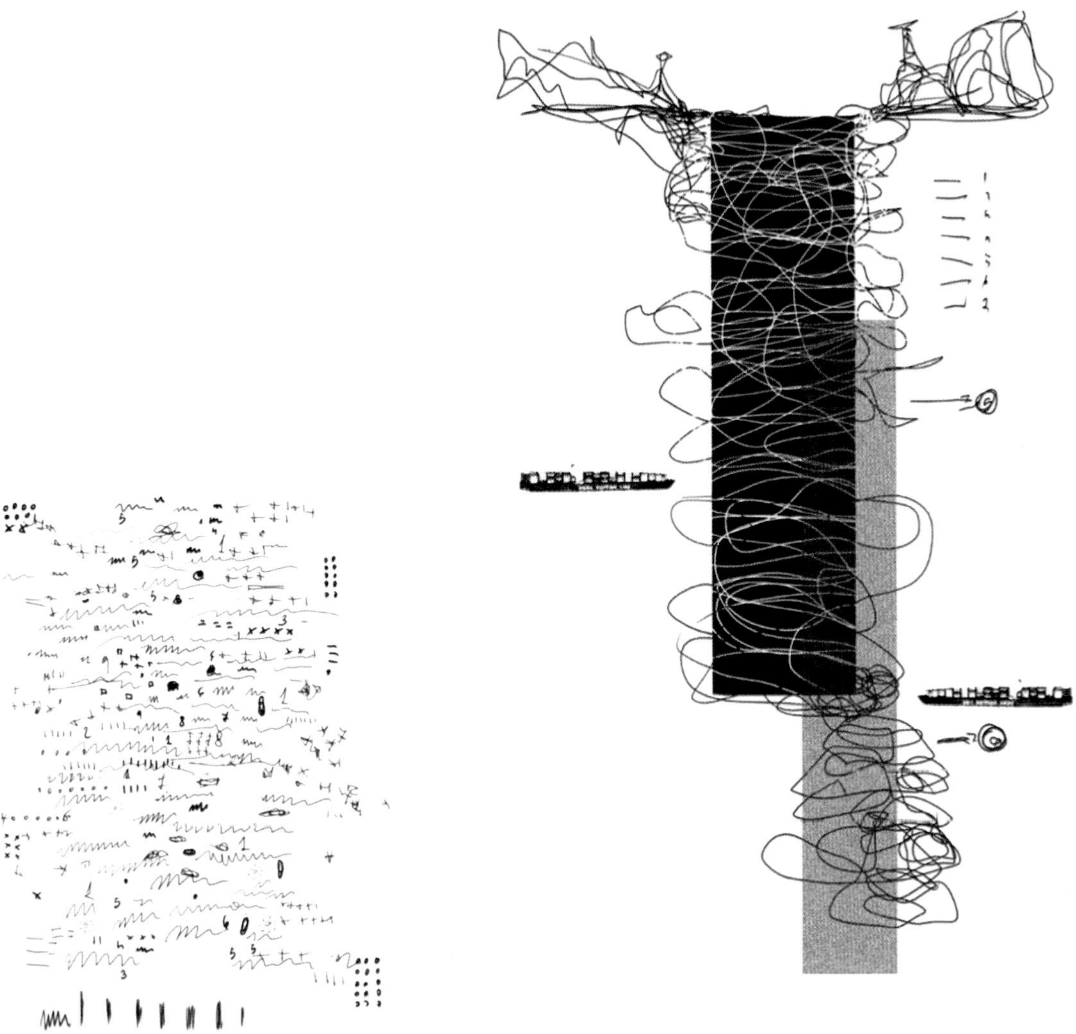

create an optical illusion using the depth of the sea that changes the paradigm of mirage. In fact, despite the three kilometers that separate Calabria and Sicily, the sea is only 500 meters deep. By drawing the sea much more profound than it is in reality, the drawings produce an illusion of perception. The distance between Calabria and Sicily seems small.

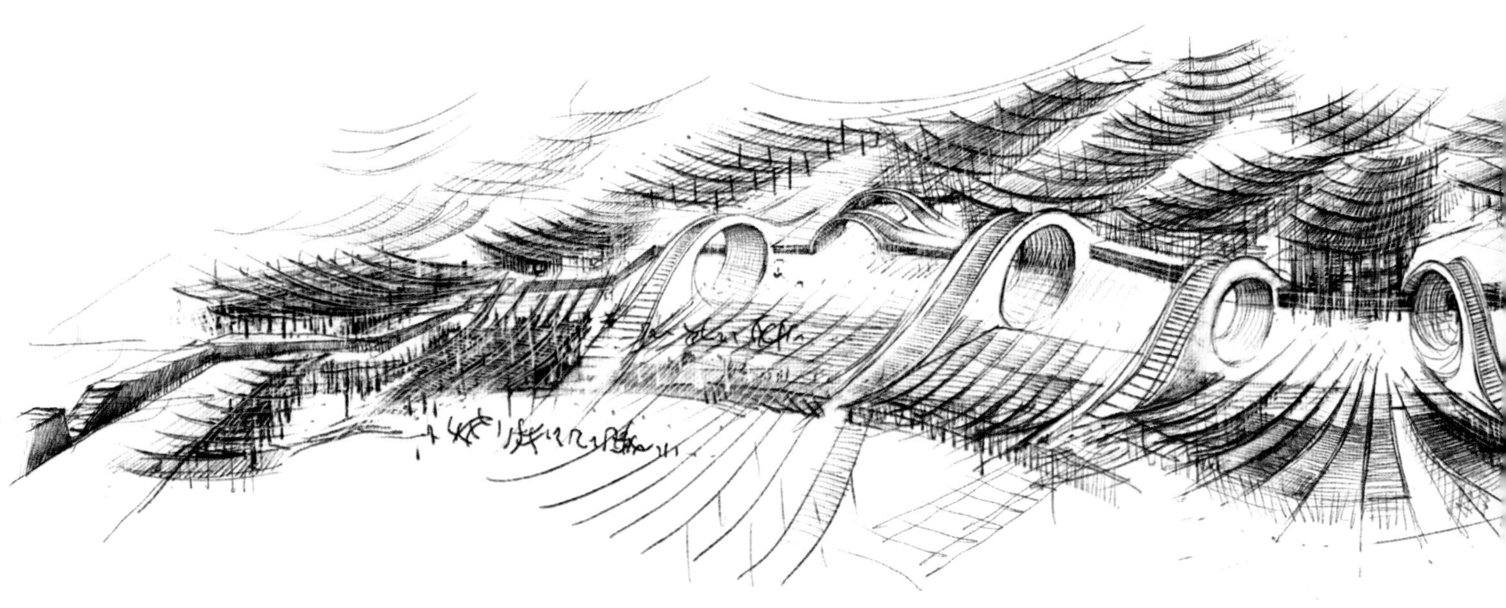

TRADITIONAL CHINESE WATER TOWN

To visit a traditional Chinese water town is one of the most impressive experiences that someone can have. When inside one of these towns, we perceive an ideal space made by two different real elements: one is the water able to go to and from everywhere, the other is the structure of the city trying to follow the water's flow. Without weight, the city can fly on the water's surface, wandering and exploring unusual geometries.

I looked for something to explain the idea of these towns, and it became evident that the bridges are capable of revealing this secret. Sewing the two elements together, they are anchor points to connect and fix a precise balance between the water's desires and the town's structure; they become the reason the city does not move on the surface of the water.

CITY OF ORNAMENT

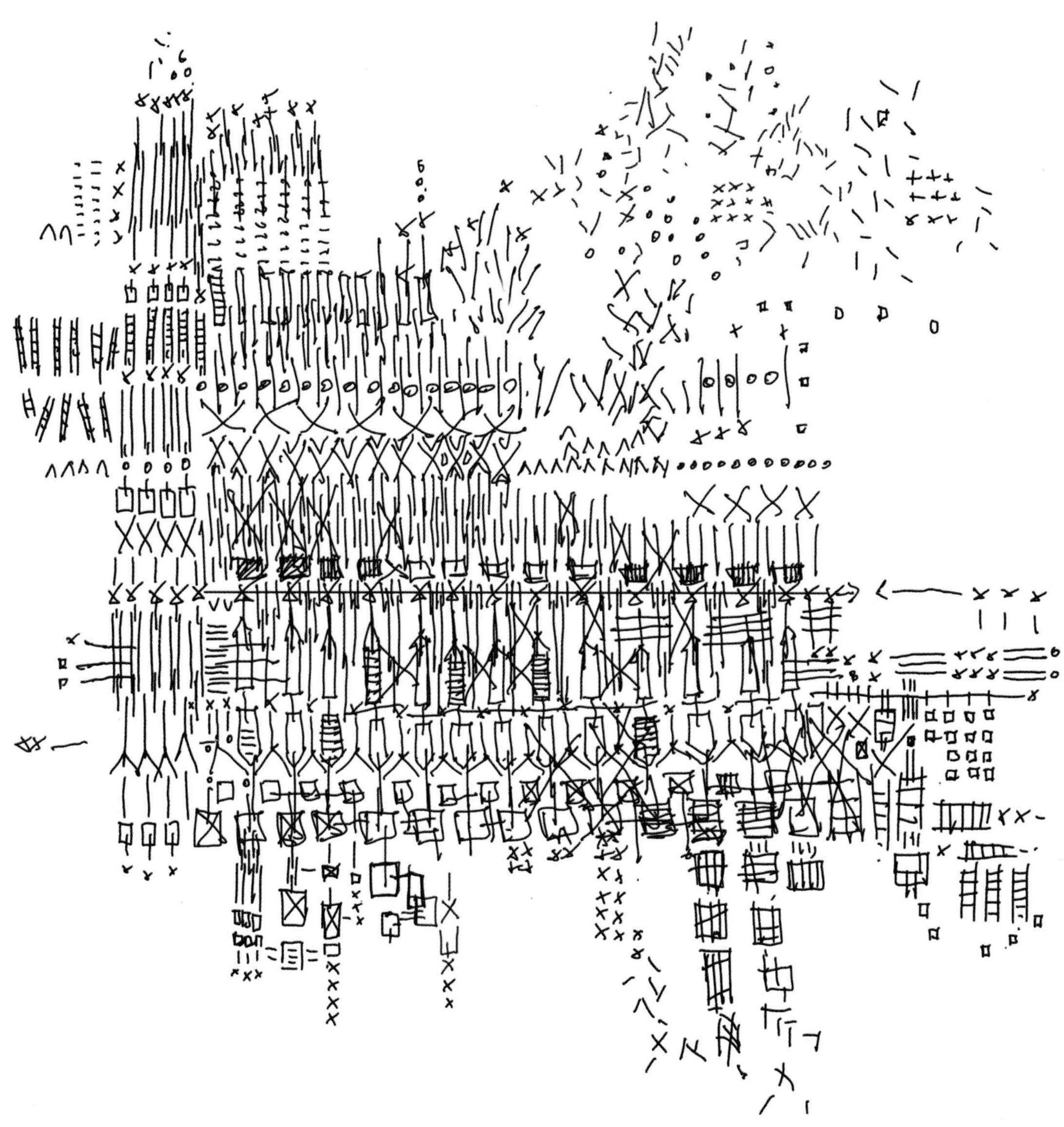

SIDI BOU SAID

Many years ago, while visiting the city of Sidi Bou Said, near Carthage in Tunisia, I bought the book *The Journey to Tunisia*. The book is a collection of many drawings and paintings Paul Klee made during his journey around the country. They are the beginning of his artistic inspiration, in which the combination of many abstract lines with real objects reaches sublime poetry. Stains of colors are disposed on canvas and paper using a geometry that pretends to be precise, but the geometry is full of errors, and colors are allowed to expand over neighbor-

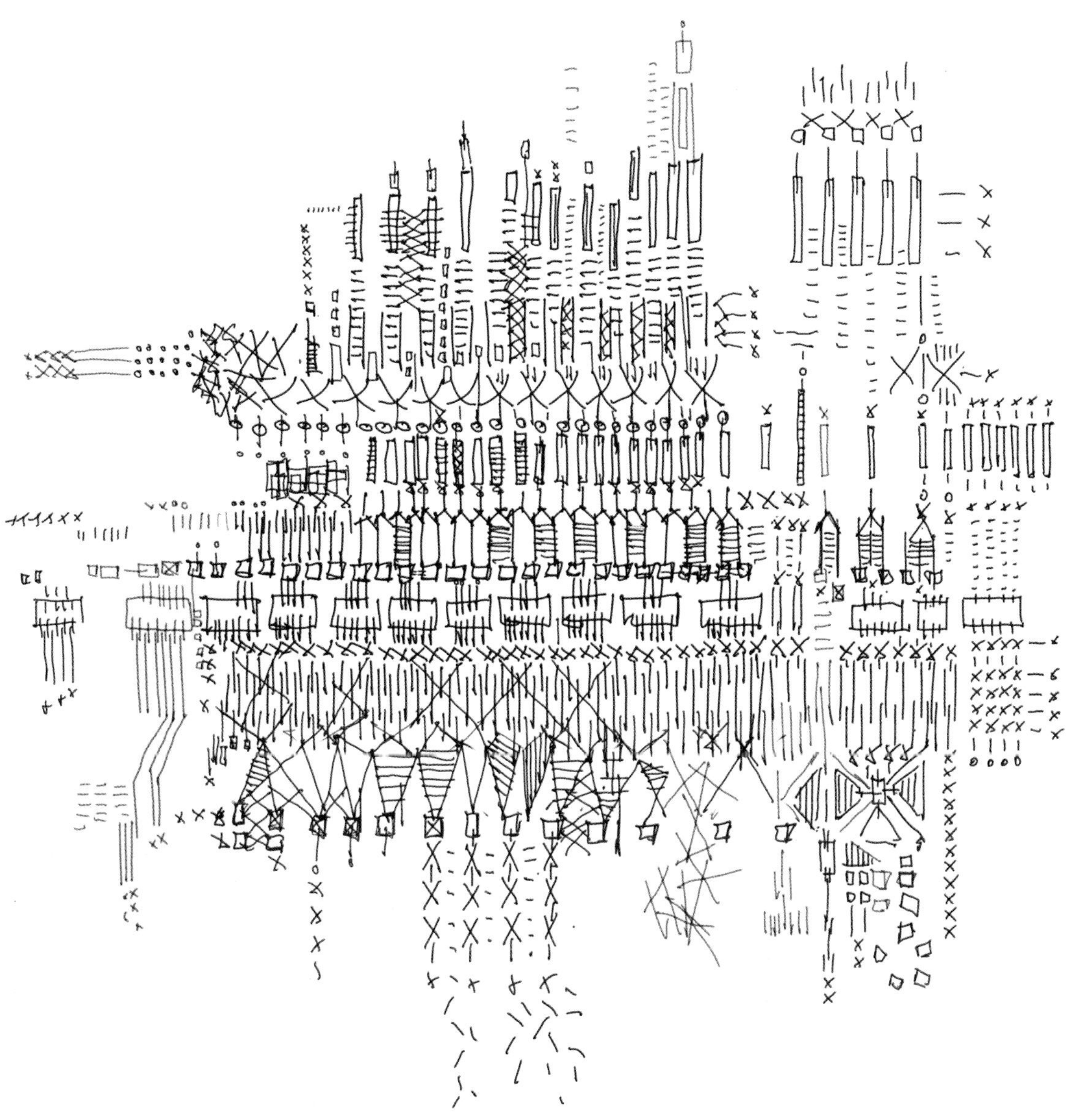

ing ones, blurring. If we see them very close, it is possible to recognize every single color; however, if we stay far from them, the colors are no longer unique elements but are part of a unique integral composition. In this case, the exactitude of representation is a particular poetic condition; errors are accepted and used skillfully. These two drawings are memories from Sidi Bou Said and a tribute to Paul Klee.

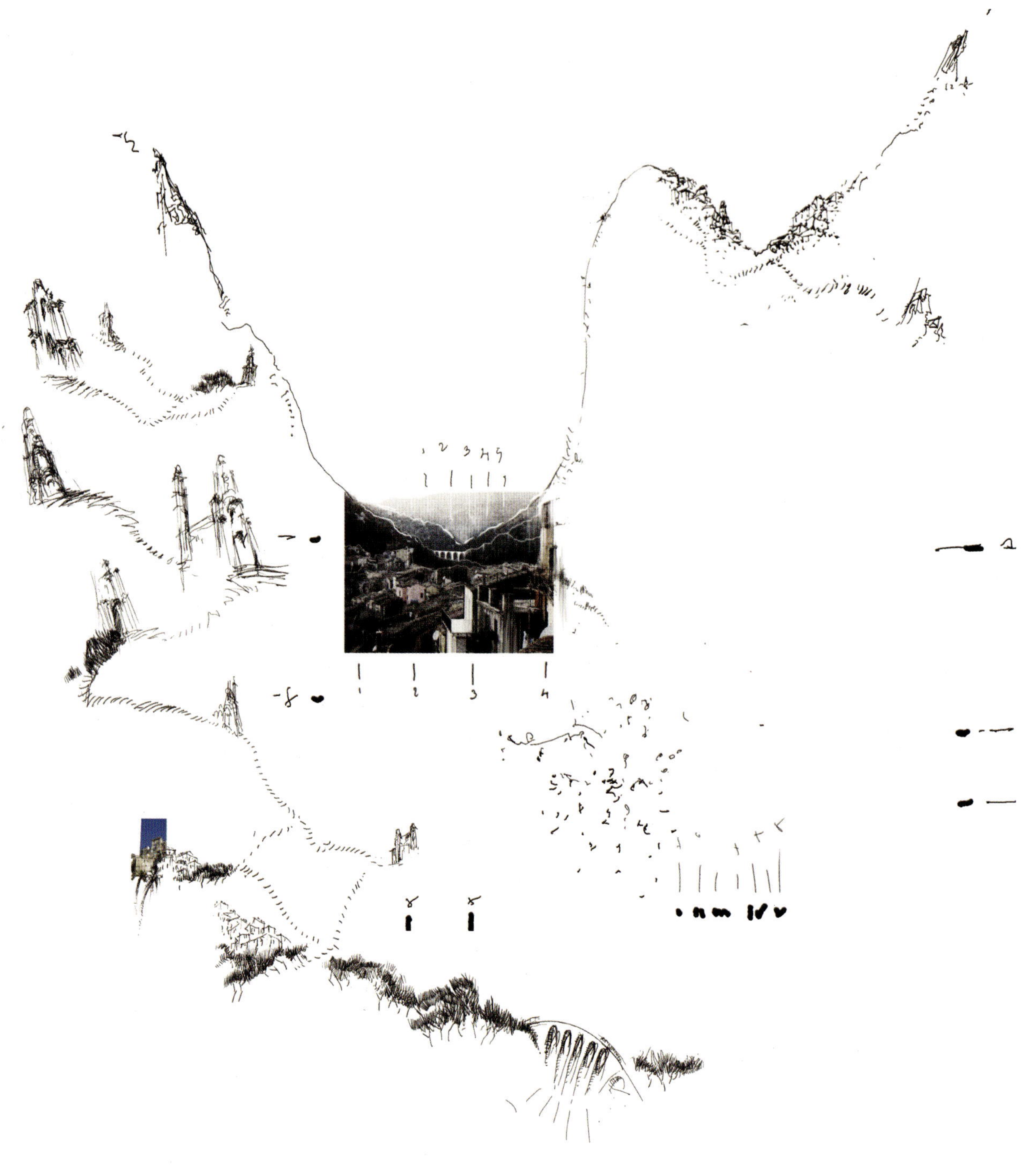

RAGUSA'S VALLEY

The city of Ragusa has two distinct areas, the lower and older town of Ragusa Ibla and the higher Ragusa Superiore (Upper Town). The Valle dei Ponti separates the two halves, a deep ravine crossed by four bridges. The most noteworthy bridge is the eighteenth-century Ponte dei Cappuccini.

ORNAMENT IN RAGUSA

The drawing presented here is a combination of sketches made while standing in front of several real scenes. One was made from the upper level of the Philadelphia Museum of Art's grand exterior staircase. It was done while looking at the Benjamin Franklin Parkway and having in mind the scene from the *Rocky* movies. The parkway's trees were bigger than those I remembered in the film's famous scene when Rocky rejoices on top of the stairs, and a series of new towers had modified the city's skyline.

The other sketches were made in Ragusa. They are of the churches of San Filippo Neri, San Giovanni Battista, Anime del Purgatorio, and San Giorgio, along with the Palazzo della Cancelleria. By adding black spaces to create links between the sketches and a unique story, it became a multi-perspective view of Ragusa, showing the impressive storytelling of its ornament.

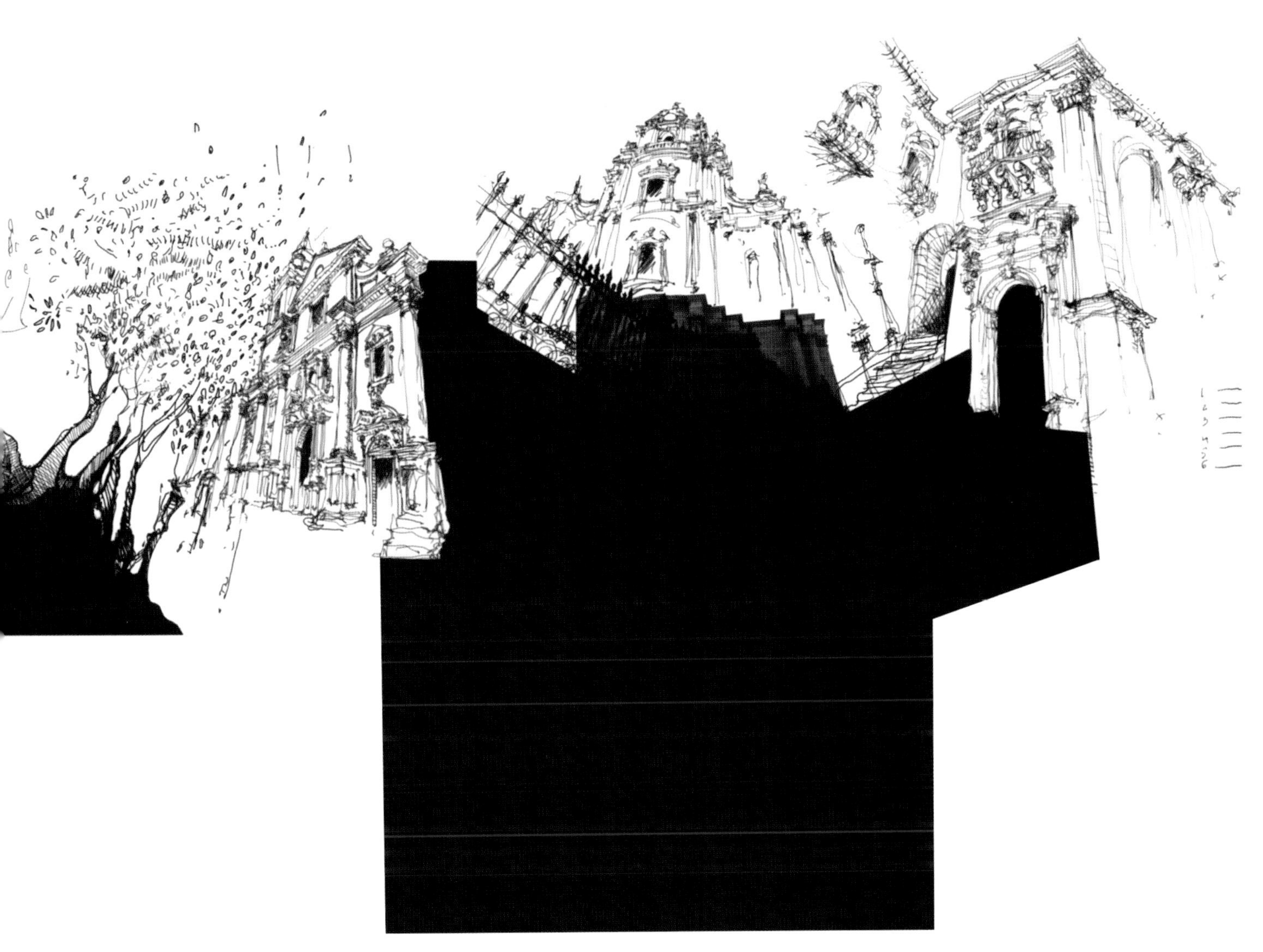

THE CONTRADICTION OF VOIDS IN PRAGUE

Prague is a city that seems to confuse and amalgamate the boundaries between interior and exterior voids. Inside a Gothic cathedral, space widens and lengthens almost without end. At the moment when its borders seem perceptible, we find ourselves, inexplicably, projected outwards. Walking through Prague, its squares, courtyards, and streets appear as a continuous repetition of external voids without interruption; deprived of

a usual perception of space, we find ourselves in one of the countless empty spaces of Prague's cathedrals. Deciding to abandon the ground and climb up a tower toward the space of the sky, we are eventually forced to look down and see voids in the roofs. Prague's condition of the interior and exterior voids dematerializes perception. It is for this reason that Prague has to be described using its ornaments.

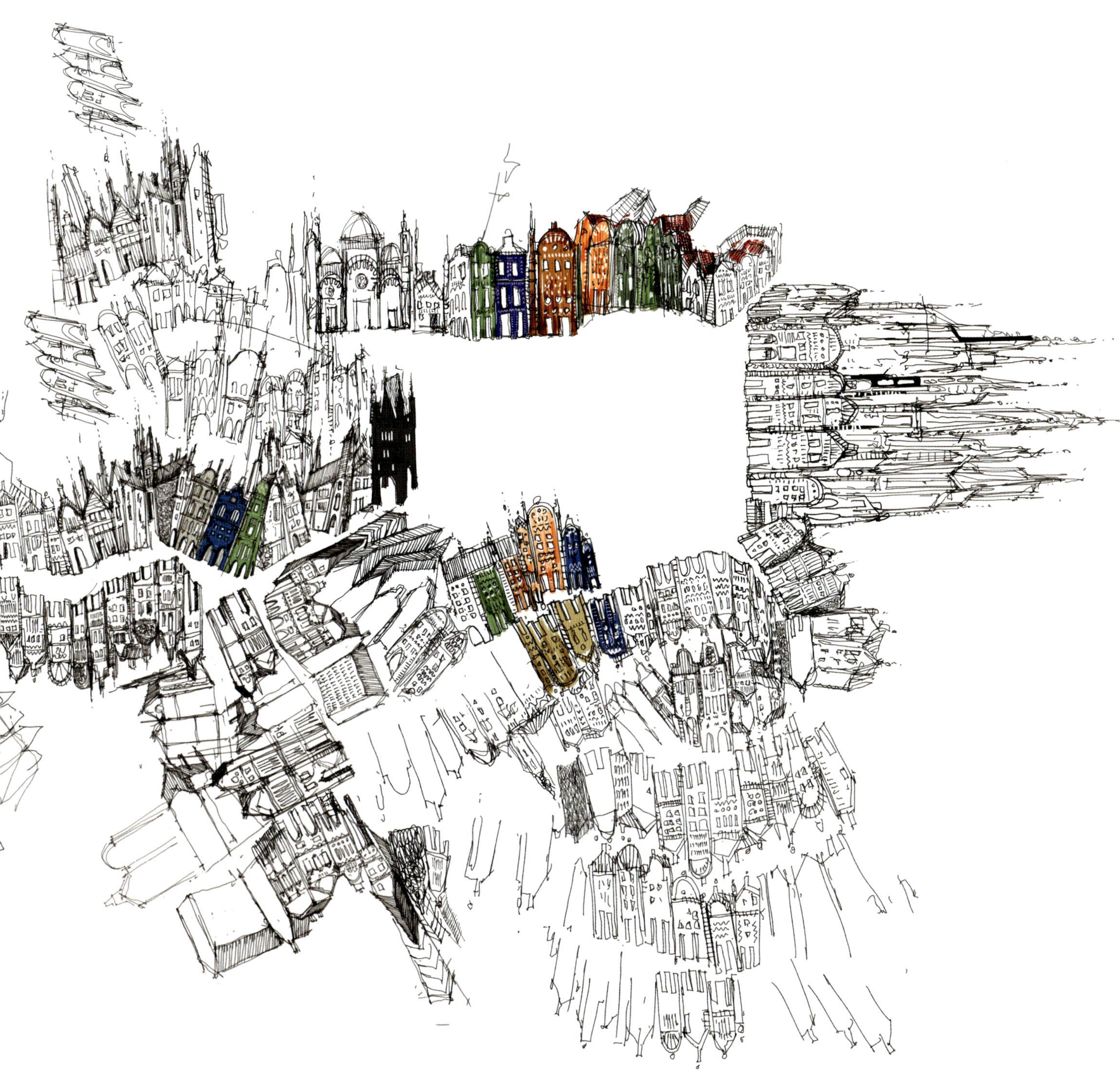

PLANNING THE ORNAMENT

Prague is a city of ornaments. Strolling by them, they appear as an endless array of secret combinations of lines and shapes. If we do not spend time to decode them and leave them climbing on the buildings' surfaces, we can perceive their efforts to escape into the sky. After a while, like cleaned wax tablets, the buildings' facades are ready to be engraved again by new codes. Prague absorbs all of them, more and more.

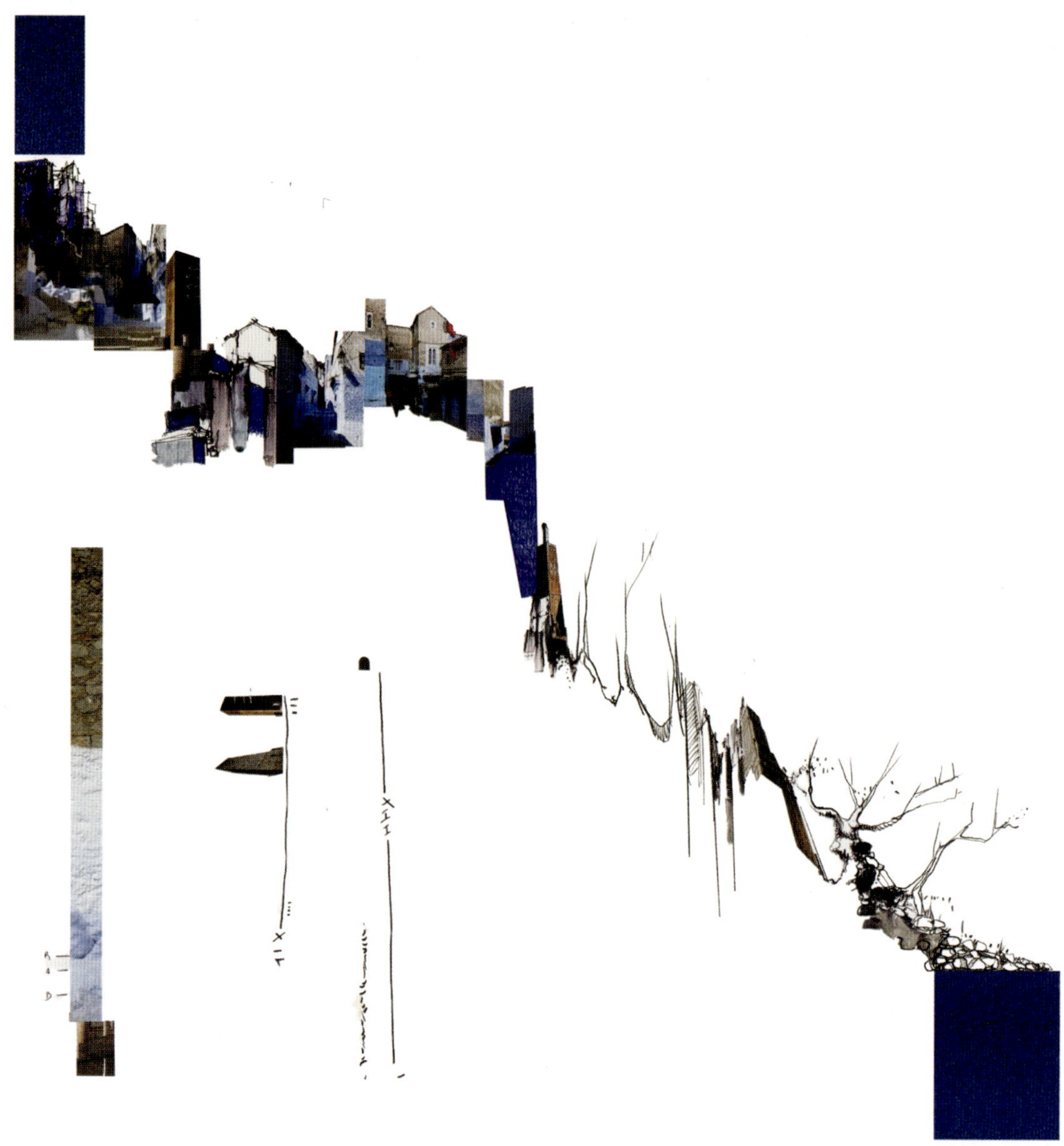

MEMORY OF CHEFCHAOUEN

Chefchaouen, also known as Chaouen, is a city in the northwest of Morocco. The town climbs along a hill, with a series of compacted tiny spaces that follow one another uninterrupted. A few trees and vines fight to conquer a living space between the narrow streets painted blue. My memory is represented according to a section that climbs the hill of Chefchaouen; along with it, objects are arranged according to a logic of continuous landscape in which space and time balance each other.

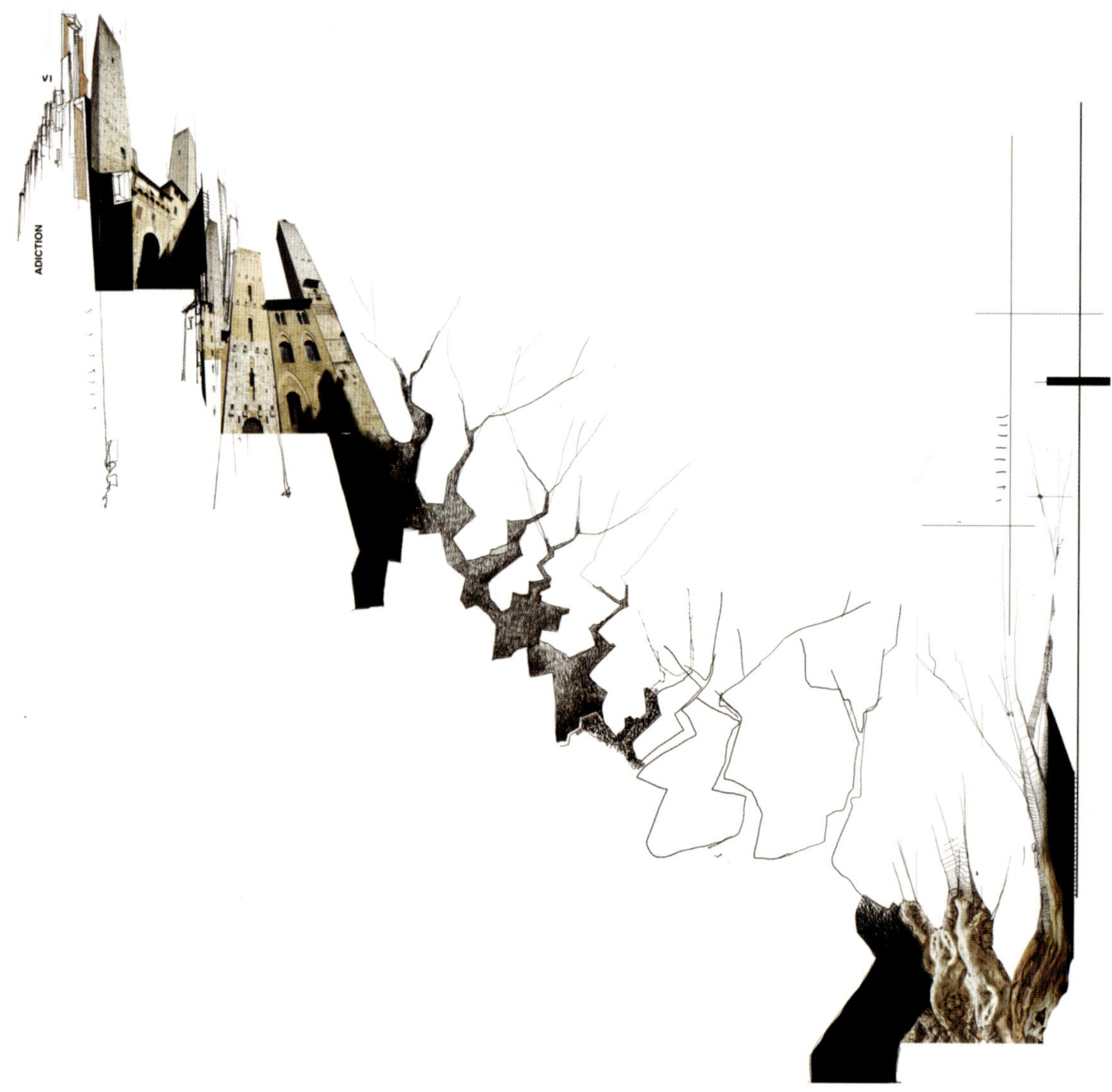

MEMORY OF SAN GIMIGNANO

San Gimignano is a small medieval hill town in the province of Siena, Tuscany, in north-central Italy. Known as the Town of Fine Towers, San Gimignano is famous for its medieval architecture and its particular skyline. These drawings are a strong relationship between the city and its surrounding agriculture. Starting from a scheme made by a ruler measuring the precision of agriculture connected with trees, the drawings are completed with the idea that memory is going up without weight.

CONTAMINATION
5

MEMORY OF BONIFACIO

Bonifacio is a city at the southern tip of the island of Corsica in the Corse-du-Sud department of France. Bonifacio is located directly on the Mediterranean Sea, separated from Sardinia by the Strait of Bonifacio. The city and its fortifications extend along the top of a cliff, about 70 meters above the sea level. There is a particular monument in Bonifacio, the Staircase of the King of Aragon, which is carved into the side of the limestone cliff.

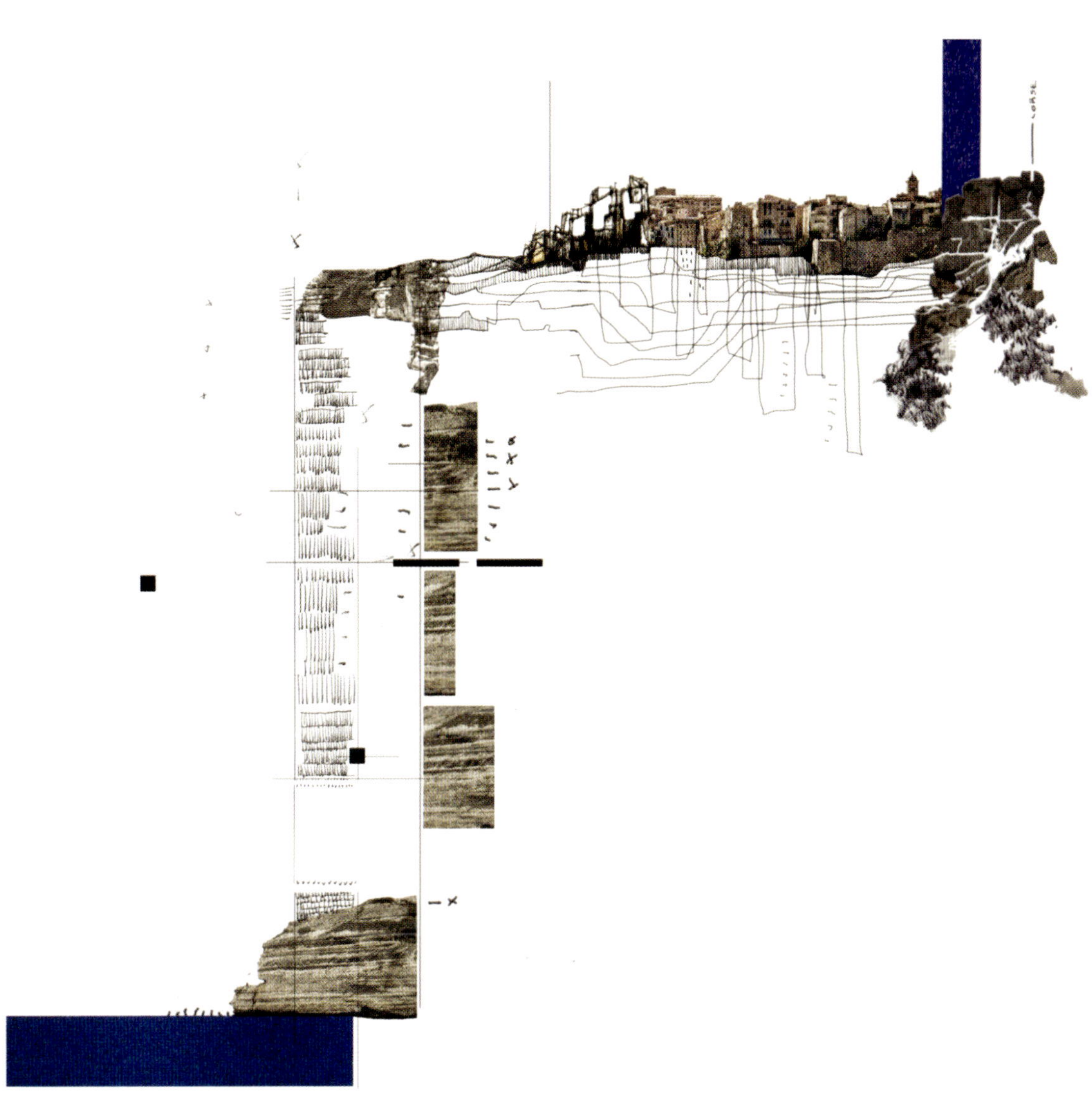

According to legend, the staircase was dug in 1420 by the troops of the King of Aragon Alfonso V in the course of a single night during the unsuccessful siege of Bonifacio. In reality, the staircase descends to a natural spring in a cave, and it is believed to have been dug by the Franciscan monks long before the troops of Alfonso V set their feet on Bonifacio. In these drawings, a ruler is added to the cliff to measure the city's relationship with its sea.

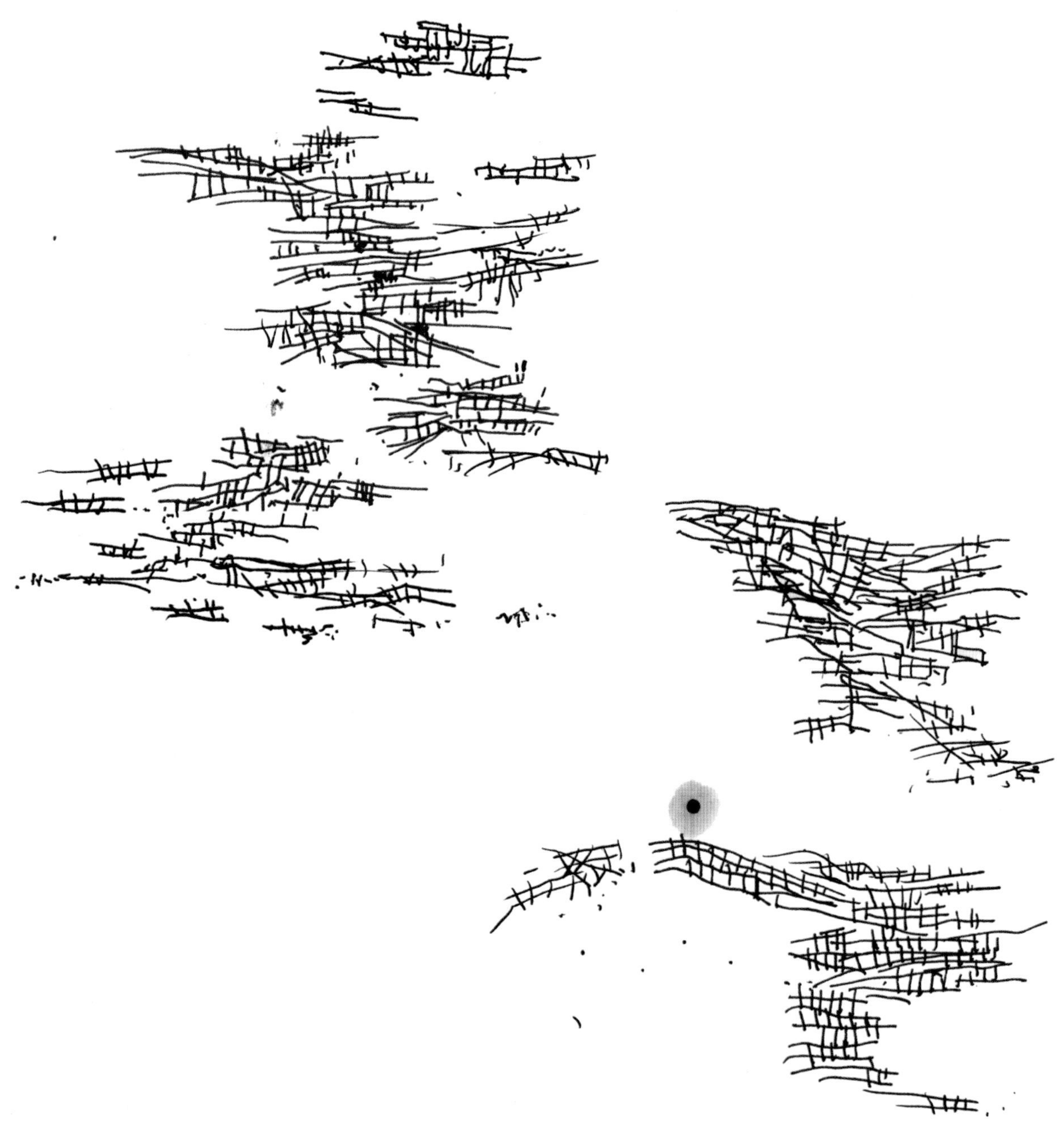

THE SOUND OF GREECE

The incredibly loud sound of crickets and cicadas overwhelms Greece during the summer. It is not music, it has no precise rhythm, but the sound produces a dense and continuous tonality. These drawings have attempted to break up this sound and write its abstract scores, from which it is possible to read the lightness of the Mediterranean coast. The sea, the hills, the islands, and the beaches are within the sound of Greece, closed and monotonous. But monotony often reveals wonderful memories.

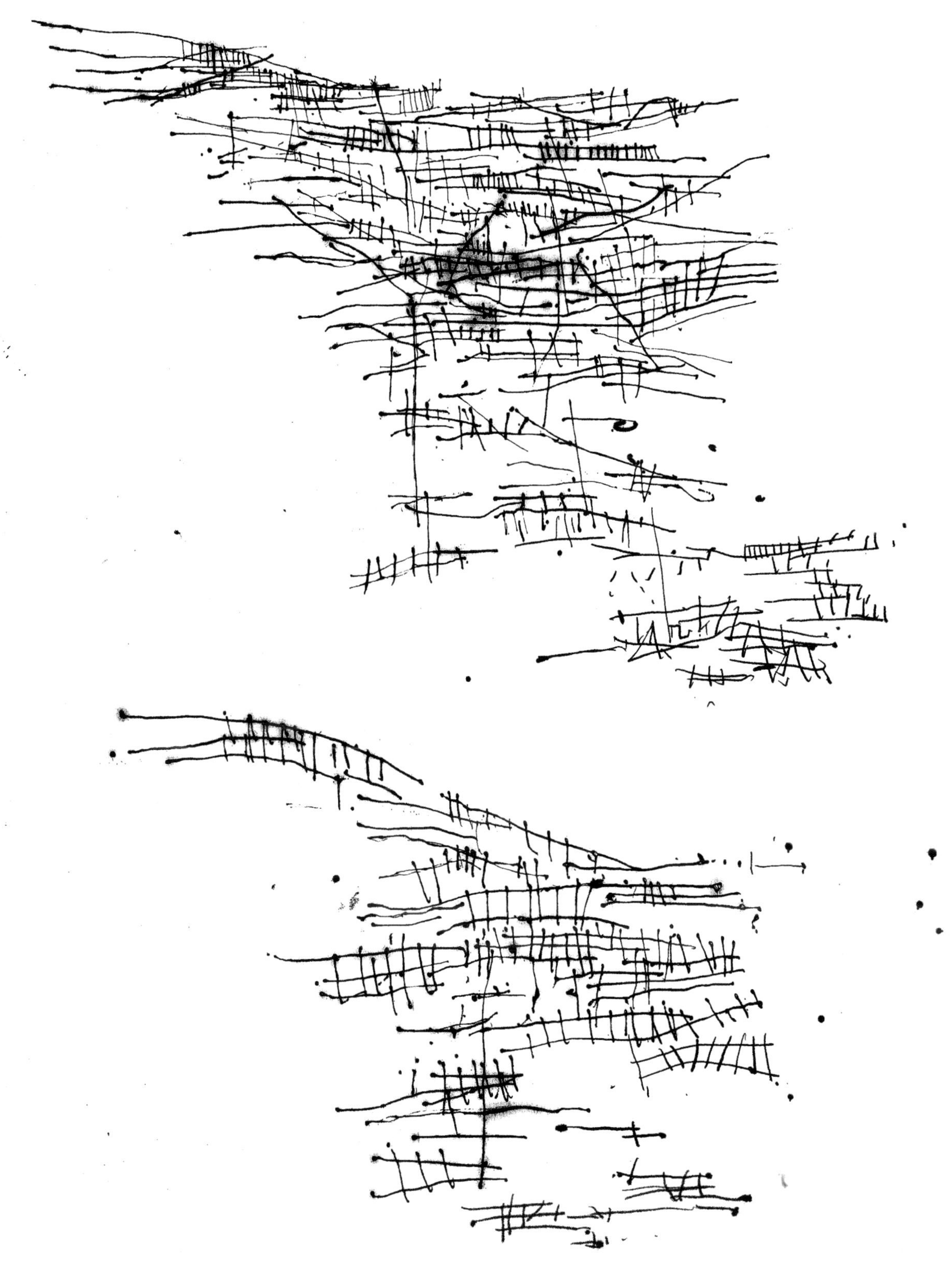

DANCING GREEK CITY

Visiting the new museum of ancient Greece in Athens, we can observe, among many things, beautiful objects used during the common Athenians' life. If we observe with attention and constancy some traditional black and brown vases and pots, we can understand that figures, ornaments, and objects represent scenes of dancing lightness.

CITY OF LANDSCAPE

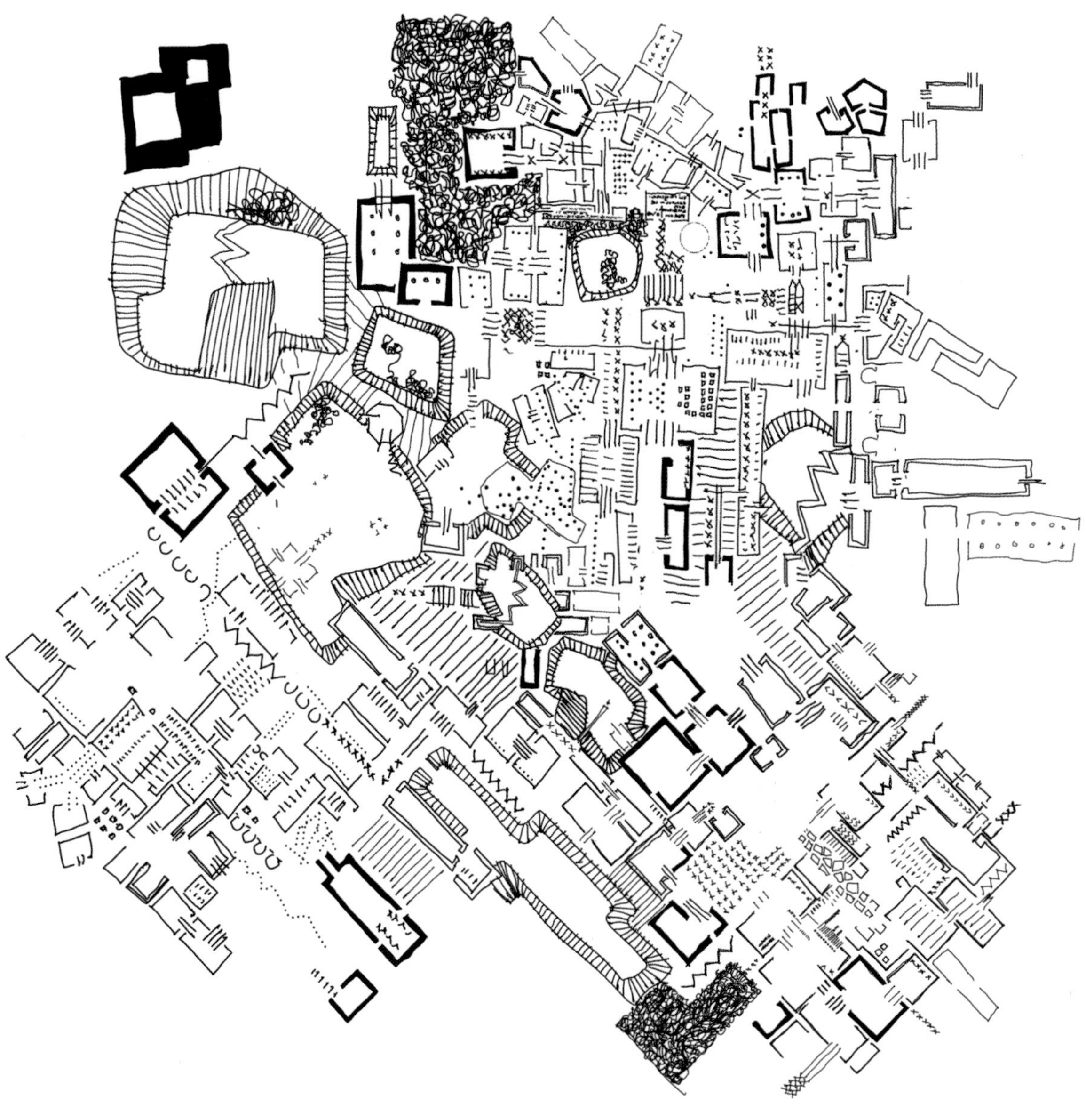

MAPPING TRADITIONAL CHINESE GARDENS

Traditional Chinese gardens are sources of endless imagination. Their space welcomes us with an incredible presence of objects and colors. Waiting for a moment to establish a discussion with them, they unfold and explain a series of secret codes to understand their very essence. The codes teach us how to deal with unexpected perspectives, dynamic compositions, repetitive layering, the loss of scale, false measures, precise ornaments, cut window frames, intelligent thresholds, oriented doors, paving with secret signs, surfaces of water,

and the succession of vegetation. Having established a personal notation to record this code, the drawings started with the act of mapping and placing all the symbols. From there, spaces followed each other and found perfect relationships, the separation between inside and outside disappearing to create a unique space. These drawings are archives; they are little pieces of memories collected from numerous traditional Chinese gardens. They are endless sources of inspiration when creativity has a lack of imagination.

INSIDE TRADITIONAL CHINESE GARDENS

I am not a thorough connoisseur of traditional Chinese painting. I cannot remember dynasties, periods, authors, nor even paintings. This puts me in a position of intellectual disadvantage every time I look at calligraphy, drawing, vase, painting, or ornament, and this disadvantage leads me to say that everything seems beautiful to me. But, when I see Guo Xi's painting *Old Trees, Level Distance* or *Early Spring,* I feel his innovative technique for producing multiple perspectives influences and becomes part of my imagination. He calls his perspective technique "the angle of totality"; others have defined it as a floating perspective. Trees, mountains, lights, voids, and other elements in his paintings help us to see ways to animate static renaissance representation. Inside a traditional Chinese garden, I can displace my eyes and see the landscape from a different imagination. This drawing is a tribute to Guo Xi without any intention to be a heroic undertaking, or to show a lack of respect for him; it is a simple exercise in loving beauty.

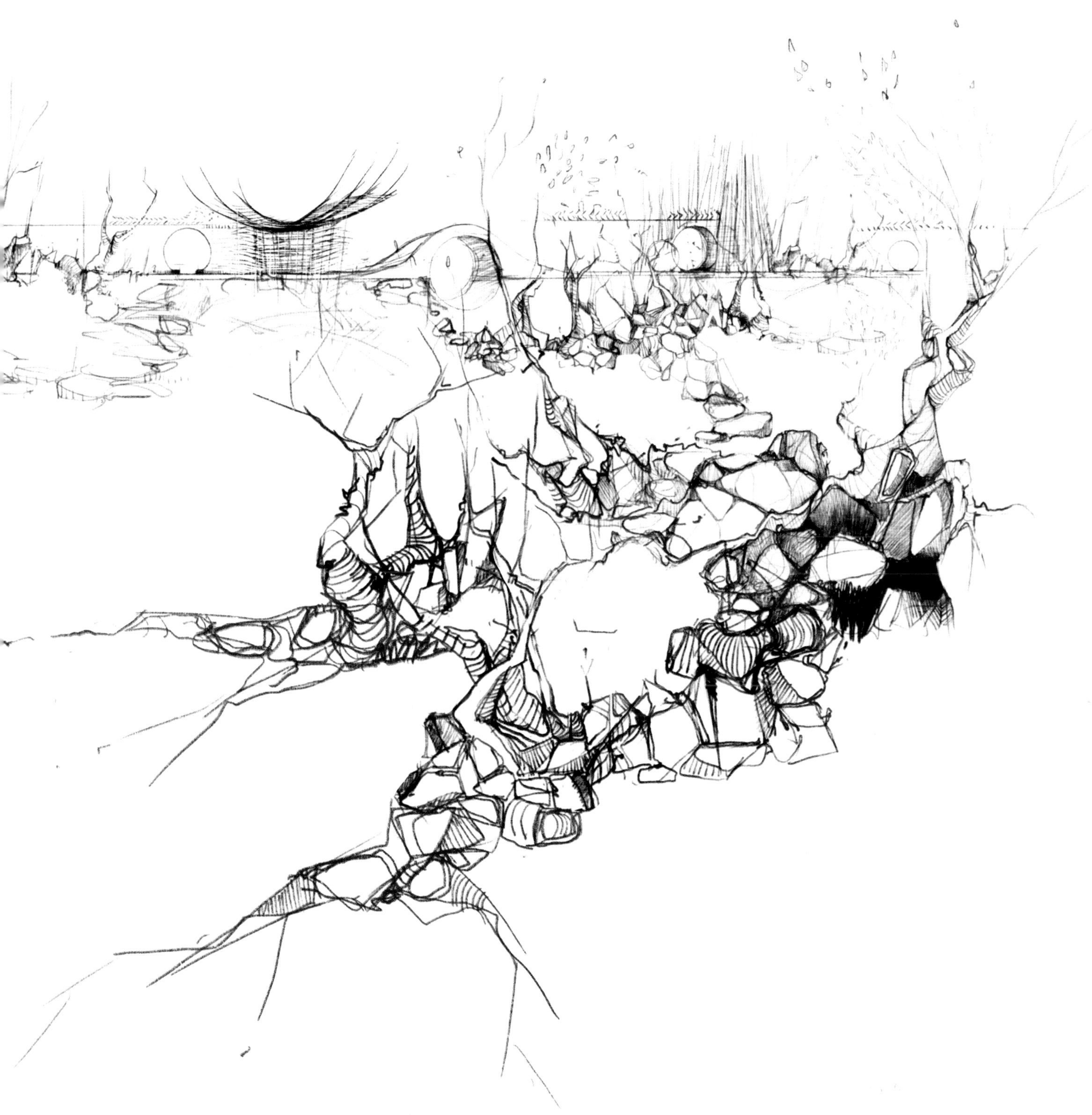

CHINESE DRAGONS WALKING ALONG A BRIDGE–CHINESE DRAGONS DISCUSSING ON ROCKS

Visiting China for the first time, I was particularly impressed by the tradition of its dragons. I started drawing them everywhere, on the pages of Chinese newspapers, on restaurant handkerchiefs, on my iPad, on every possible surface. They don't correctly follow the dragons of the Chinese tradition. They are free interpretations of my particular idea of China. In my drawings, they are the expression of a culture imbued with ornament.

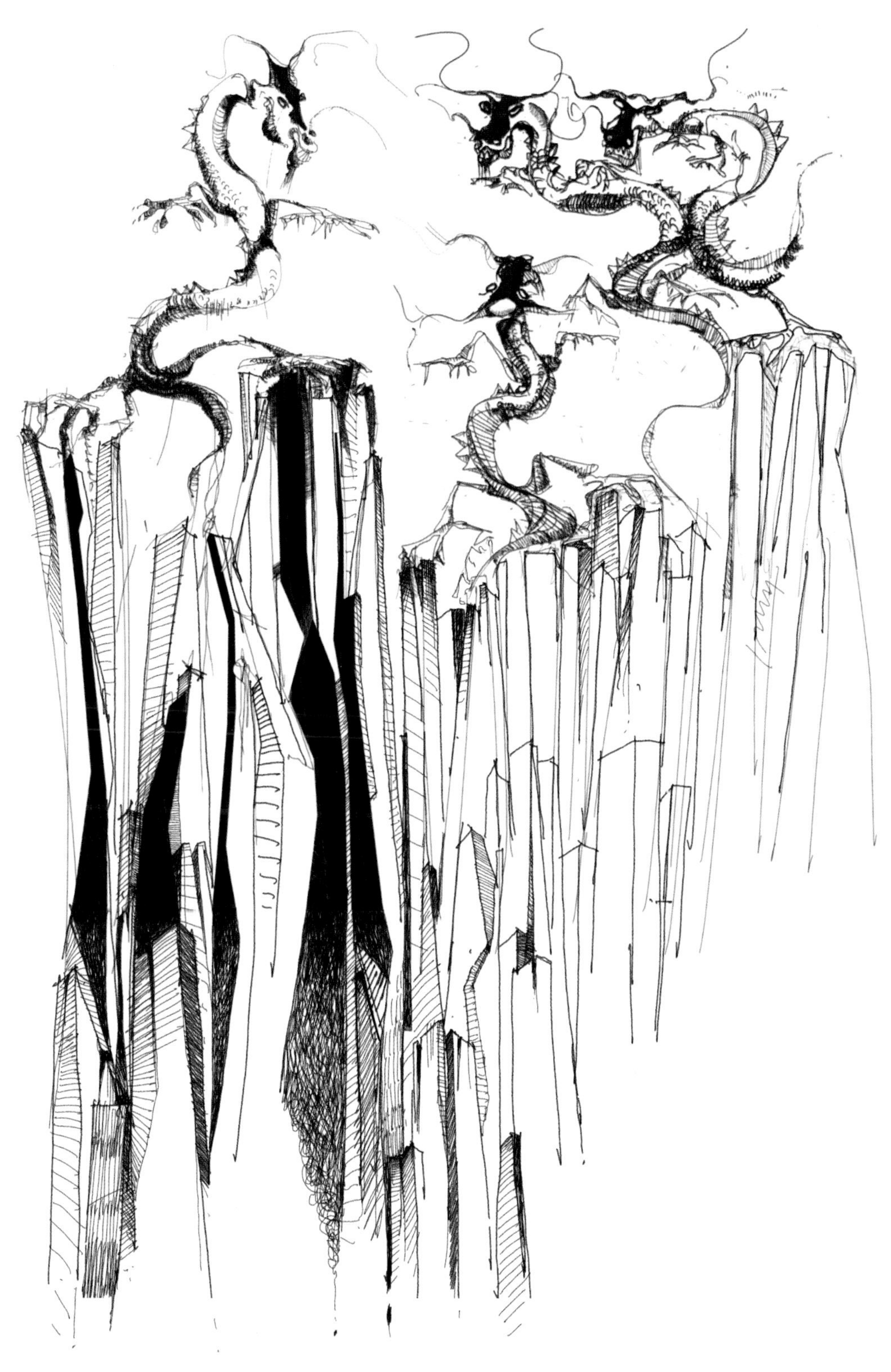

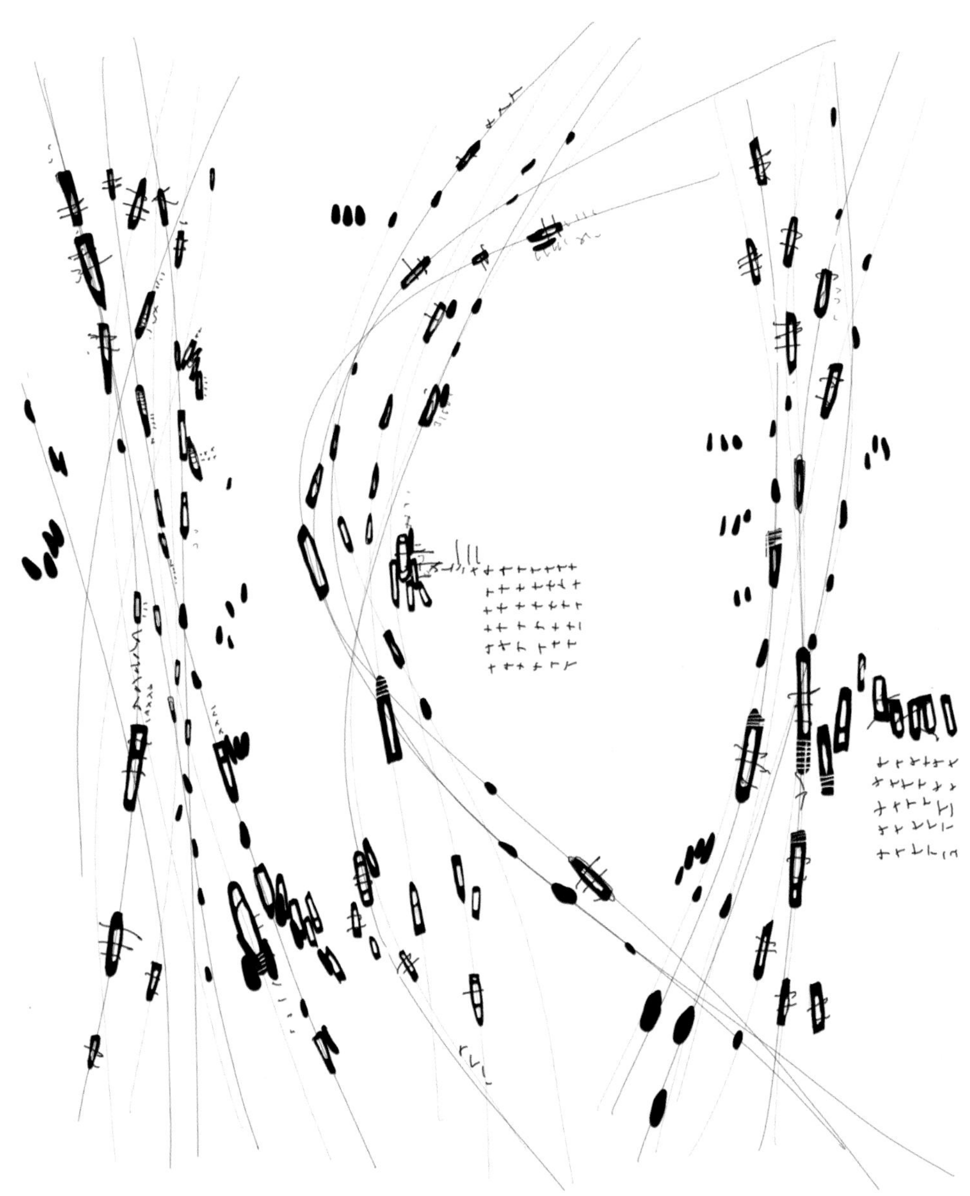

ALONG SHANGHAI RIVER

Sitting in front of Shanghai's river during the night; counting the numbers of black boats passing and discovering the number is endless; measuring the small space between two of them; understanding the weight they transport is in relationship with the waterline; comparing the different mass they have; judging the beauty of their shapes and forms; at the end, I was sure that they were the soul of Shanghai. It took me a long time to figure out how to draw this Shanghai soul.

I tried to make sections, to draw the city skyline with the boats on the river, and to draw the boats and ships as they were. However, none of these drawings represented the idea of the soul of Shanghai. I decided then to draw the ephemeral traces the boats leave on the surface of the water and some abstract shapes that somehow recall the form of the boats of Shanghai. In a way, it seemed to me to draw the soul of the city, its flows, strategies, thoughts, and desires.

LANDSCAPE CITY OF SHANGHAI 1

Before visiting Shanghai, I drew the first Landscape City of Shanghai. I expected to see a city in which there was a strong relationship between the city and its landscape. I still imagine that Shanghai is a landscape city.

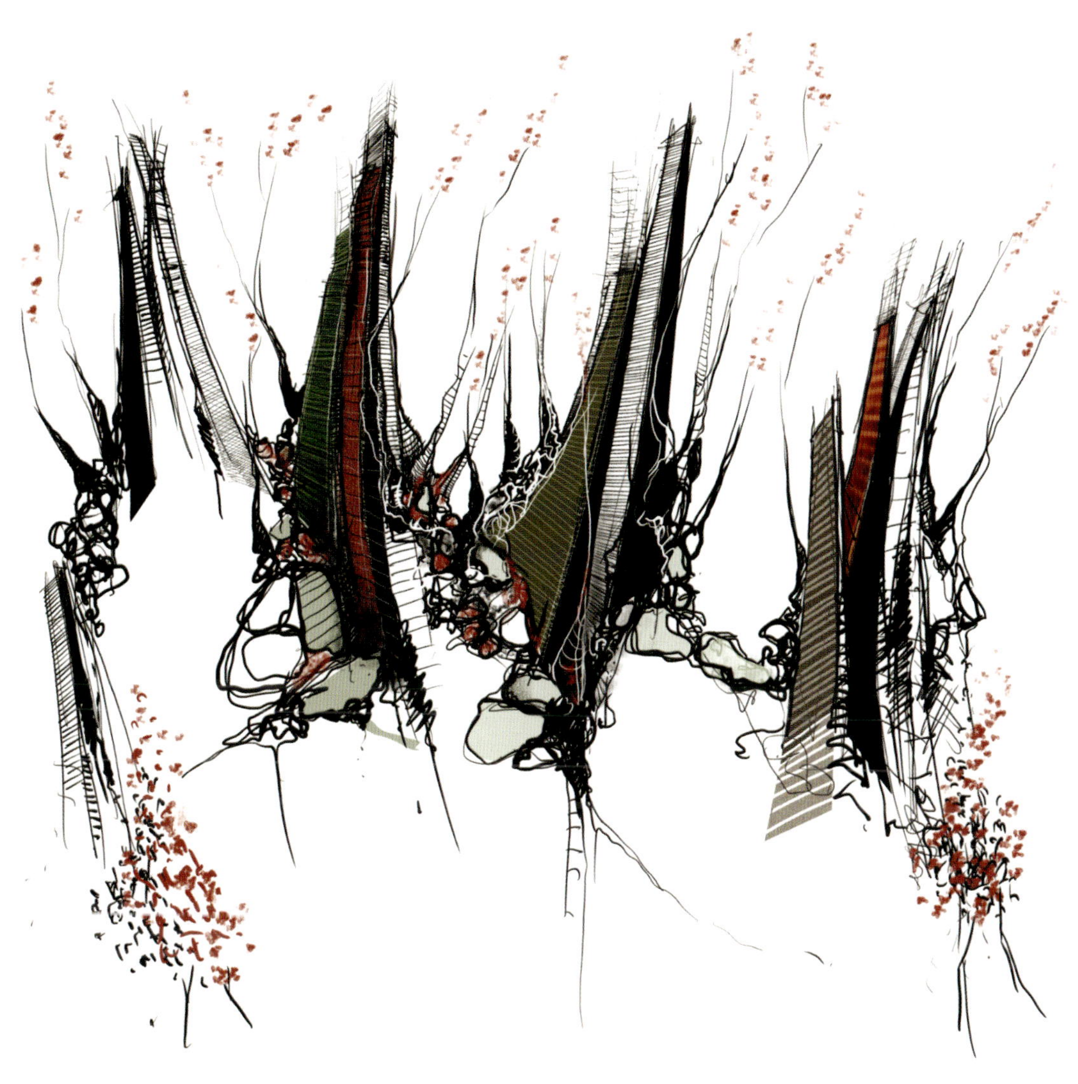

LANDSCAPE CITY OF SHANGHAI 2

LANDSCAPE CITY OF SHANGHAI 3

LANDSCAPE CITY OF SHANGHAI 4

FROM SHANGHAI TO HANGZHOU

Hangzhou is the capital and most populous city of Zhejiang Province in East China. It settles at the head of Hangzhou Bay, which separates Shanghai and Ningbo. Hangzhou is the southern terminus of the Grand Canal and has been one of the most renowned and prosperous cities in China for much of the last millennium. This drawing represents a long walk from Shanghai to Hangzhou.

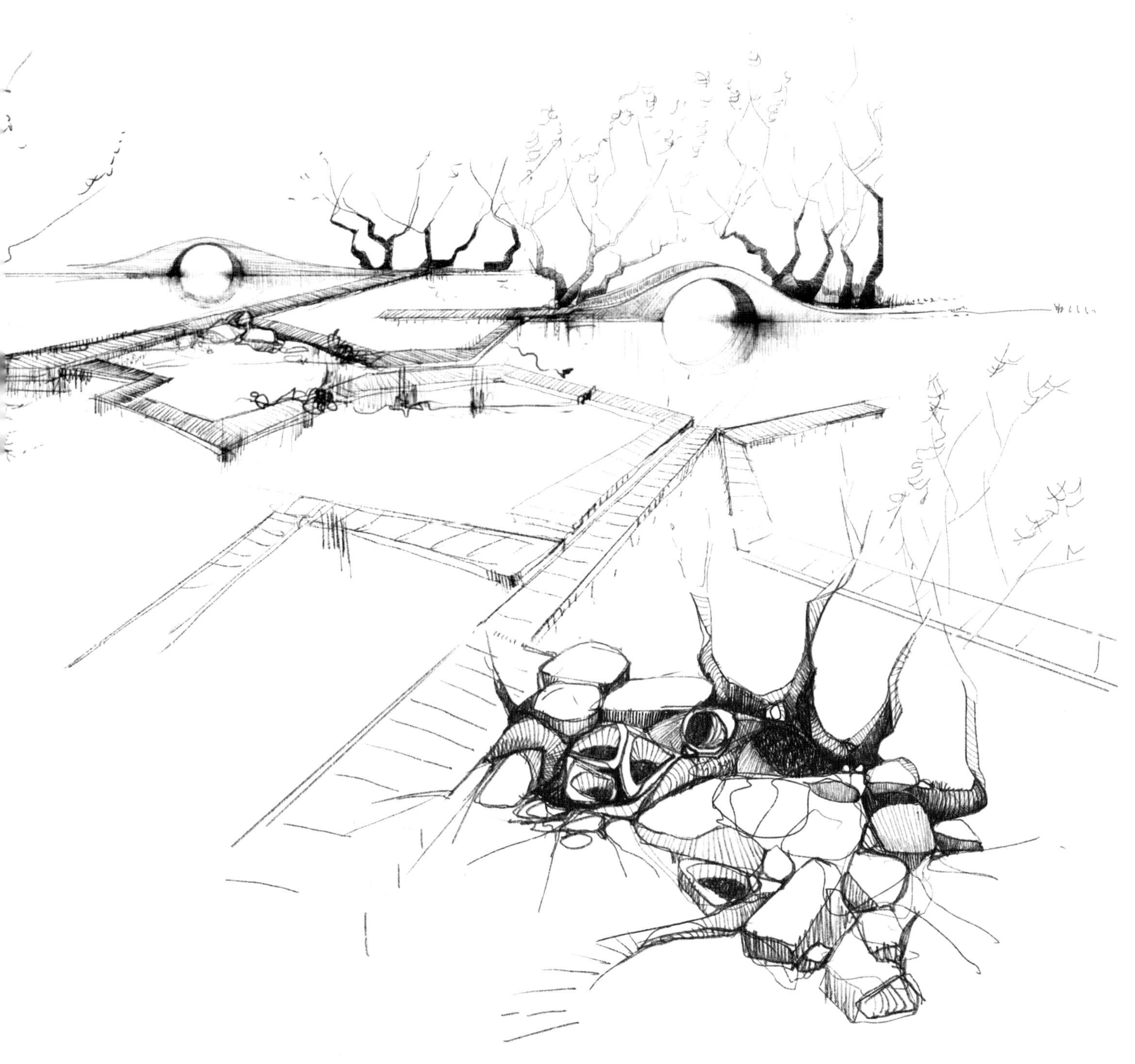

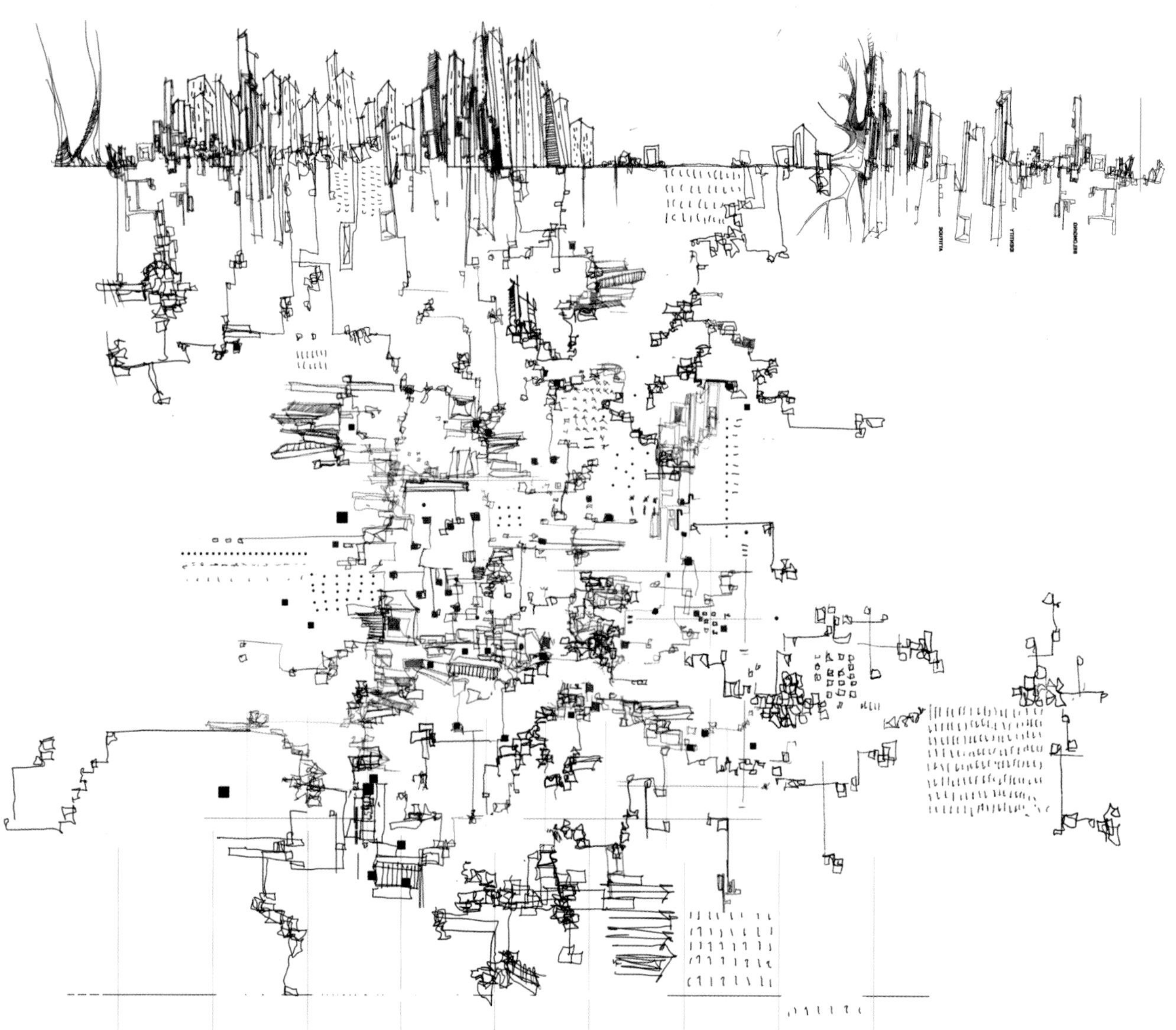

NANTOU VILLAGE THINKS IT IS BIG

In the parks of some Chinese cities master calligraphers paint poems on the stone paving using brushes dipped in water. After a while, as the water evaporates, these stories vanish. However, their traces remain in the memory of those who saw these stories appearing and disappearing. A similar process seems to involve the small Nantou village in Shenzhen. It is a medieval village, once mighty, with a significant territory under its control. Nowadays, surrounded by the new city of Shenzhen, Nantou is an ill-preserved village. Its urban structure is made by a combination of new buildings and a few old monuments. The only thing well preserved is its original footprint. New buildings are piled one on top of the other, compact and high, following its medieval urban structure. Sometimes ideas do not change even if the ink used to write them is evaporated. Nantou was rebuilt many times with different inks, and, in spite of everything, its idea is still there. It is because of this that the small Nantou village thinks it is more significant than Shenzhen.

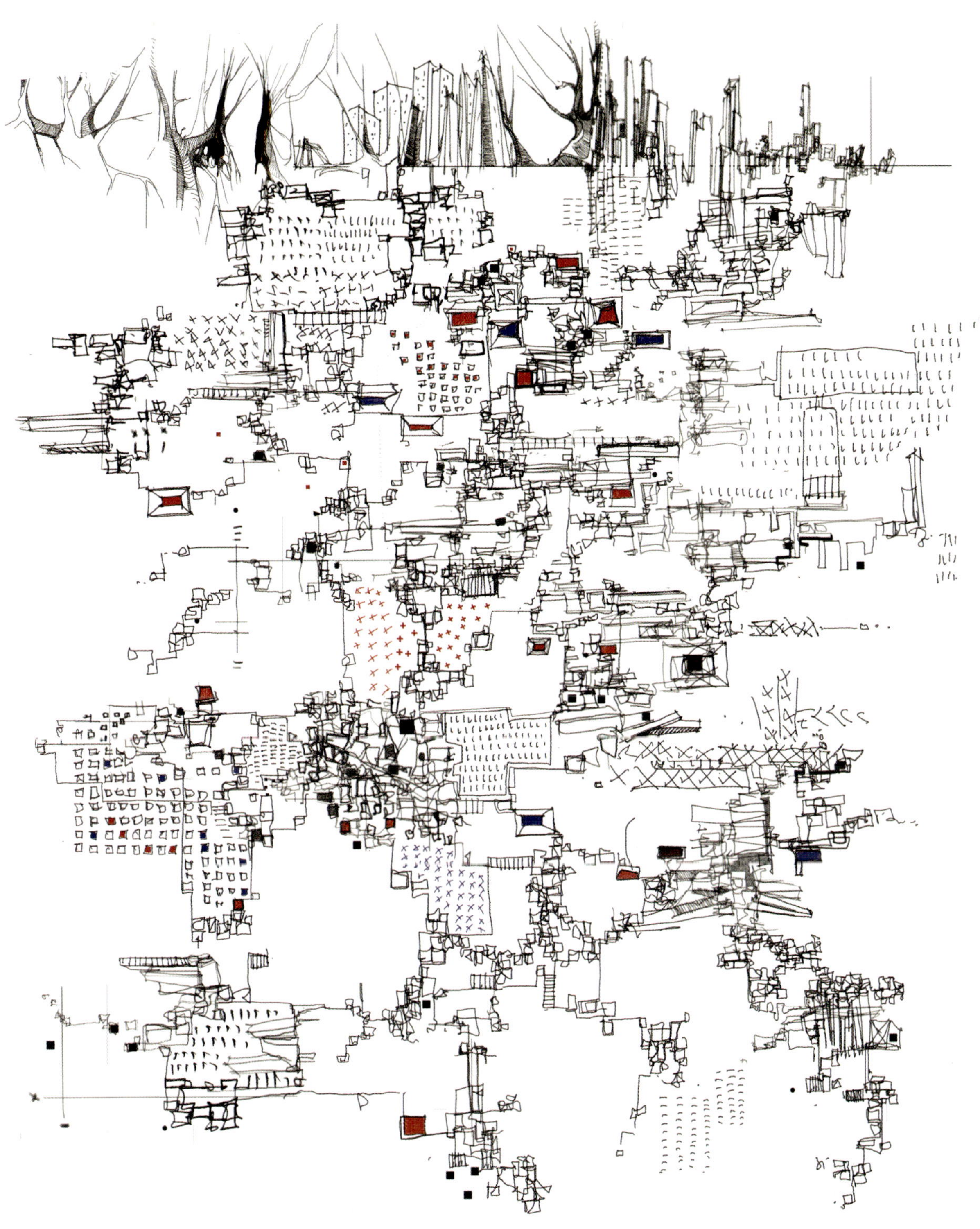

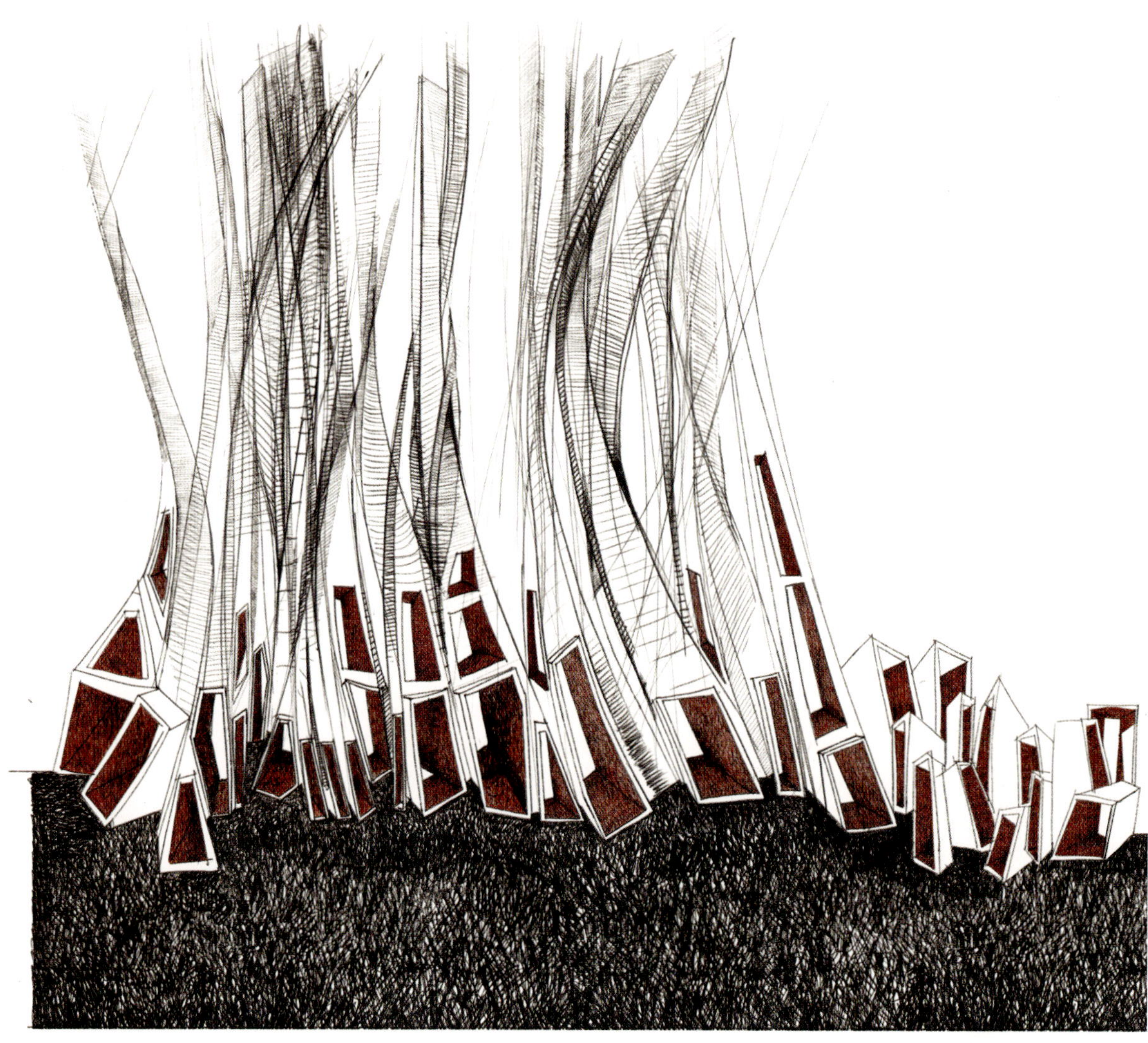

DANCING CITY OF SHENZHEN

Shenzhen is not a city I have become well acquainted with. I visited and enjoyed the Nantou village it subsumed, but I barely explored the larger city. From what I saw from taxis or walking along a new promenade, it seemed to me that all around a new and old architecture was dancing nonstop. Then I visited a magnificent park near the village of Nantou and was impressed by the huge ficus trees. I started to draw the trunks of these trees, which then became architecture. After, I added a series of abstract volumes between the ground and the trunks of the trees.

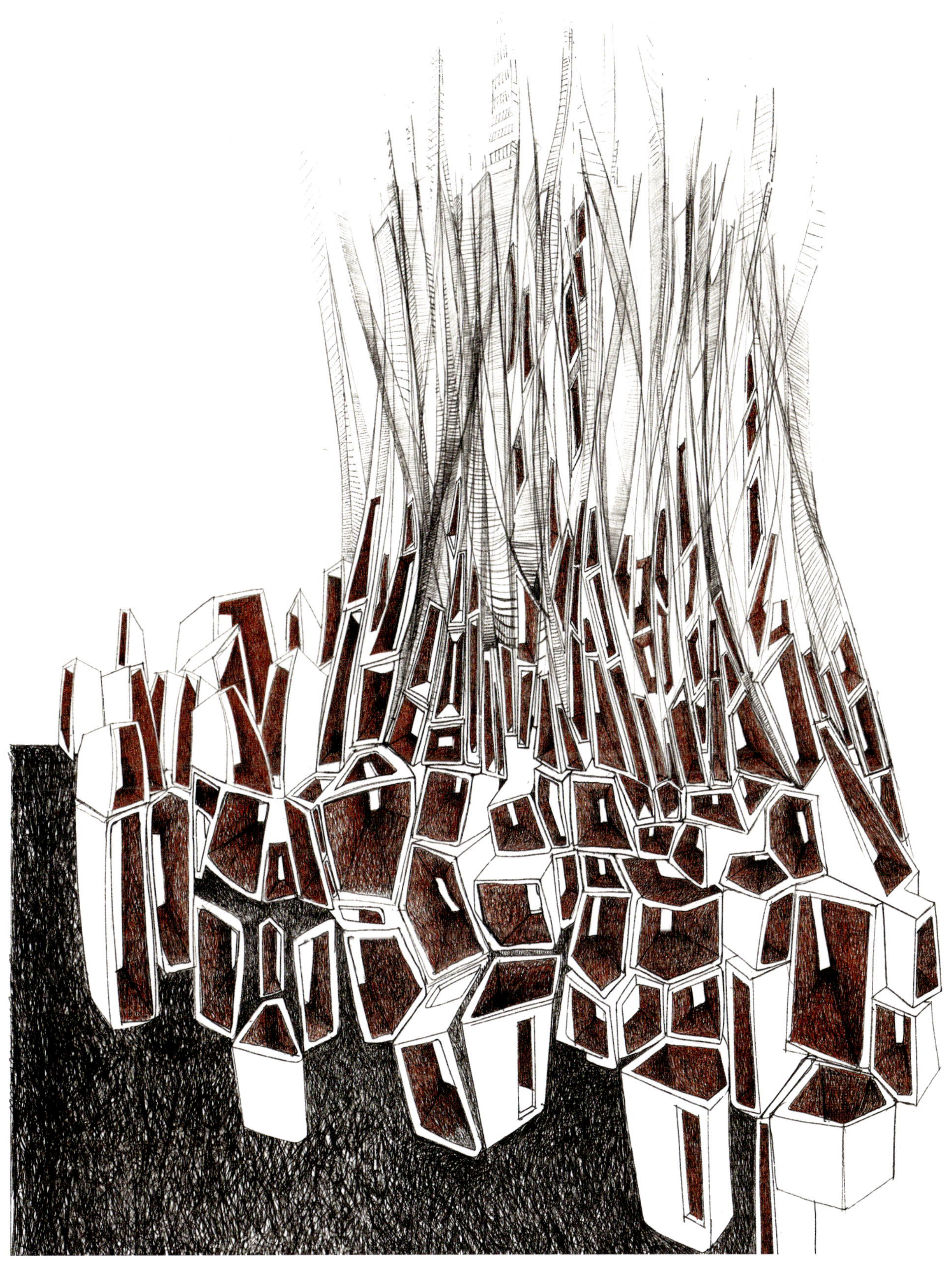

CITY OF SQUARE

COLLECTING PLATFORMS FOR ITALIAN SQUARES

Italy has a strong tradition of urban squares. Squares are voids in the urban structure. The buildings around them, therefore, characterize the empty space. In medieval cities, the square space had a very particular connotation, inseparable from the urban context and the morphological conditions on which the city was founded. The square is a symbol of the Italian cities, many events have had squares as their ideal setting.

The drawings that follow are reflections, even ironic, on this public place par excellence of Italian urban life. Paradoxically, these drawings have their inspirational trace in an industrial area of Pittsburg. By photographing rusty metal plates and modifying them to a square shape, they were placed and overlapped on paper. From this position, they welcomed a series of urban elements around them.

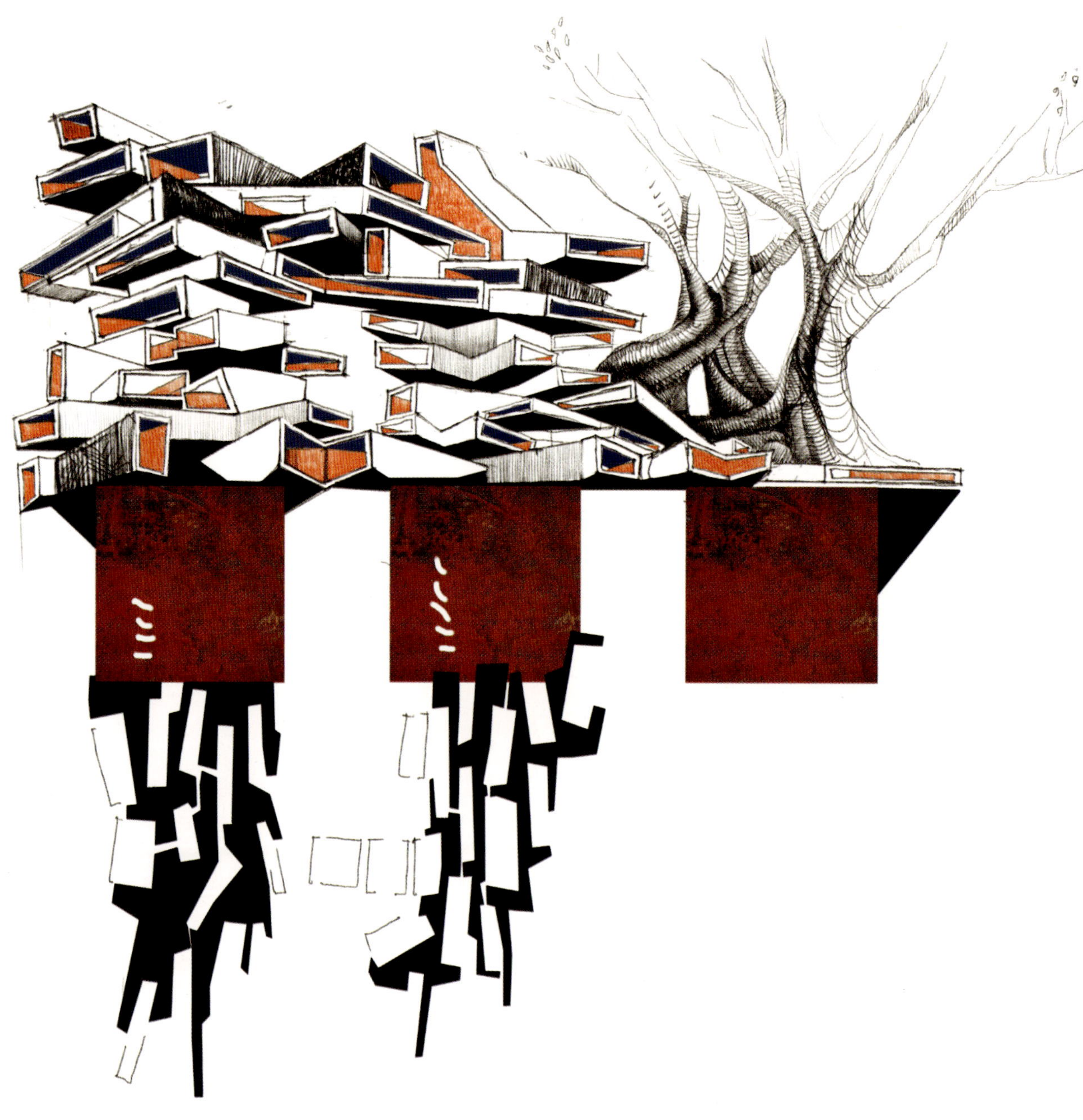

THE THREE ITALIAN SQUARES

Three square spaces in the center were the first step in founding a city drawing. On two of them, the city extends in height and according to a logic of elements in addition. One square is dedicated to the presence of some large trees. The trees try to invade the space of the city, and the city attempts to invade the space of the trees. In this case, the city landscape is an apparent conflict of roles between the artificiality of the buildings and the naturalness of the trees.

THE TWO ITALIAN SQUARES

The design of these two squares represents a continuous de-bate on Italian cities' historical identity. For many people, the landscape of traditional Italian cities is a landscape of stone, which excludes the presence of trees or green areas. In reality, the landscape of Italian cities has always been a continuous relationship between artifice and nature.

THE STRIPS

In the Frankfurt Art Museum, there are two small drawings made by adhesive strips of paper glued on white cardboard. Unfortunately, I don't remember the name of the artist or the name of the works, but the obsession with these two beautiful pieces of art follows me constantly. Here I tried to copy them according to my memory. I think they interpret the city of Frankfurt.

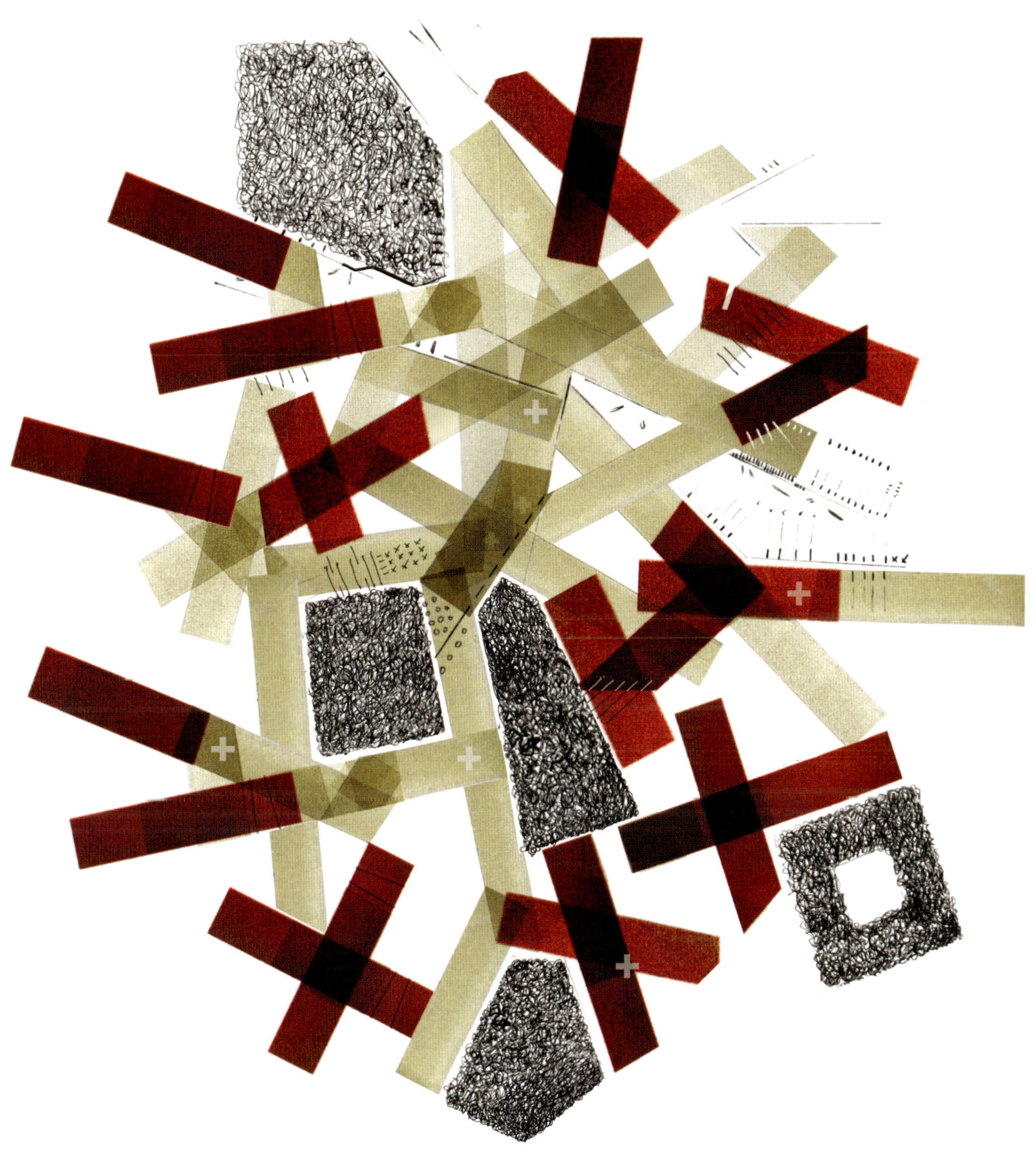

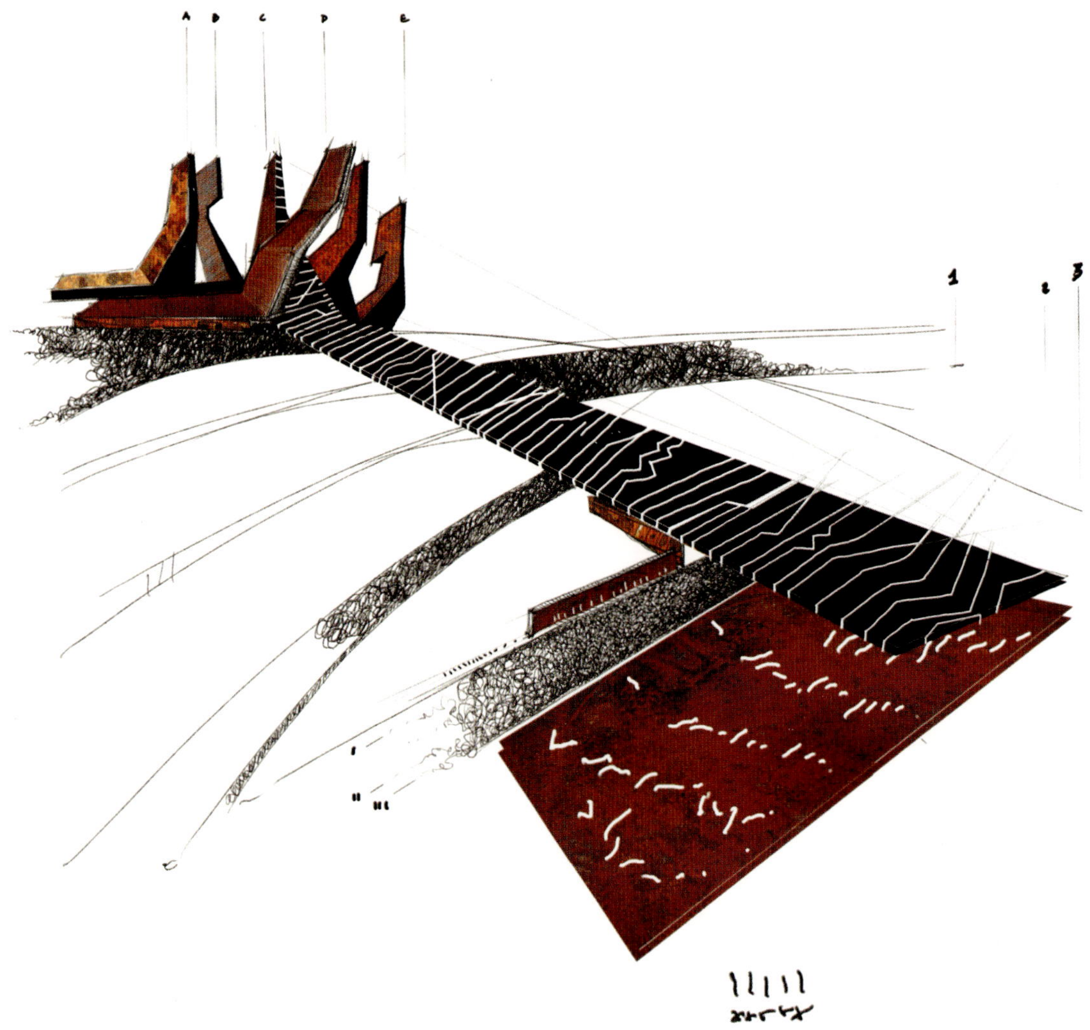

CITY OF PITTSBURG

This design has its relations with the city of Pittsburgh. A few years ago, on a trip led by Professors Cindy Sanders and David Gouverneur, I traveled with students from the Department of Landscape Architecture at the University of Pennsylvania to Pittsburgh's abandoned industrial area. This vast area was developed along the river. Following its edges, we saw containers for transporting materials along the river, piers, and small groups of industrial buildings I assumed to be control towers or offices. The surfaces of many of the docks and elevated paths were made of thick rusted metal planes, which projected outside the line of the river and often involved tiny buildings. Seeing these photos of the metal surfaces again after a few years, an idea of the city came up. By using these rusted surfaces as main squares, putting them far from the industrial buildings, and then connecting these two different parts of the city with long paths and pergolas, the city of Pittsburgh appeared.

PHILADELPHIA NORTH/SOUTH MAP

I have several sketches of Philadelphia's buildings, each a small, slender colored shape through which I have tried to synthesize the idea of the old city. I have tried many times to collect them in a single entity, having the desire to give them a place where they can stay. Sometimes sketches or doodles are lost from our memory; looking back, I discovered two similar such efforts. Both had been drawn as exercises in using my hand to react intuitively to memory. The maps were similar but still differentiated by small details. For instance, in one, the

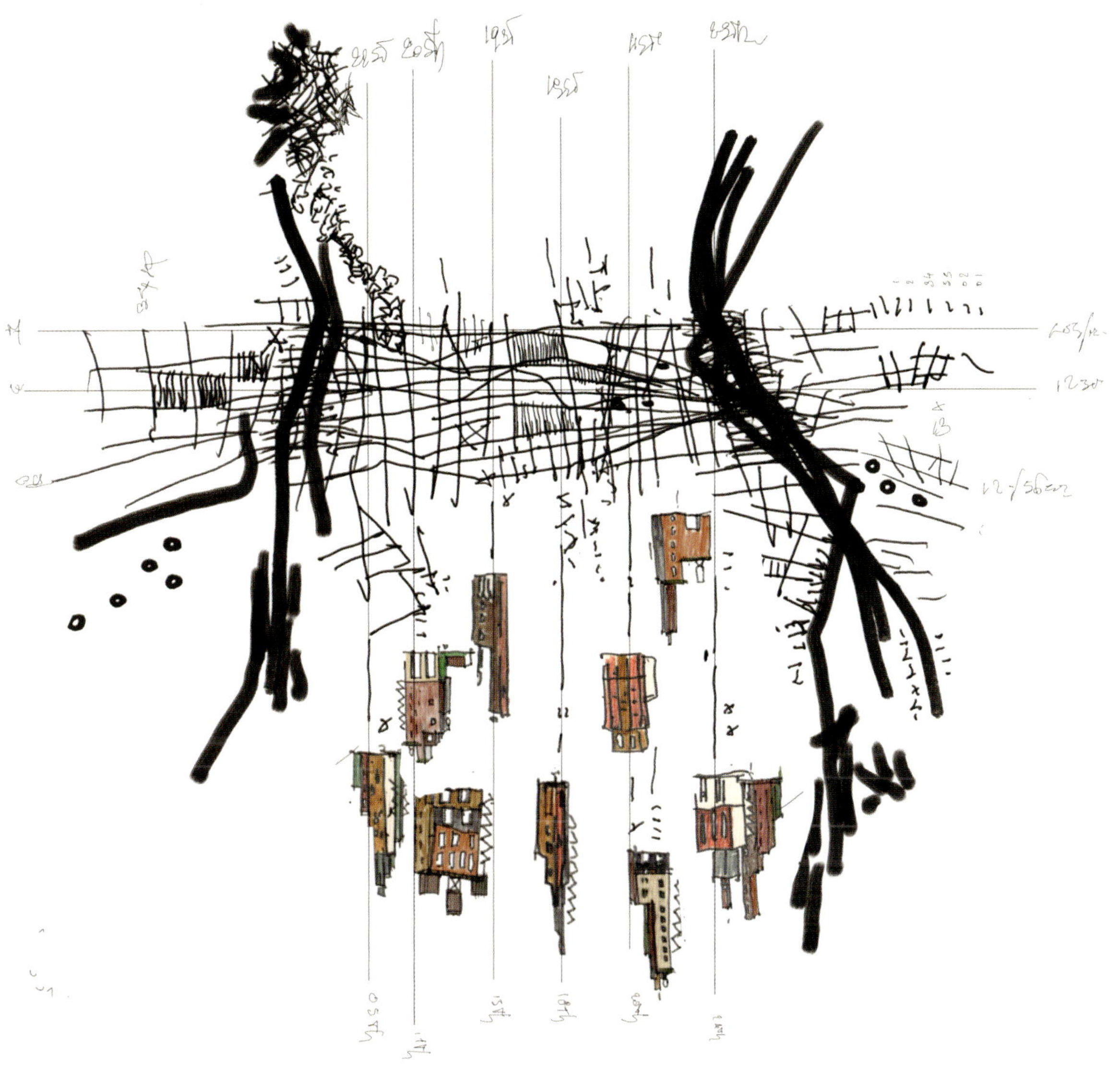

rivers were stronger, and in the other, the urban structure was more evident. Taking into consideration that Philadelphia's center city is divided into two parts–the north and south one–a few buildings were oriented to the north, and a few displayed on the south, the combination generating a simple double city. Frequently, maps show monuments. In contrast, these two maps show ordinary buildings that together generate the urban structure of regular events.

SQUARES OF PHILADELPHIA

Finding the way to put together my sketches of single Philadelphian buildings was a long process that, starting with the previous two maps, ended with the imagination of these two drawings. After mapping Philadelphia, it was easy to zoom into the maps and represent the core of Philadelphia's soul: its squares. When inside one of these squares, surrounded by buildings and sinking into their " nature," one has the feeling of being in a room. The ceilings are canopies, tall, and transparent; the walls are painted brown, red, and green by the buildings'

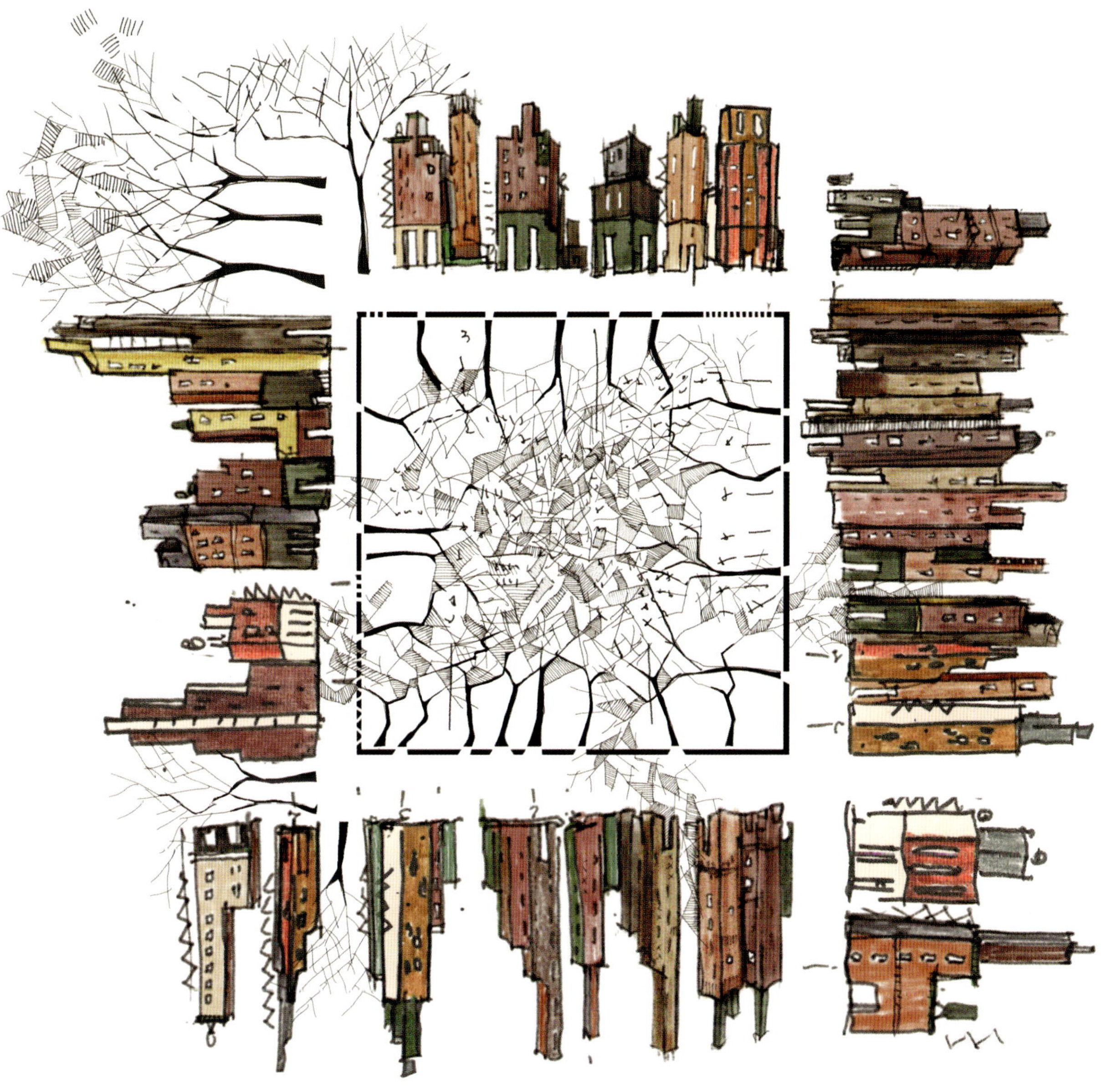

colors; the windows are streets offering opportunities to explore more and more rooms. Inside of Philadelphia's center city square's, one feels protected. The big trees take care of us. Sitting on a bench or laying on the lawn allows us to establish a special relationship with the city: friendship. We feel like friends of Philadelphia, a daily common and simple friendship that everyone can experience to improve social significance.

CITY OF WATER

ALONG THE RIVER

It is often forgotten that the first language with which we communicated, and which we have handed down from the first moments of our history, are drawings. We have painted and engraved on many rock walls since we started to be sapiens. We have left our hands' imprints in the form of rock art. Sometimes the prints are of an entire palm, while others are restricted to the palms' contours. These drawings are the same everywhere, even in the most remote corners of our planet. Over 75 million prehistoric images on the exterior or cave rocks are documented. They span 170 countries on five continents.

Collectively, humanity has put a lot of effort into collecting materials to paint and sculpt these forms of art. The site where the materials came from, their landscape and nature, has always had an important role in the artistic creation. Over time we turned these drawings into signs, then signs into spoken words, and eventually into written words. The hands on the walls reproduced our thoughts, moods, and relationships. Through them, we found links with deities we believed lived in other worlds. Each drawing in this book emanates from words without words, sentences without words, and concepts without words.

MAPPING DOCKS

The Docks are an enormous water landscape entering into the city of London. These drawings are an attempt to imagine a space in continuous evolution; space that modifies the city by digging, cutting, and designing places according to increasingly complex requirements. Looking from another point of view, they can be interpreted as an attempt by the city to enter into the water's place to conquer new power, draw new relationships, and

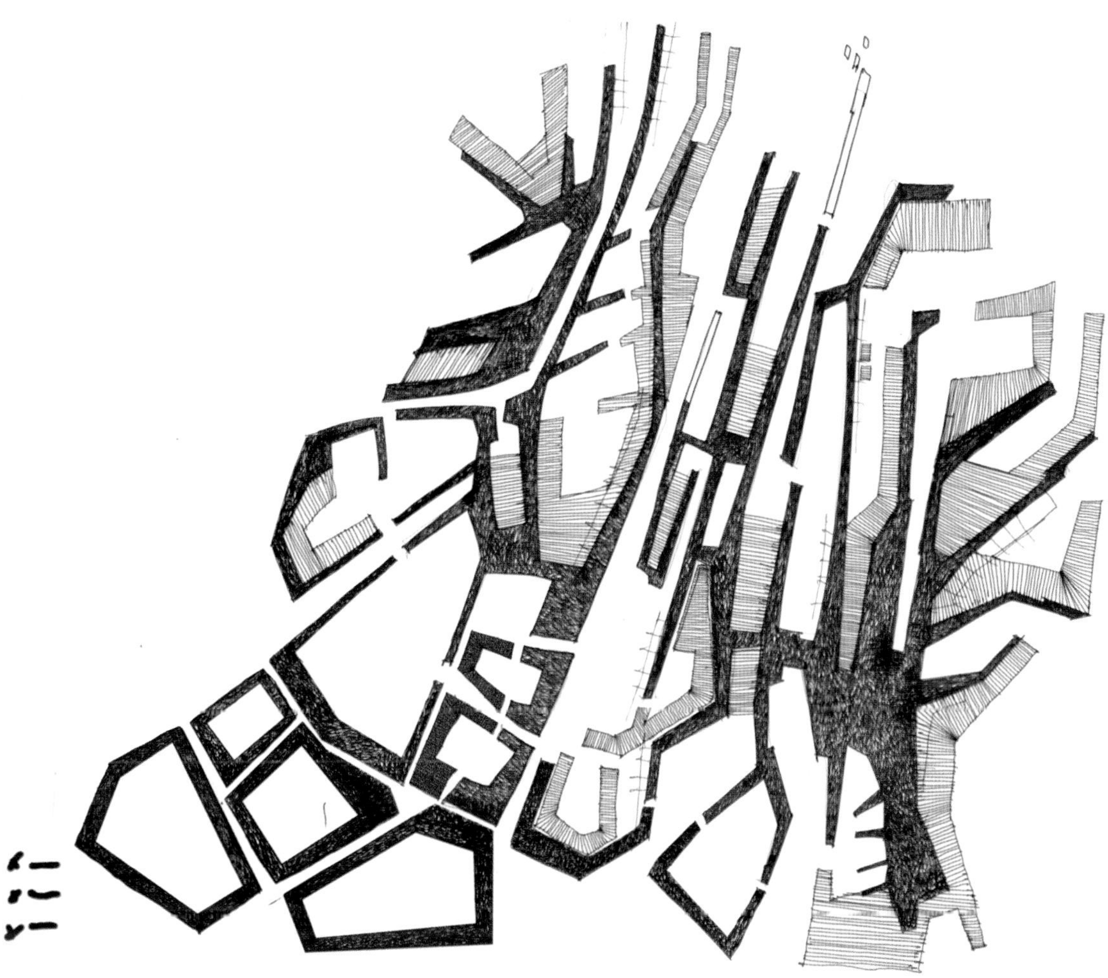

design new boundaries. In any case, the maps' spaces are divided into many sites, specialized functions, and built using a technique of additions or subtractions. The Docks' are a place of arrival and departure, a place of exploration and commerce, and a place where the imagination demands to discover its new cities and its new landscapes..

LEAVING DOCK 1-2

When I saw the London Docks for the first time, it was a space undergoing an incredible urban transformation. In that period, the many new buildings that now front them had not yet been built and the area was empty and immense. Some huge cranes were sentinels that seemed to contain undecipherable secrets. Walking among this impossible space to draw, a lot of stories rose in my mind. They were stories based on ships that left these

places in search of other sites, looking for other cities. The only possible way to draw the Dock's was to imagine large ships departing behind new buildings that were also moving together with the ships. These two designs were chosen among many others.

LEAVING DOCKS - 3

LEAVING DOCKS - 4

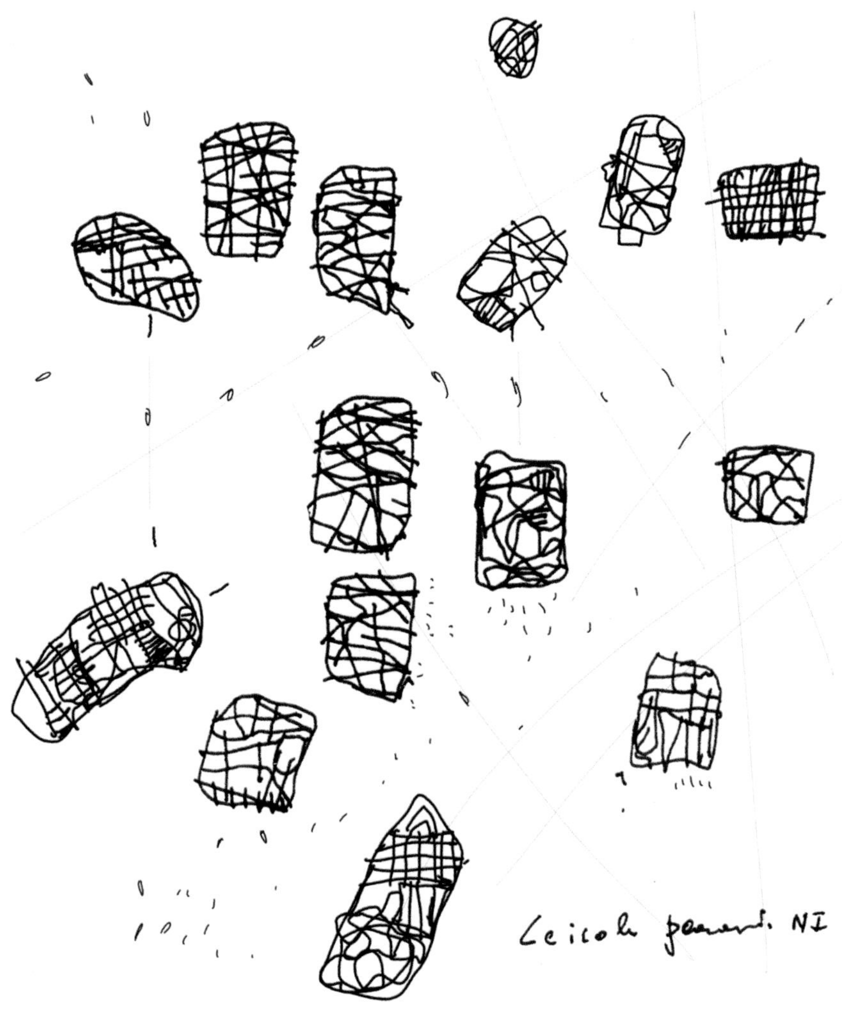

CITY OF ARCHIPELAGO

These two archipelagos are a free interpretation of the Canary Islands. The Canary Islands played a fundamental role in traveling to the "so-called" New World, in exploring new lands and trades. The island of Lanzarote has an especially particular and unusual landscape made by a repetition of volcanic stone circles.

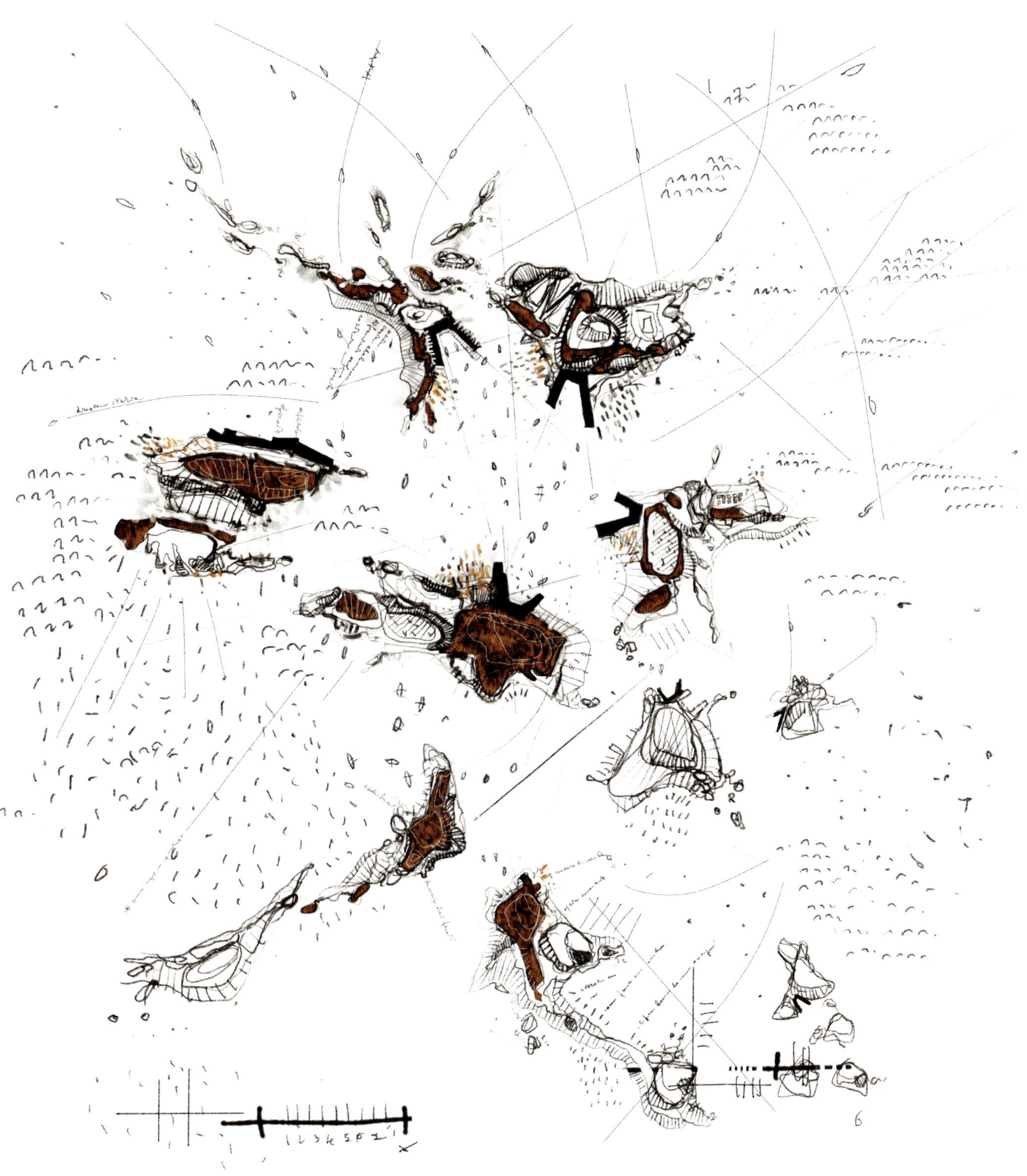

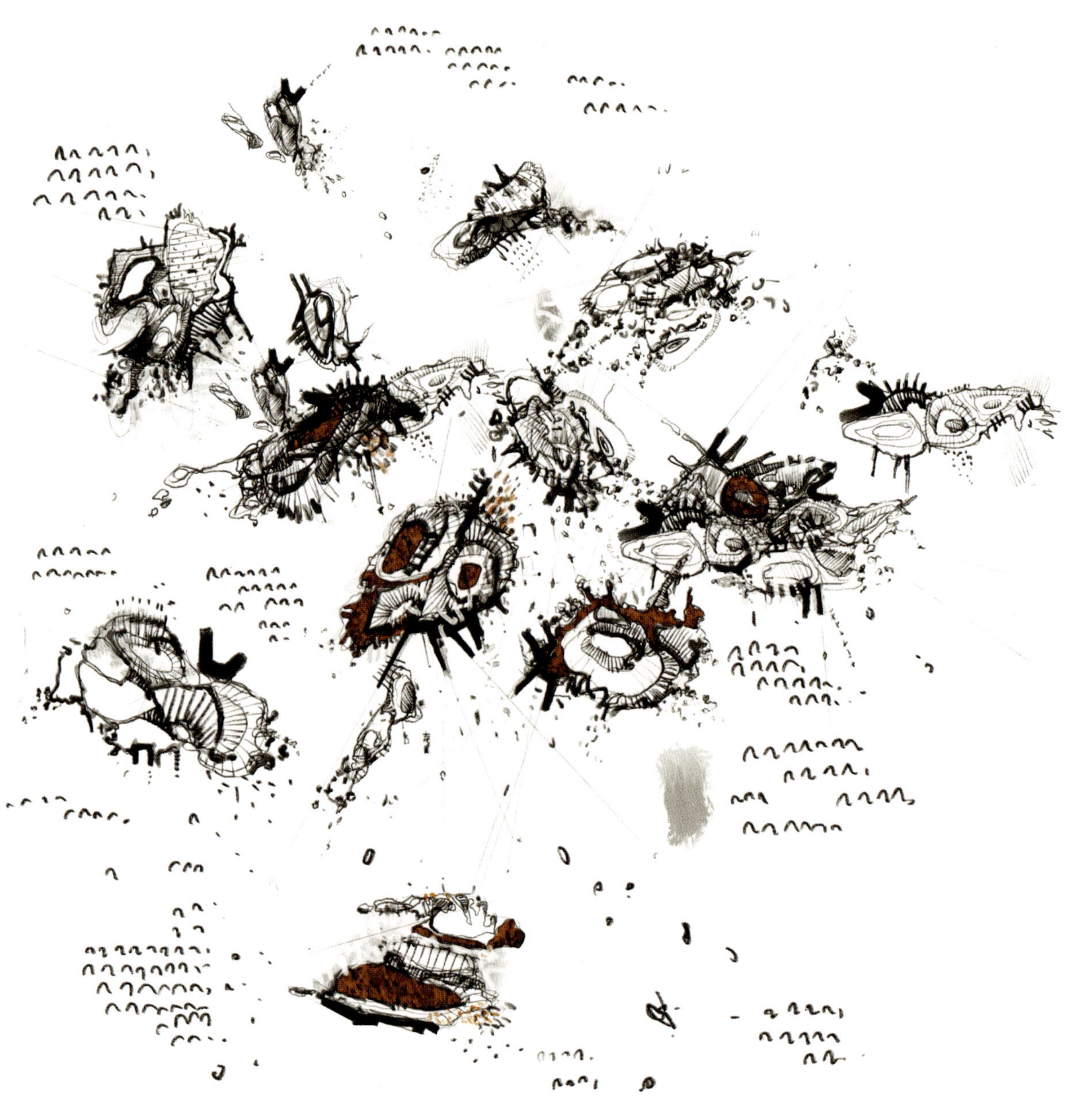

MOVABLE ISLANDS

"Here, we came to the Eolian island. Aeolus lives here, son of Hippolyta, pleasing the lords of Olympus. That island was a wandering island. A large bronze wall surrounded it, unbreakable, with a series of smooth stone walls. Twelve children lived with him inside the palace; six young women and six young men in their prime. Eolo gave his sons to his daughters as brides; all of them spent their time together with their father and mother, having a lot of feasts. Thousands and thousands of dishes were always ready, and during the day, the house was invaded by vapors and sounds of songs. At night they slept with the brides on rugs and beds with magnificent decorations." (*The Odyssey,* Homer)

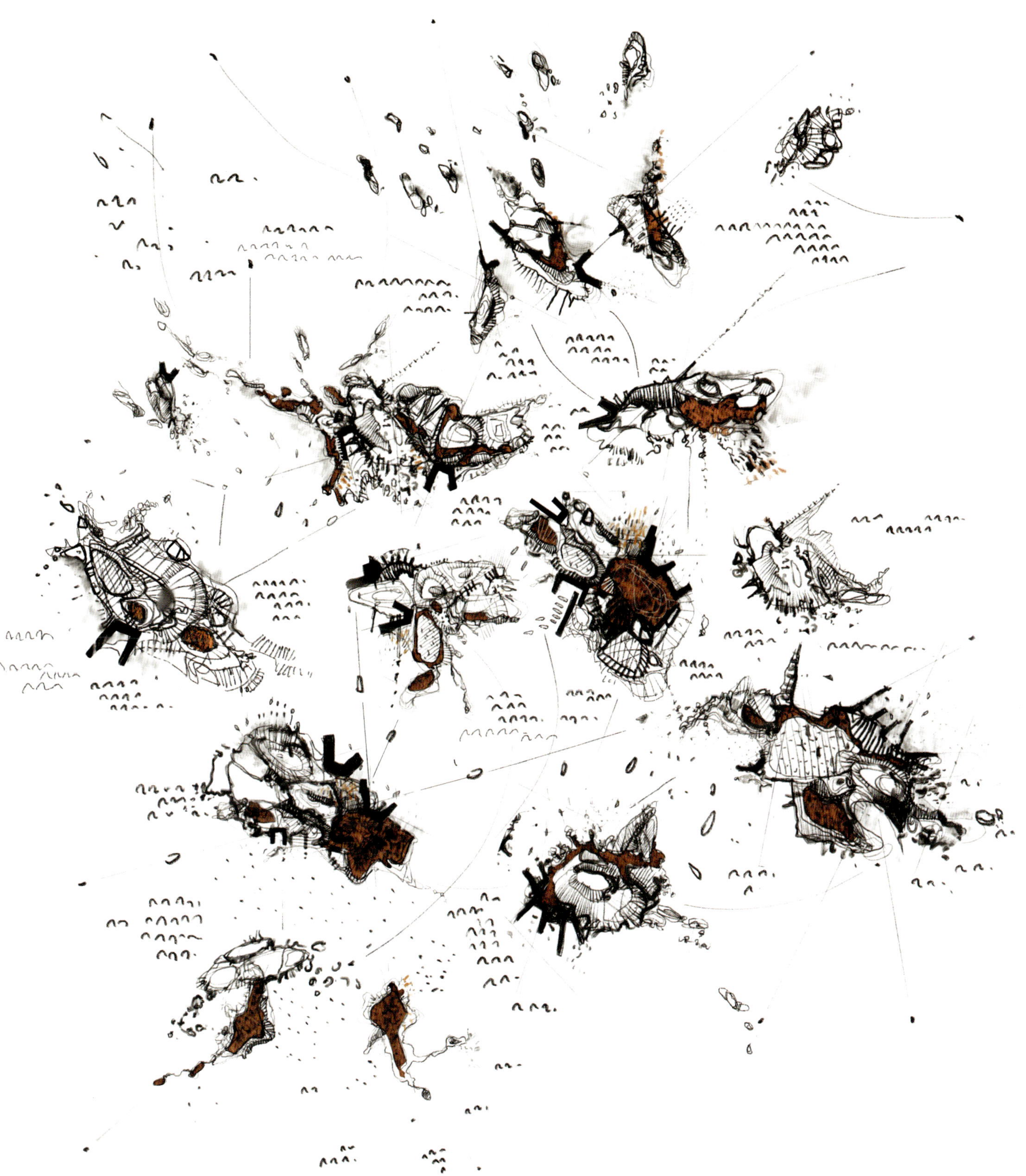

MAPPING THE WATER

Sometimes drawings reach an unexpected shape considering their starting points were visits to particular cities. With a slow process, they move from their originating places toward unpredicted representations of non-existing cities. Apparently, during this process, they lose any real shapes from the original cities. Hidden inside a new imaginary appearance, the original form of the place survives as immaterial ideas, fixed into the memory from what was perceived as particular, engaging, and denoting principle.

These waterfront drawings were born from visiting Venice. It is one of the most beautiful cities in the world, represented countless times with its buildings, bridges, streets, water channels, and churches. These drawings cannot compete with any of these representations. Instead, using a process of removing reals shapes, I have opted to represent Venice based on ideas formed from the continuous relationship that the water has with its city.

CITY OF WATER

Many years ago, I bought the Yann Arthus Bertrand's book *Earth from Above.* Among the beautiful images of natural and artificial landscapes, one photo of a watermaker found in Arab countries stood out. A big building produces a flow of water on the desert sand, reproducing a natural river delta. This drawing is a representation of a city made by buildings that provide unsalted water and release it, designing a landscape of water.

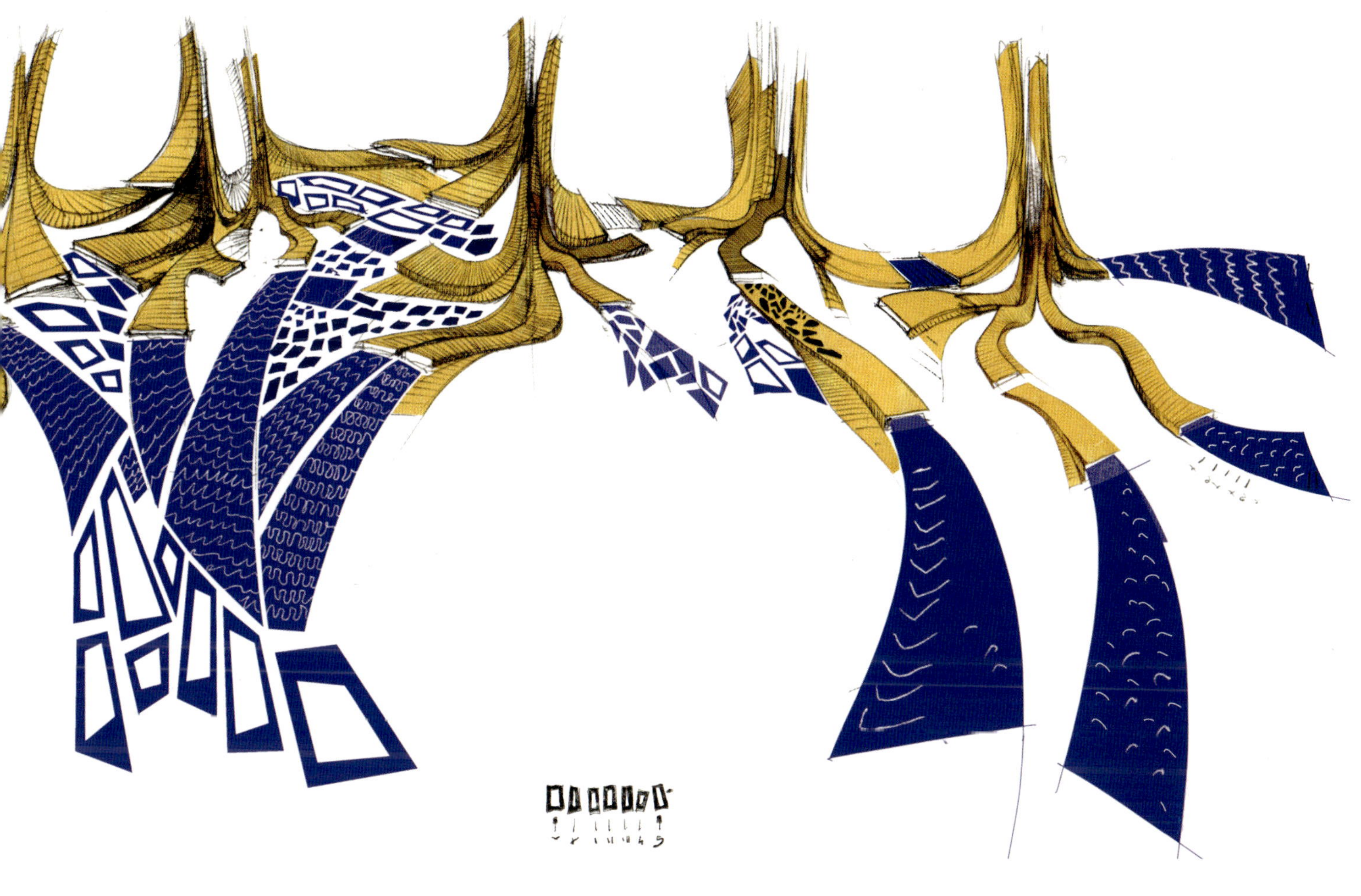

WONDERLAND CITY

A few years ago, at MOMA in NY, there was an exhibition on Tim Burton's work. The exhibition presented a particular idea of the landscape and showed an intriguing space full of countless inventions of characters and objects. In this landscape, each object and character contributed, together with the other objects and characters, to the creation of a rhizome-shaped network, which transformed the landscape in a fantastic narration of stories without beginning and end.

This idea of the landscape was transferred into these two wonderland cities, in which the buildings have spatial and formal continuity with their context. It is not possible to understand if the buildings came before the vegetation or the vegetation traced lines for the buildings' shapes. In any case, they all imagine a landscape of homogeneous connections, as if it was a network in the form of a rhizome.

CITY OF PARKS

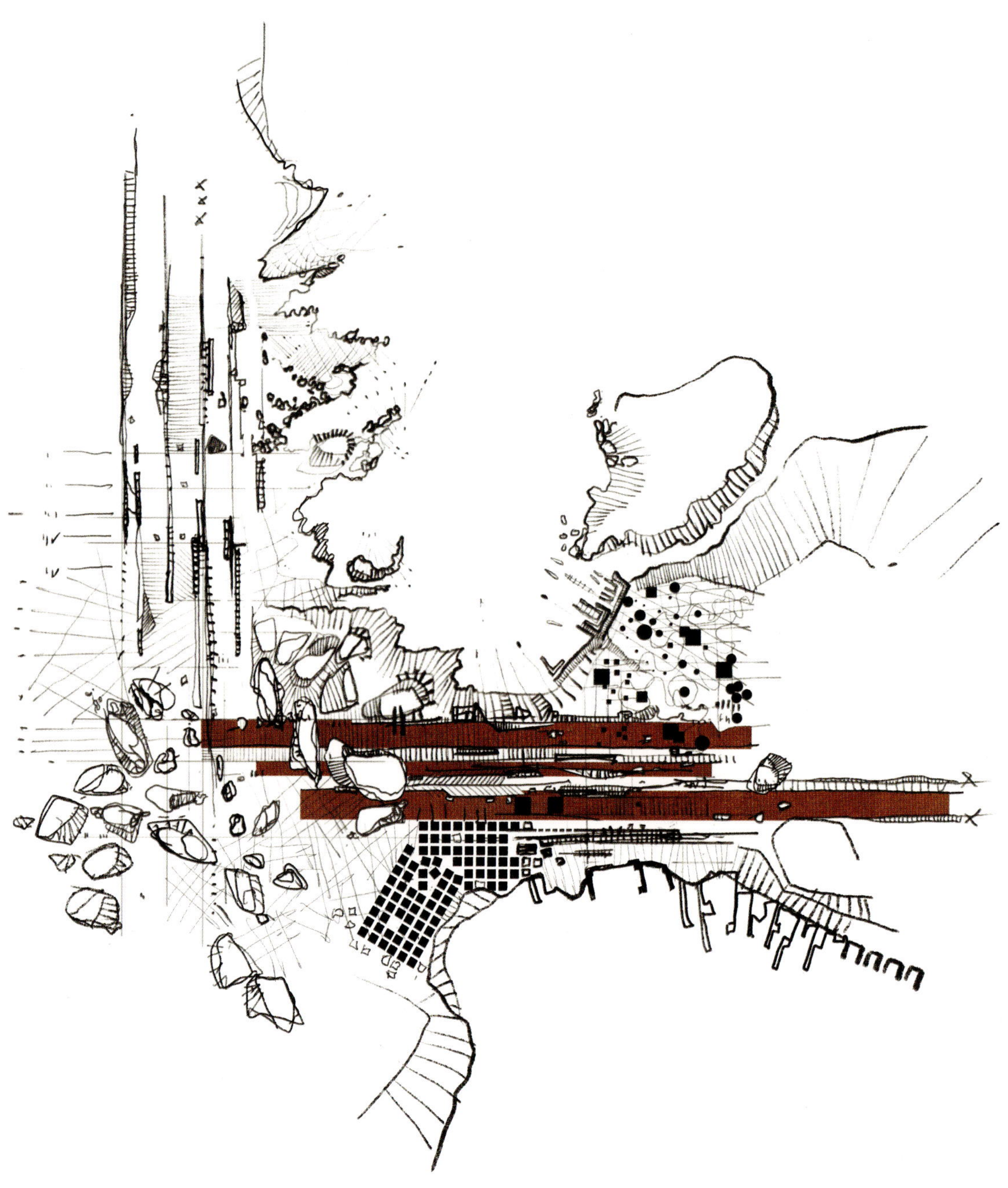

LINEAR PARKS

In the mid-nineteenth century, under the direction of Napoleon III, Baron Haussmann initiated his program of cutting grand boulevards through Paris, making the city less compact and giving it a more modern, open, and monumental quality. In many parts of southern Italy in the past years, we have frequently witnessed the construction of cities with illegal buildings, unfulfilled city plans, and industries located in the wrong places. This development has created a fragmented, inhomogeneous, uneven landscape with no good qualities or identity. This design is a reflection on the possibility of applying the same methodology as Baron Haussmann but overturning his strategy: to use a line to compact, reunify, close, redefine and structure spaces rather than open and monumentalize.

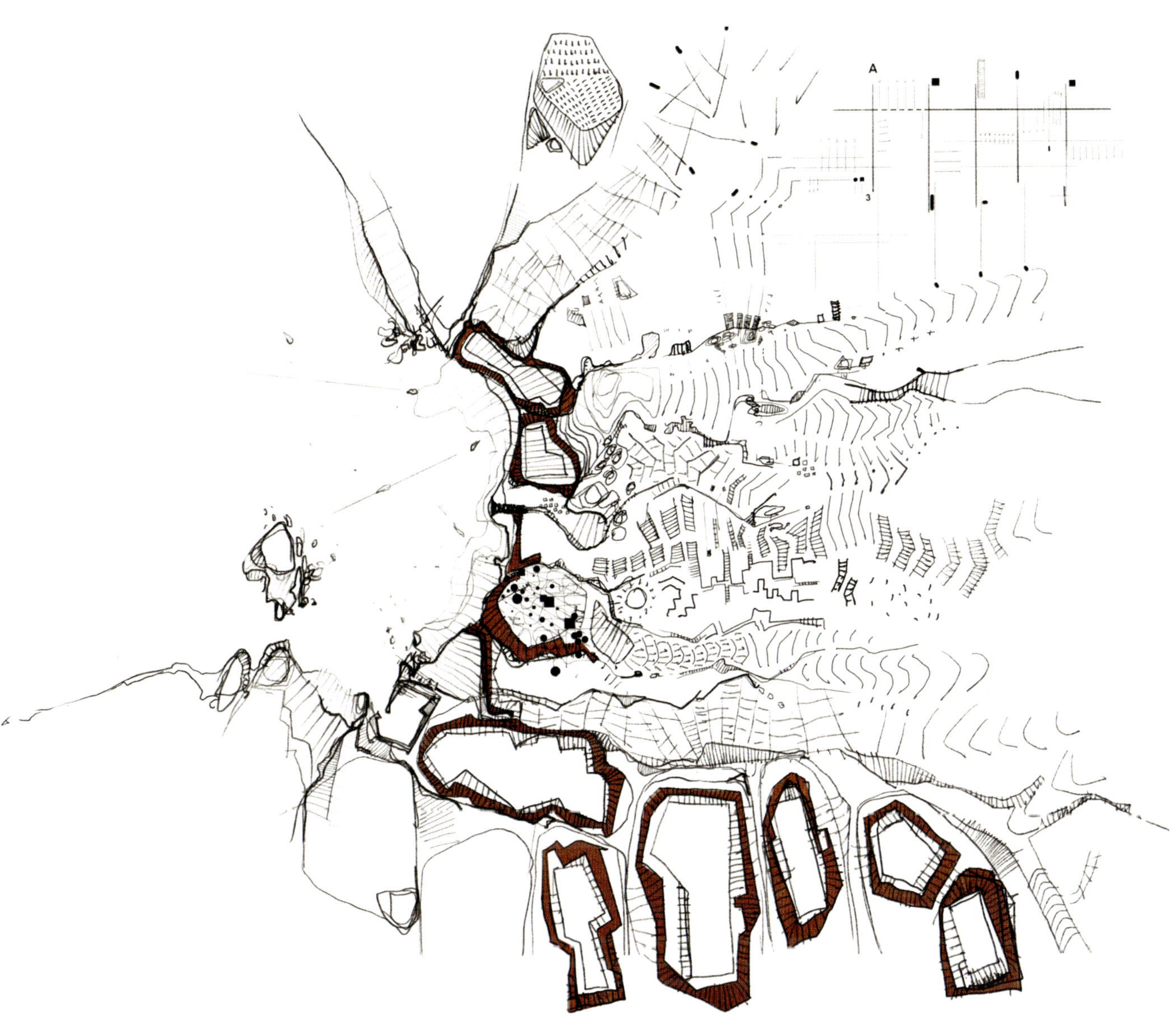

GREEN INFRASTRUCTURES

In Morocco, I designed a few green belts that tried to reconcile agriculture outside the cities with urban activities, recreational spaces, and more. They were not the usual compact green belts often made with only one type of tree, but were dynamic and flexible landscape structures able to combine different needs. This drawing is a free interpretation of how green belts can connect spaces outside cities with urban spaces, creating string-like systems of landscape infrastructures.

GREEN BELT FORMS

These two drawings are tributes to Giuseppe Capogrossi. Capogrossi was an Italian painter, and, after World War II, he embraced an abstract style, becoming one of the leading exponents of Italian informal art, together with Lucio Fontana and Alberto Burri. His main idea was to paint significant elements with "fork" shapes that he combined in different and dynamic compositions. These two drawings represent two cities surrounded by big green belts in the form of big paintings. They are modern landscape walls and doors, active and connected with the urban structure, its activities, and social spaces.

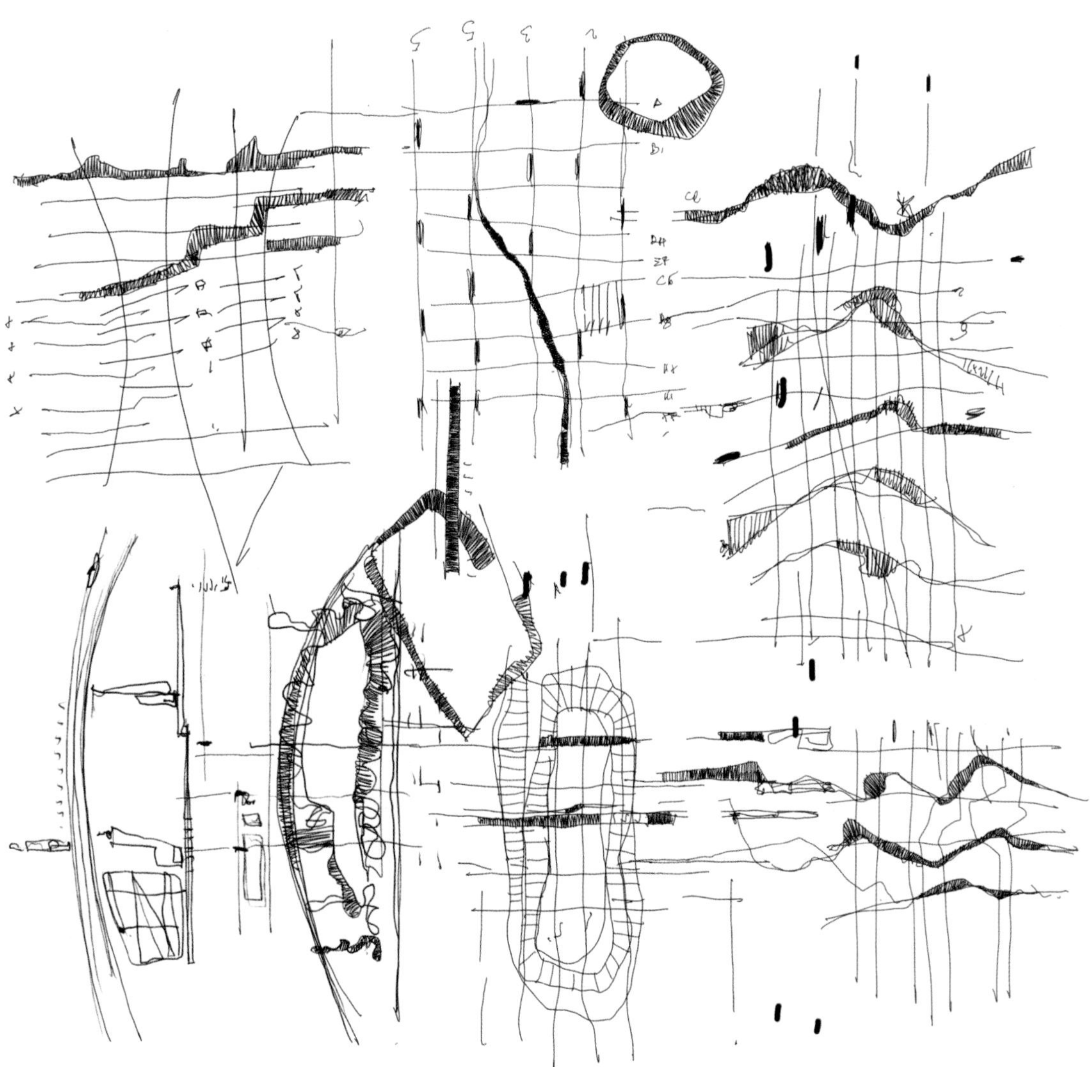

URBAN STRUCTURES COLLECTION

This drawing collects a series of experiences I had during many visits in Morocco, especially coming from my observation of new unfinished cities. Many times, these cities have been built without taking the site conditions and morphologies where they are settled into consideration. The consequence is an abstract approach to landscape. In tracing these urban structures near cities like Rabat, Tataouen, Marrakesh, and so on, the sketches contain suggestions for new layers of landscape architecture. They are, more or less, linear landscape strategies made by a combination of urban agricultural gardens and public parks. Entering into the existing urban structures, they link cities with their surroundings and suggest new ways to define ideas for these almost anonymous cities.

URBAN PARK IN FORM OF FREE SHAPES

This drawing, like many others, is an exercise in composing forms influenced by each other. A series of vertical lines with different thicknesses adapt to a series of almost circular shapes. These latter forms enter into the vertical linear scheme, modifying it and reforming them to it.

COLLECTING URBAN OBJECTS

In one of the three stories from Paul Aster's *The New York Trilogy*, there is a man who, after a series of personal difficulties, decides to collect objects that have been abandoned or thrown away along Manhattan's streets. The objects, no longer used, have lost their original function, and the man decides to give them a second life. In doing it, he formulated a new vocabulary used to assign a new name to each of these objects. In the same way, these drawings collect small geometric shapes, resembling memories of African ornaments. As in Aster's book, these objects are cataloged and arranged according to a structure that, giving them new names, becomes a small pocket dictionary.

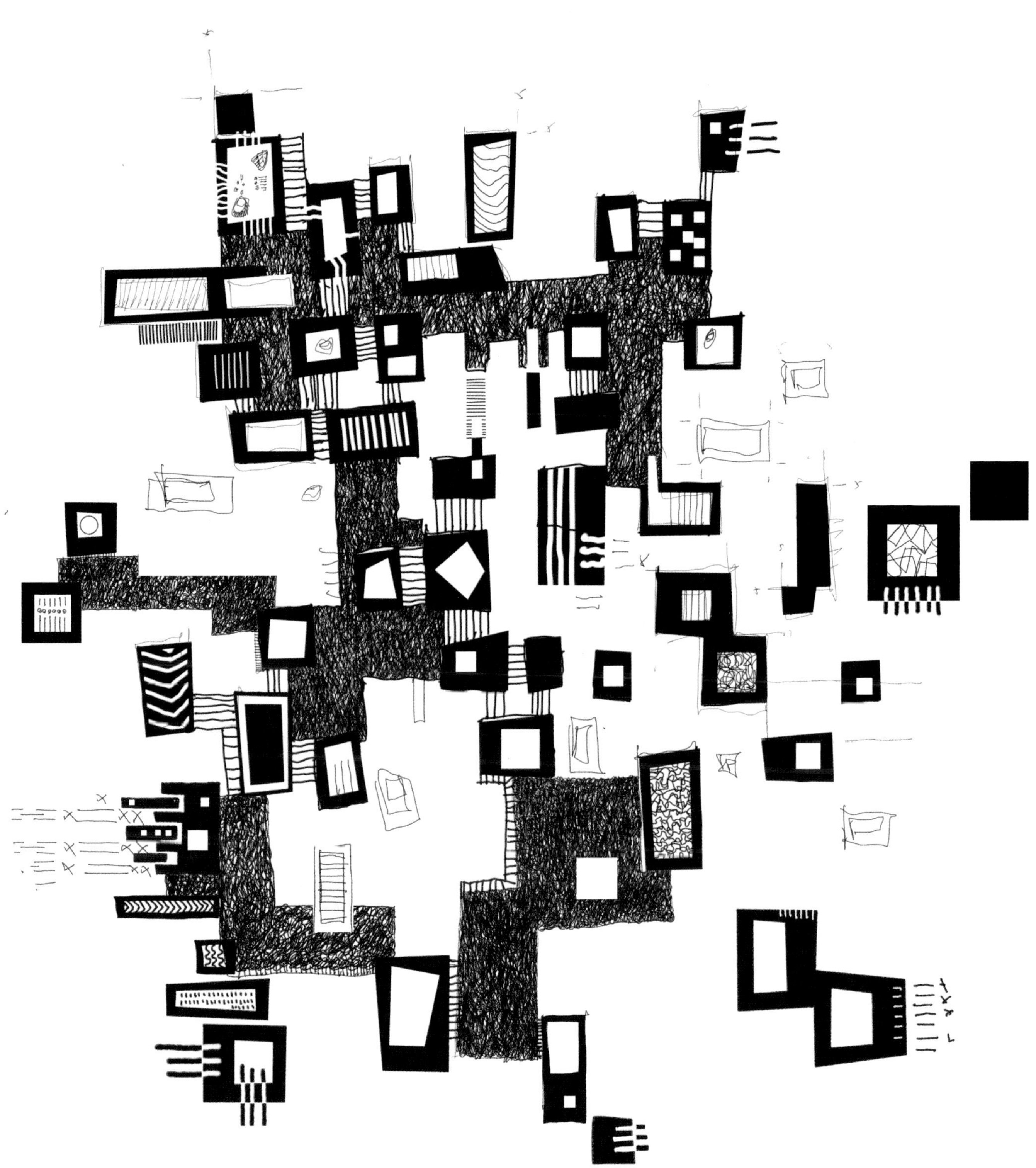

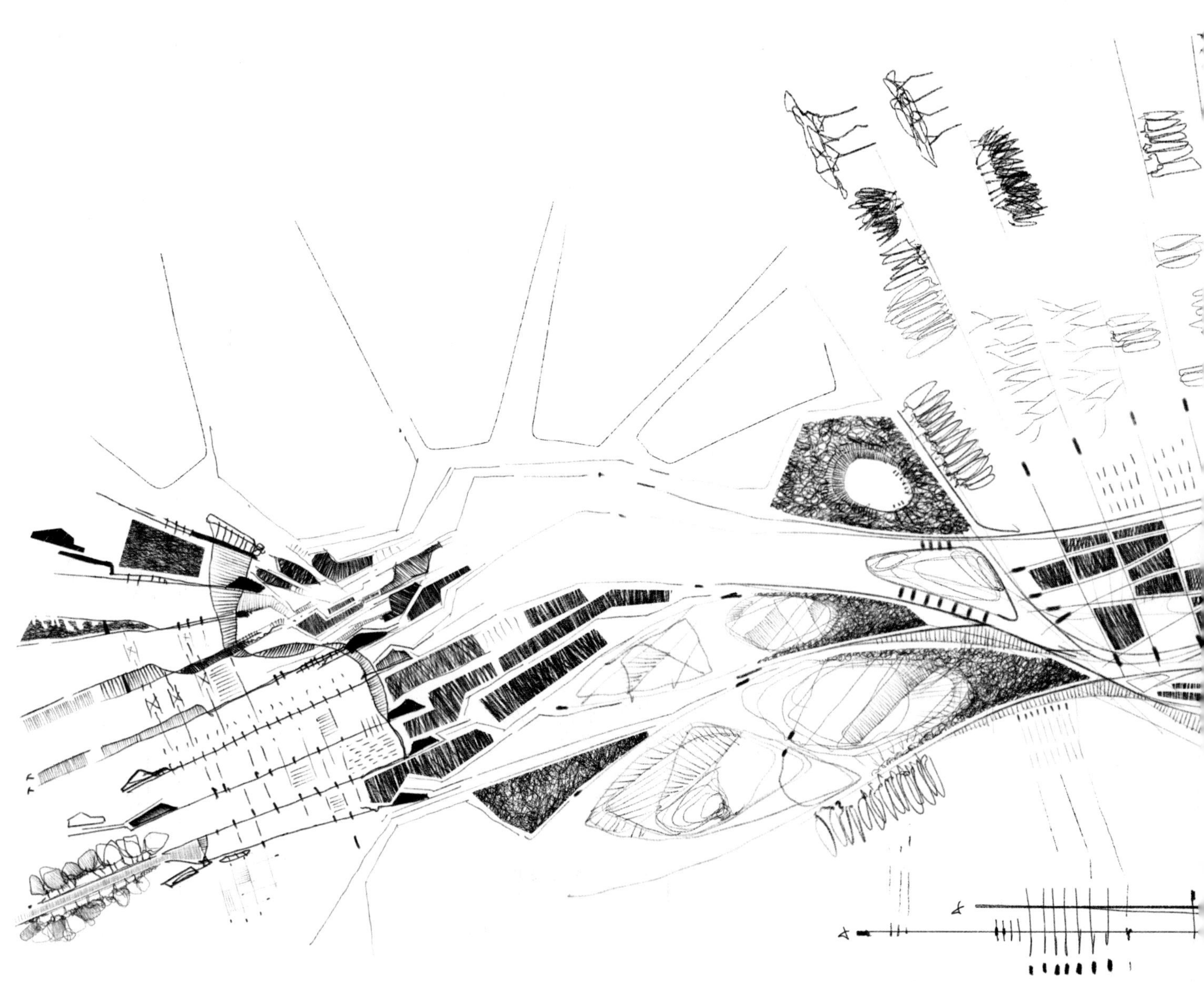

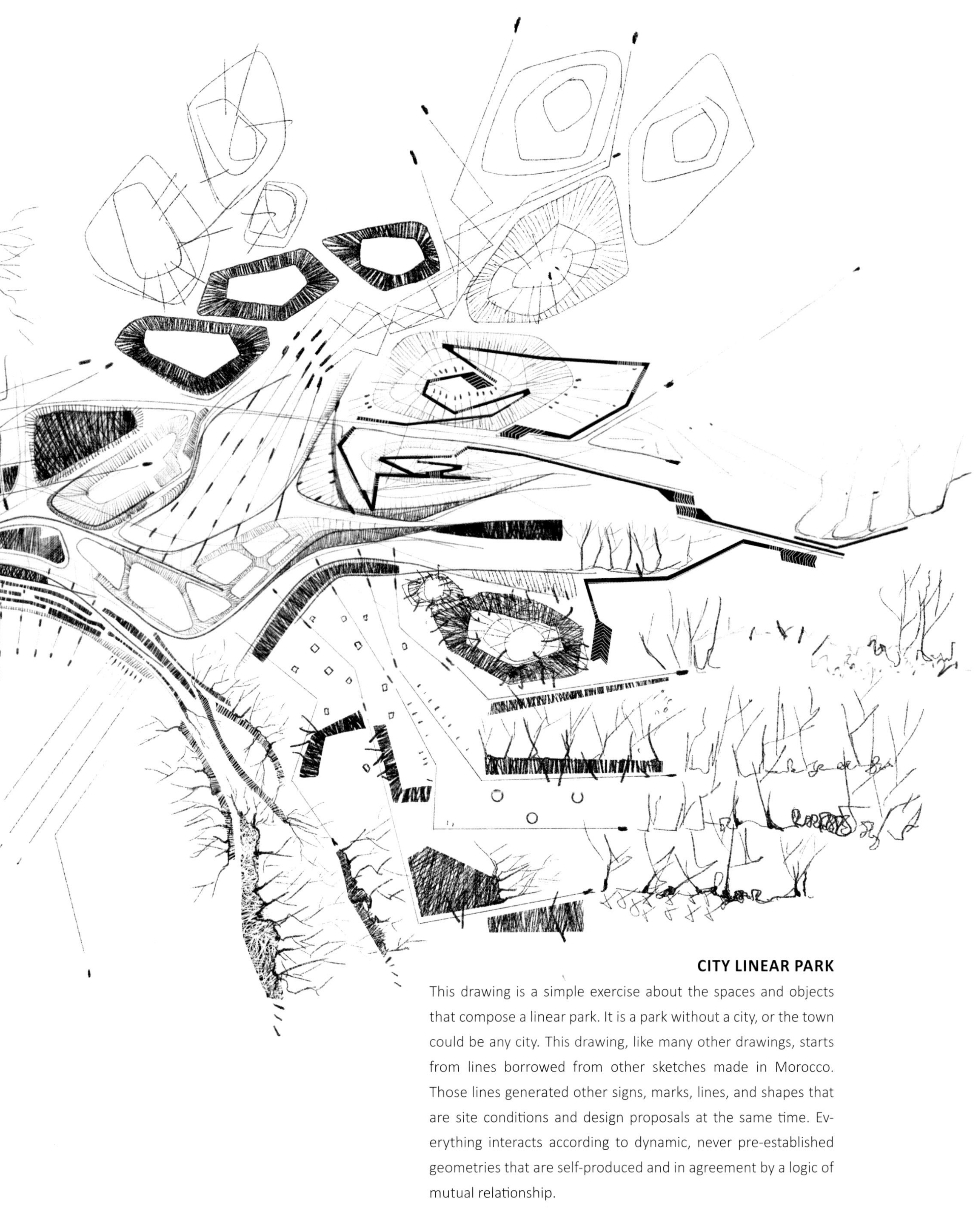

CITY LINEAR PARK

This drawing is a simple exercise about the spaces and objects that compose a linear park. It is a park without a city, or the town could be any city. This drawing, like many other drawings, starts from lines borrowed from other sketches made in Morocco. Those lines generated other signs, marks, lines, and shapes that are site conditions and design proposals at the same time. Everything interacts according to dynamic, never pre-established geometries that are self-produced and in agreement by a logic of mutual relationship.

CITY OF TREES

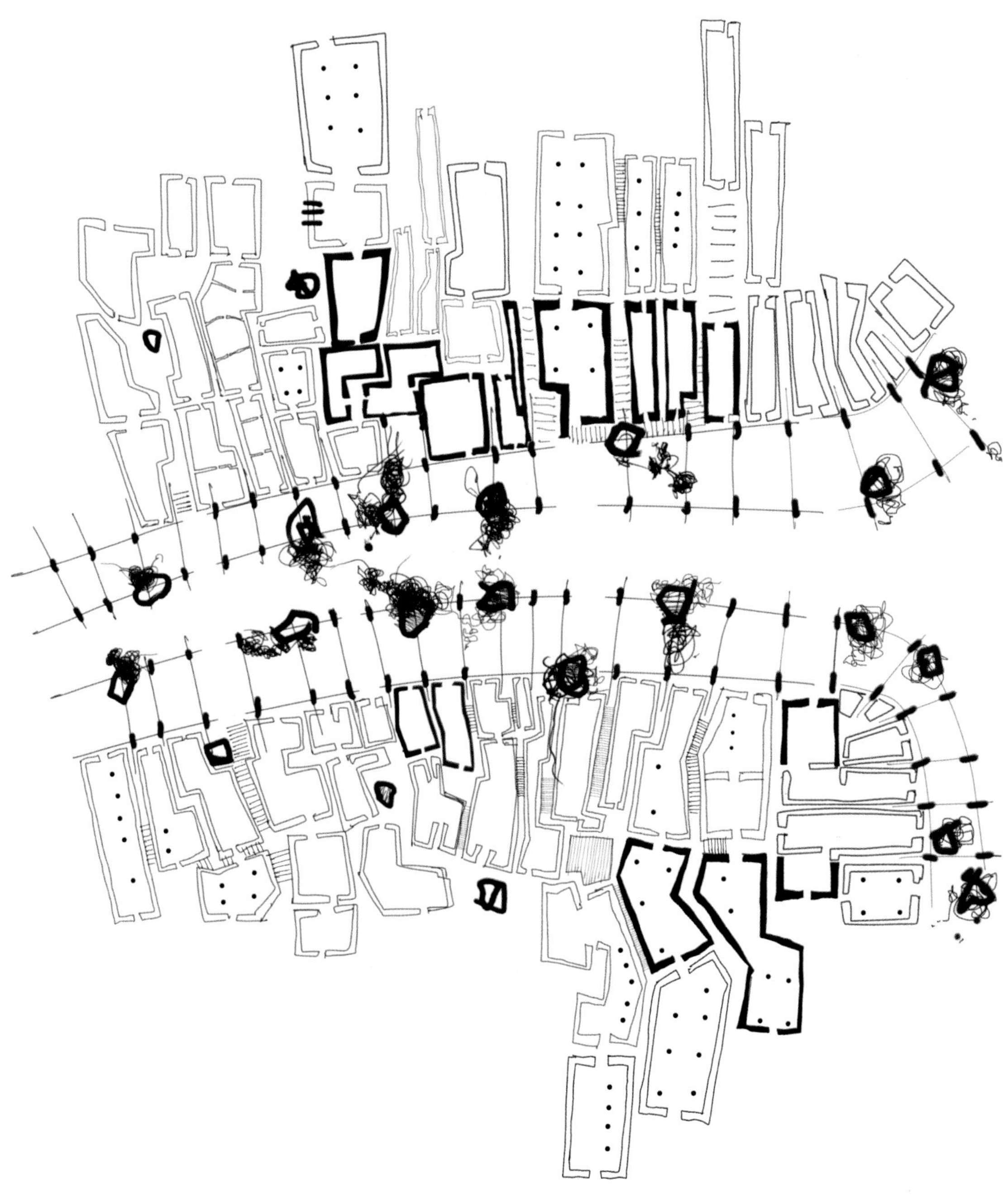

MAPPING GUANGZHOU'S OLD TOWN

Visiting the ancient city of Guangzhou, it is possible to see a particular competition for conquering space. Along the main streets of the traditional colonial urban structure, we can walk under a porch, whose composition seems to have been added after the construction of the buildings. Along with the same linear space, we can see big trees in intense competition with the porch. They push its pillars, break the porch's ceiling, and occupy space along the sidewalks in competition with the porch and the urban activities underneath it. We could in-

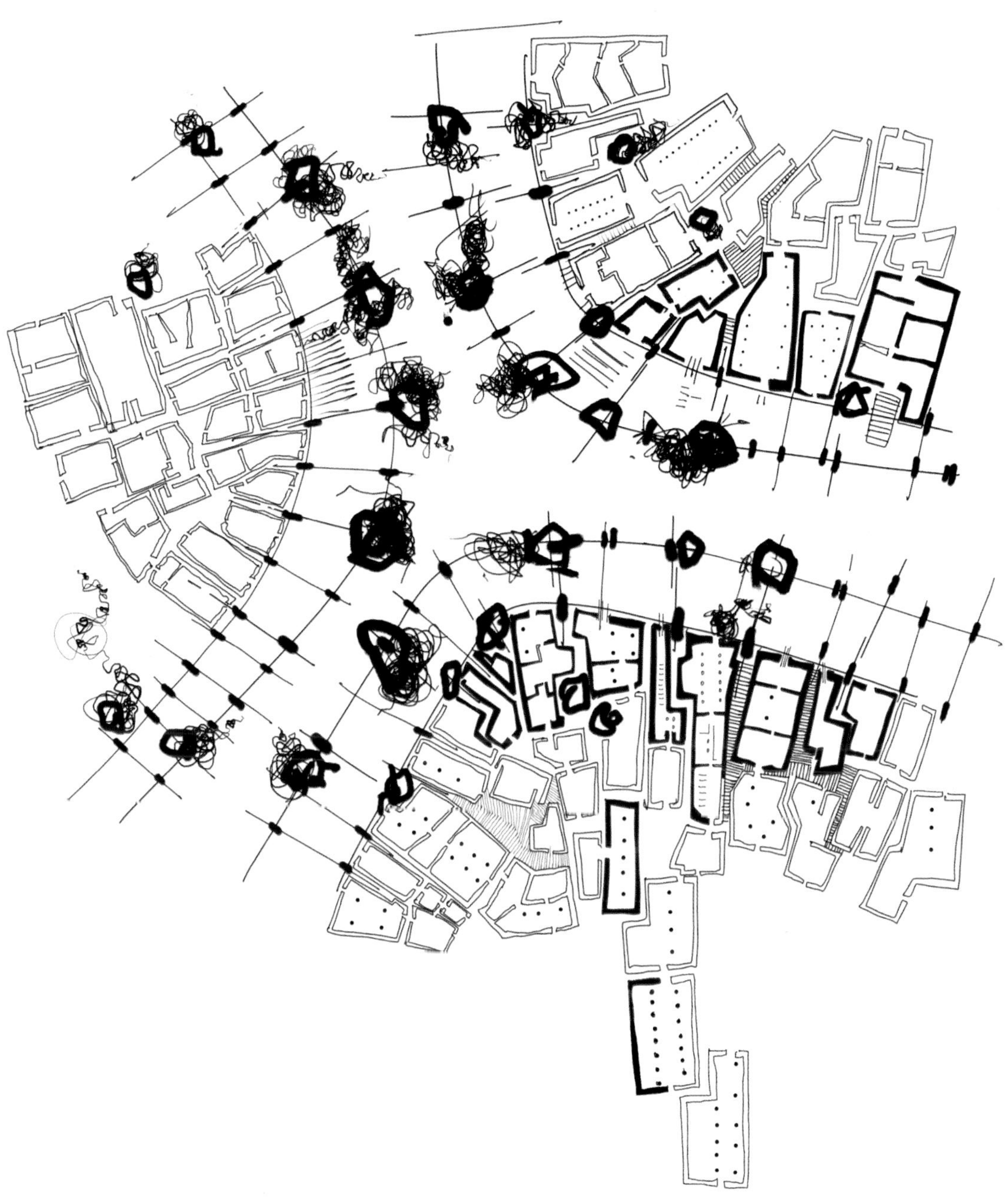

vent a story in which the trees were planted before the porch was built. Due to the trees' slow growth, and thus their incapability to produce shadow immediately, someone decided that the city needed an artificial element to accomplish the function of protecting people from the sun and rain. Today, the trees, big and strong, are claiming their original purpose and places.

BUILDINGS AND TREES

These two drawings are symbolic of my idea of the relationship between architecture and landscape, between buildings and trees. The trees are deliberately drawn on a large, non-natural scale, and they define the space in which the buildings can be located. The complex structure of the trees, with their dynamic shapes, are free to move in different spatial directions. Meanwhile, the buildings, thought static, present themselves in their repetitive and self-celebrating monumentality.

THE EXTENDED CITY OF TREES

The competition between trees and buildings is often extreme, especially in many urban situations where space is compact and rare. It is not about cities where trees are part of the consolidated urban fabric and have their autonomy, in composition and function. It is about all those trees that are forced to survive in residual urban spaces. The examples are endless: in Guangzhou, there are some examples as previously mentioned; in Montpellier, there are some tiny squares that host large trees which try to occupy the entire sky; in Reggio Calabria, the magnificent ficus magnolias compete with the street space and engulf benches and sidewalks; in

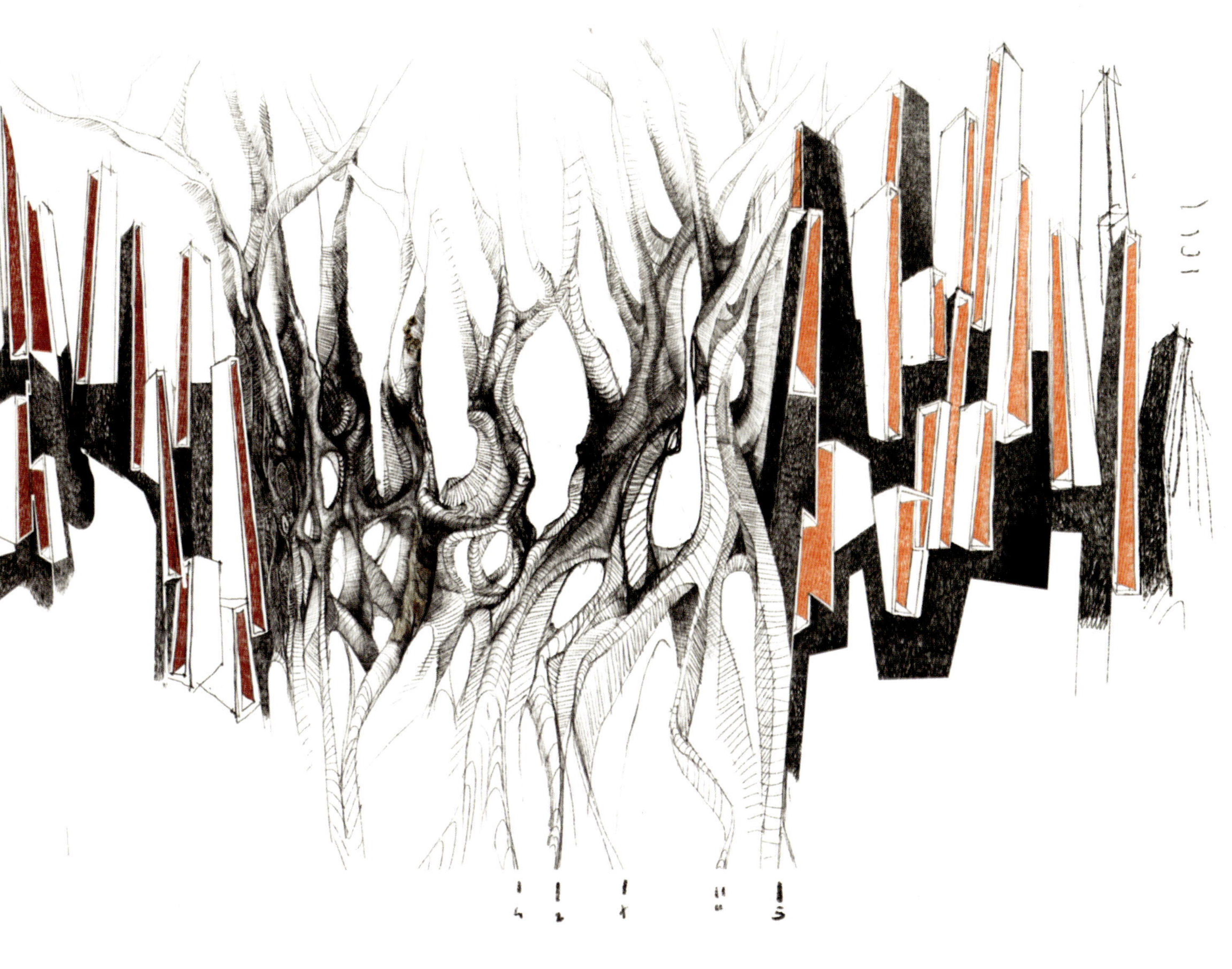

Fes, some trees are used for market activities in narrow and cramped spaces; in Nantou, there are a few places where trees have to share their space with scooter repair activities; and in Chefchaouen it is possible to see a huge old olive tree so integrated with the blue buildings' walls that it is hard to understand where its roots are. This drawing is a tribute to all the trees that have to compete and survive in our uncomfortable yet fascinating city environments.

CITIES OF VISIONS

This series of drawings, concerning landscapes of visionary cities, was born from a sketch I made about the French visionary architectures. It was a prelude for lithography (I have the original print of it) regarding an exhibition that was never made. In the same way as that lithography, the landscape of these visionary cities estab-

lished a new relationship between trees and buildings. While in Étienne-Louis Boullée's visionary architecture the trees are silent and follow the symmetrical geometries of the buildings, in these drawings trees modify the symmetry and proportion of buildings, to contribute in creating dynamic, visionary landscape spaces.

VISIONARY LANDSCAPE CITY

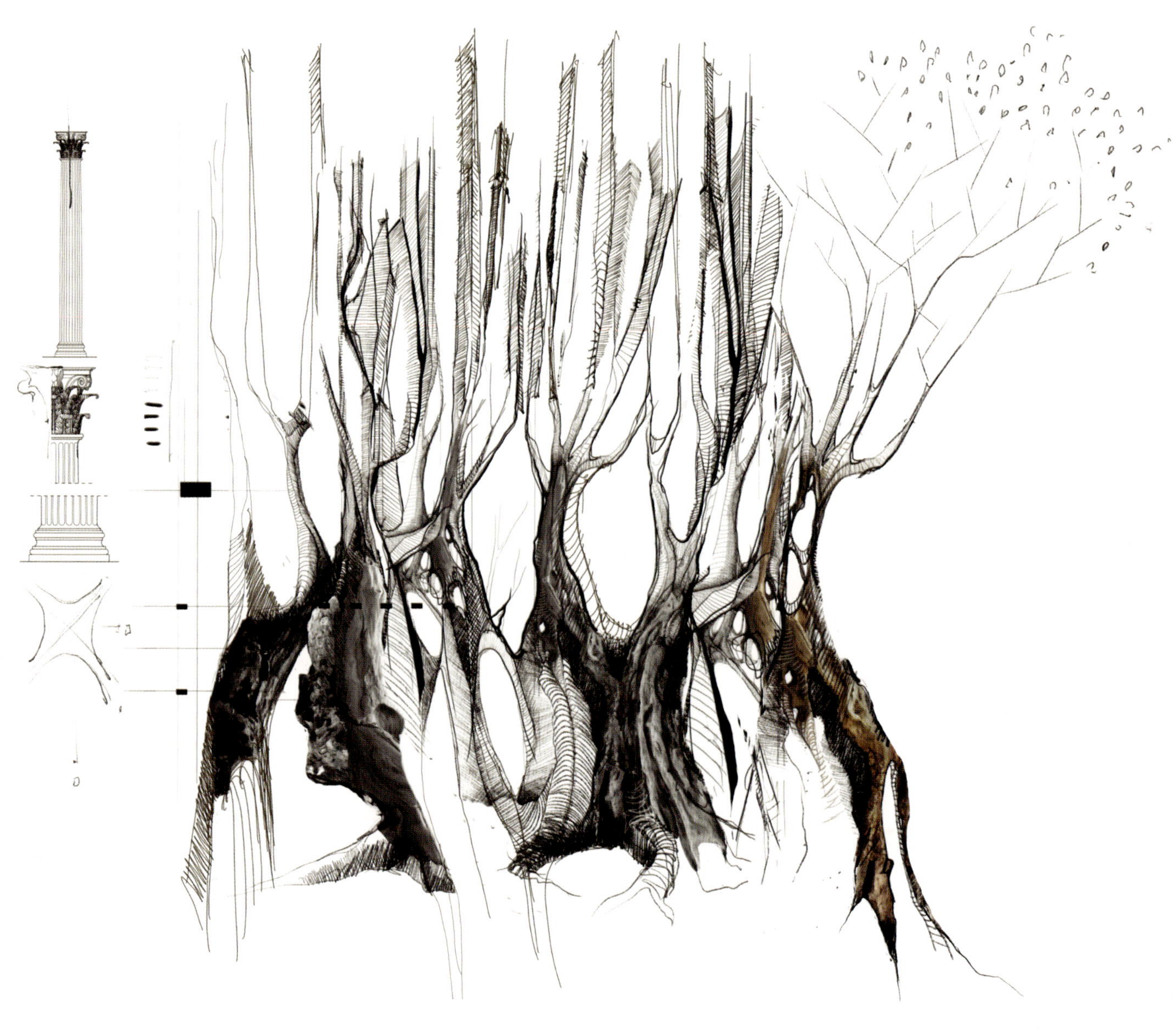

MILAZZO'S LANDSCAPE CAPITAL

This drawing is a combination of small pieces of wood picked up from the beach of Milazzo and hand-drawn lines. The wood had been smoothed and transformed by the Mediterranean Sea, cleansed of their stories and places of belonging. After composing the different wood pieces in one photo, the drawing followed the wood's lines to create an imaginary city of Milazzo.

RABAT'S LANDSCAPE CAPITAL

Photos of cork tree trunks from the "Forest de la Maamora" near Rabat, Morocco, was the base used for representing the city of Rabat in the form of capital. The red-brown trunks support a brown combination of volumes, generating an abstract idea of the traditional Arab cities. These cities are made through the addition and aggregation of volumes in a way that organizes a democratic space, a space in which the hierarchies among public spaces, monuments, and buildings seem to disappear. For those not accustomed to walking into these spaces, to do it could be an ancestral experience of loosening one's common sense of orientation.

PALERMO'S LANDSCAPE CAPITAL

Palermo's capital combines a ficus magnolia tree from the city's botanical garden and the idea of gold coming from the Cappella Palatina, the royal "golden" chapel of the Norman kings of Sicily. The capital is a piece of jewelry, an expression of the richness of Sicily's political landscape.

REGGIO CALABRIA'S LANDSCAPE CAPITAL

The massive trunk of the magnolia ficus tree is the foundation of this drawing. It comes from a multitude of ficus trees living in front of the Strait of Messina and represent the dramatic paradox of the city's memory. The city, destroyed by earthquakes and seaquakes many times, planted these trees after the last disaster. In this way, it created a distance between itself and the sea. The huge trees are sentinels defending the city and rooting it to the past.

THE CITY OF MANGROVES - 1–2

Many years ago, while on a beautiful beach in northern Cuba, I saw mangrove trees for the first time. I was coming from the town of Pindar Del Rio that smelled of gasoline due to the continuous maintenance and upkeep of old cars. For years I thought about this diversity between the untouched nature and the city with the smell of gasoline. Recently, I thought of translating this duality into some drawings, and these drawings represent the force of nature that now dominates human beings. It is

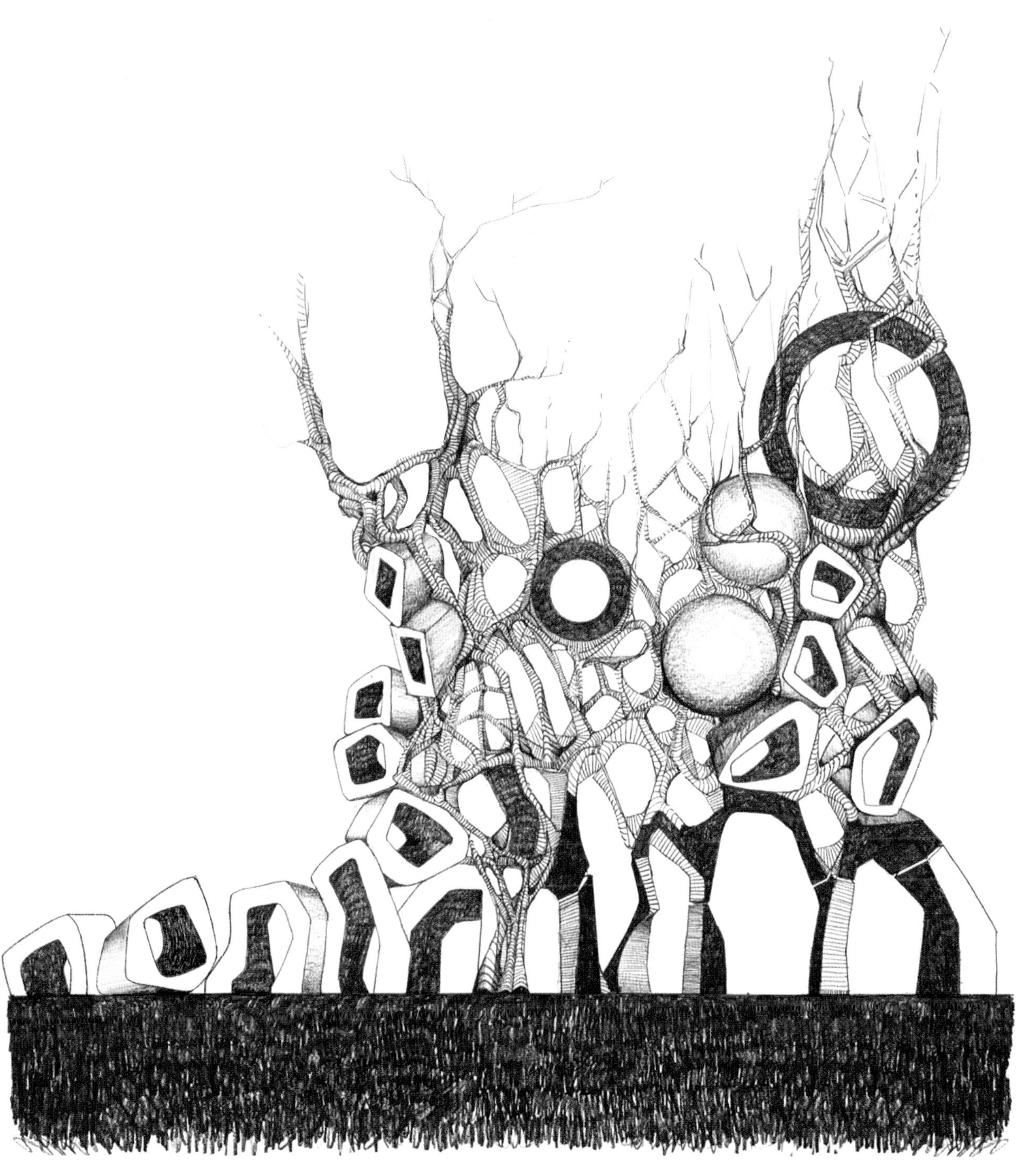

a new and different idea of domination, in which the forces of nature transform the climate, making useless everything we have created until now. Nature is not aesthetic; it doesn't care if a wolf has two or three eyes. It only cares that the wolf survives, not the human being.

CITY OF TIME

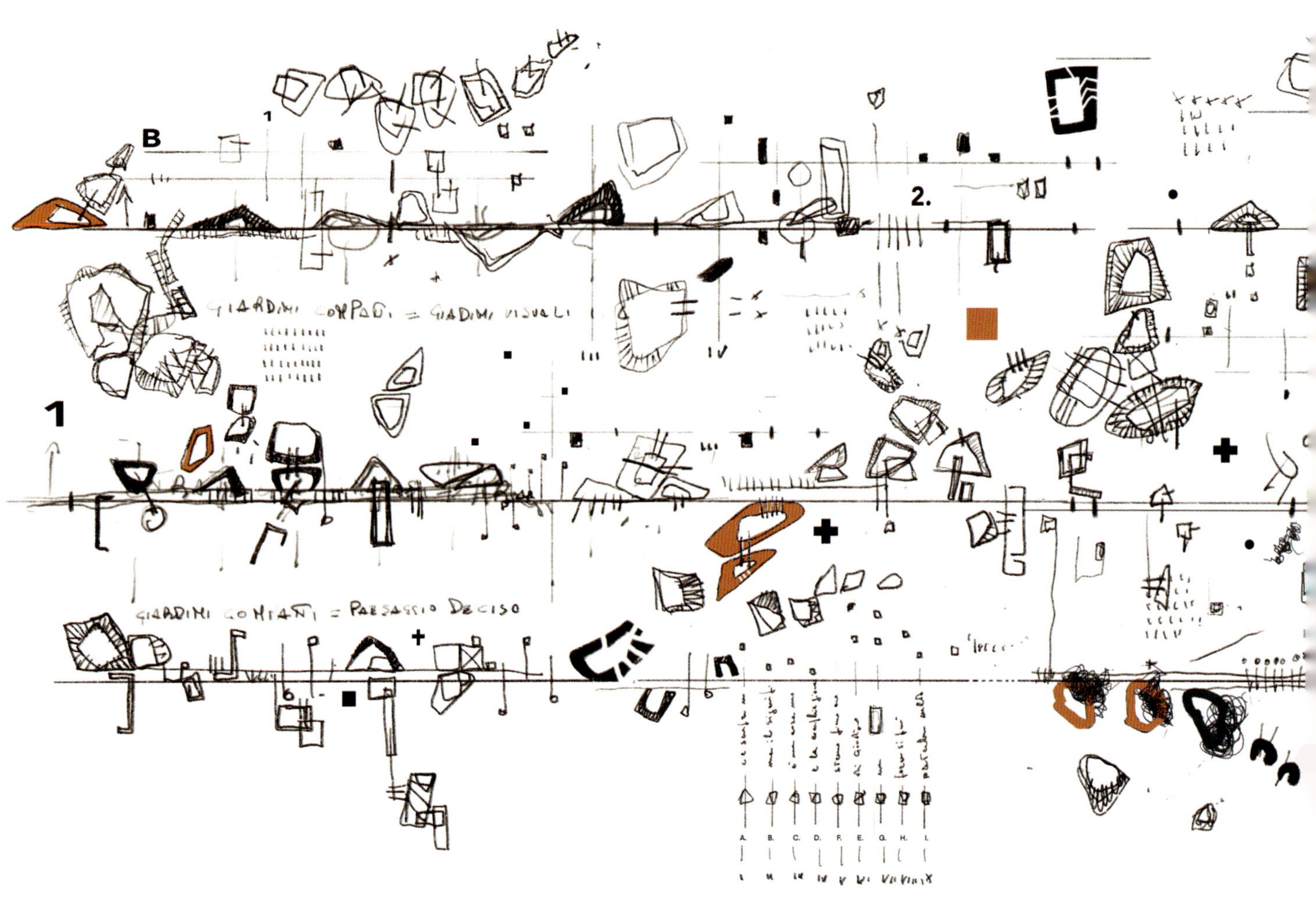
B
1
1
2.
A. B. C. D. F. E. G. H. I.

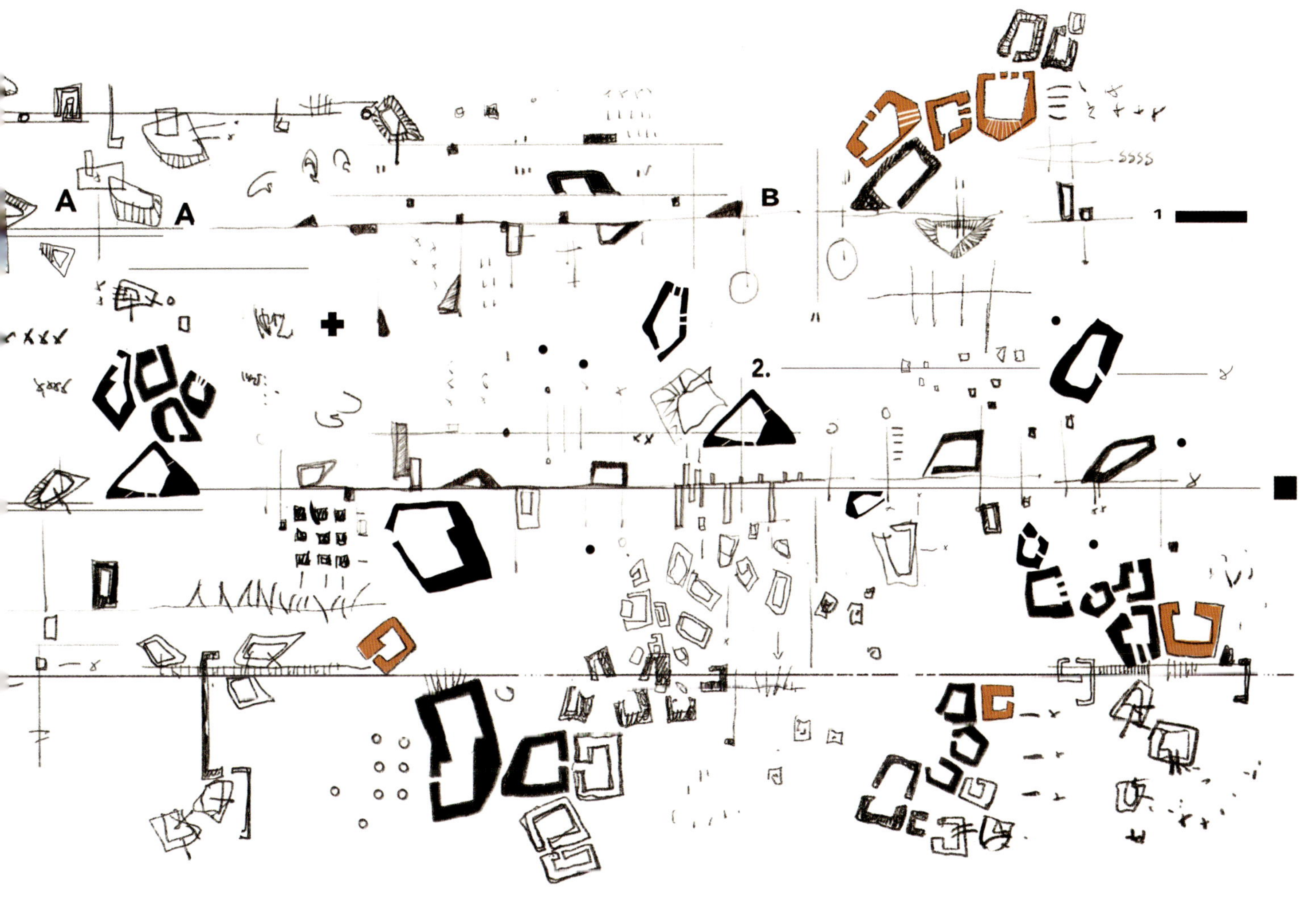

ATOMS OF TIME

Many scientific theories affirm (or imagine) that time does not exist if the elements present in space do not change their state. In the same way, the traces in this memory map are motionless, waiting for something to happen. Therefore, this immobile time could be called the zero-time of imagination, which precludes the use of other times in imagination. In this map, the narrative of space is suspended like a primordial state where things, without matter, wait for something.

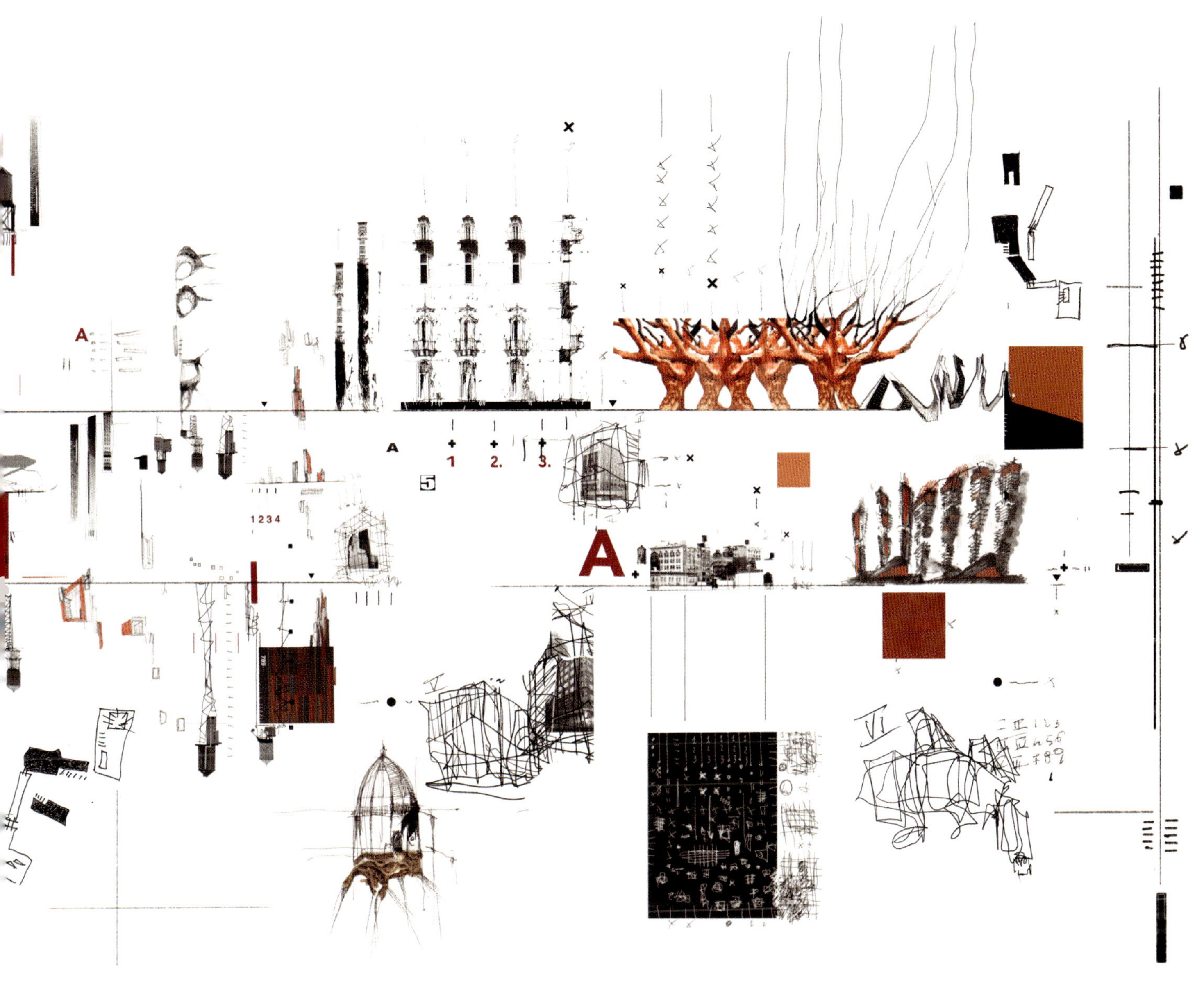

RESIDUAL CITY OBJECTS IN TIME AND SPACE

This map resembles ancient Greek wax tablets. Like them, it is engraved by small residual objects, encountered and collected during different moments. Coming from stories, paintings, photos, landscapes, and cities, they were small traces dispersed across many note books, iPad digital paper, little pieces of newspapers, napkins, and recycled paper. They are elements without time.

THE CONSISTENCY OF TIME

Whence things have their origin,
Thence also their destruction happens,
As is the order of things;
For they execute the sentence upon one another
- The condemnation for the crime -
In conformity with the ordinance ***"consistency"*** of Time.
Anaximander c. 610–c. 546 BCE.

I have been attempting to draw time through the catalysts of language and memory for many years. In this case I have taken a fragment of Anaximander's poetry and replaced his use of "ordinance," which seems too authoritarian, with the word "consistency." I've imported "consistency" from the title of the last unwritten essay in Italo Calvino's *Six Memos for the next Millennium.* Along with its literal definition as "an agreement or harmony of parts or features to one another or a whole," when I think of consistency and Calvino's death, an unexplored and unknown space opens up before me which I then fill, or rather, outline with drawing. I draw infrastructures (represented by the title of books, and words), parks, buildings (combinations of high buildings, ancient and modern), real and unreal space of ideas (fragmented tissue), real and unreal realities (grids, numbers, dots, lines), and true or false ecologies (fake trees with fragments of real ones). It is necessary to take into consideration a combination of intuitions and mistakes that turn into one another and compose them precisely to register the consistency of the time.

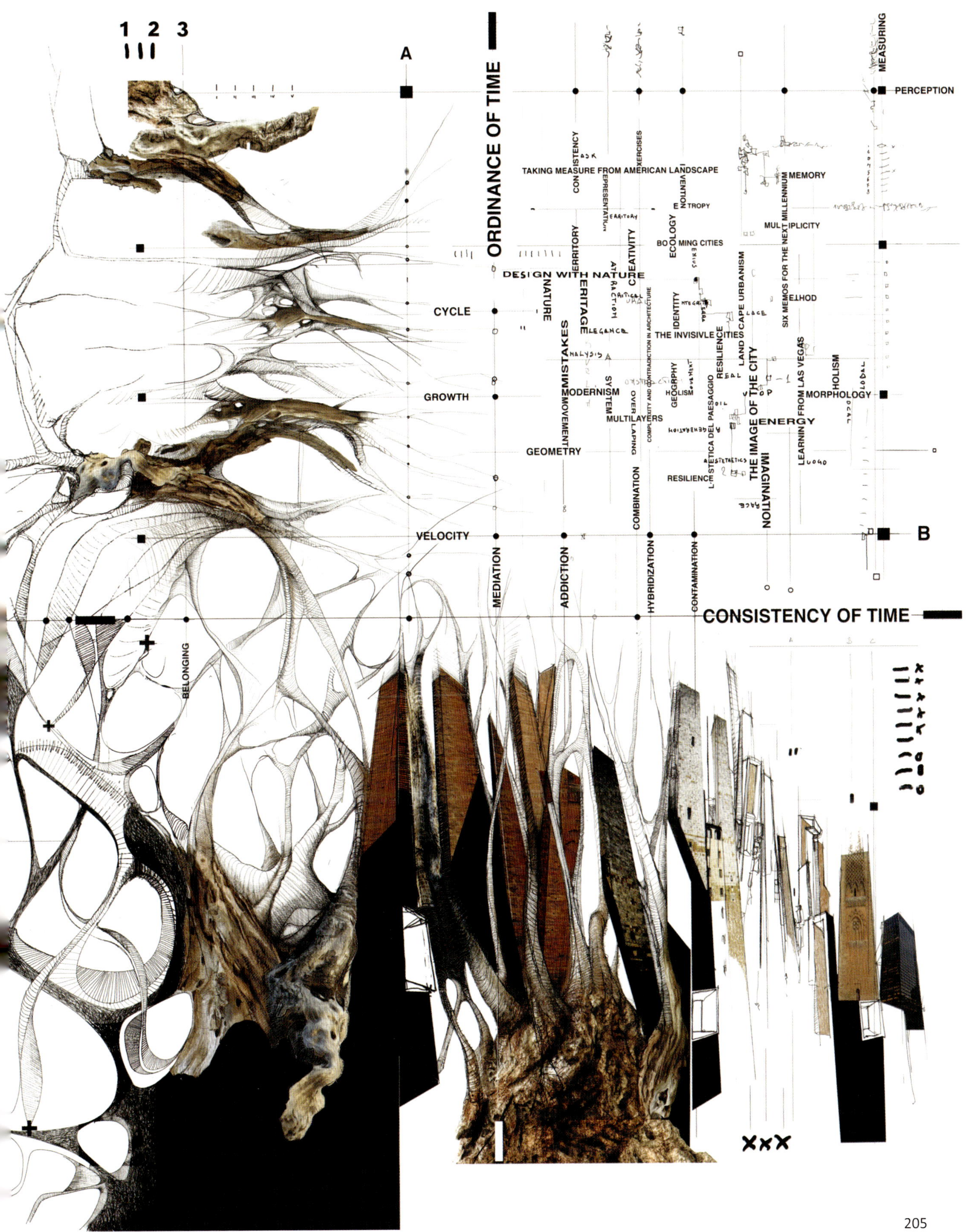

1 2 3
A
B
ORDINANCE OF TIME
CONSISTENCY OF TIME
PERCEPTION
MEASURING
CYCLE
GROWTH
VELOCITY
MEDIATION
ADDICTION
HYBRIDIZATION
CONTAMINATION
BELONGING
TAKING MEASURE FROM AMERICAN LANDSCAPE
DESIGN WITH NATURE
MEMORY
GEOMETRY
MODERNISM
MULTILAYERS
RESILIENCE
MORPHOLOGY
THE IMAGE OF THE CITY
IMAGINATION

"In order to be significant, architecture must be forgotten, or must present only an image for reverence which subsequently becomes confounded with memories."— A. Rossi, *Scientific Autobiography*
"Places Remember Events."— J. Joyce, Note sheets for *Ulysses*.

Louis I. Kahn once wrote: "While drawing I'm always waiting for something to happen: I don't want it to happen too quickly, though." While waiting, his hand lingered on essential topics, sketching was a way of abiding with primary questions. Valerio Morabito likewise lingers on the pages of this book, in much the same way, expectantly, on the verge of sense. Sketches such as these are typically described as free hand. One doubts that our draftsman would object to the term. Of course free in this case does not mean undisciplined, even though none of the lines we see were ruled by a straight edge.

The authority that presides over each drawing's development is a pencil-fisted hand, both highly disciplined and versatile, thanks to regular exercise and native talent; that is also thoughtful, though not exactly reflective, and entirely internal to the process of representation, which is to say less prosthetic, like a ruler or compass, than personal, like a mannerism or habit. But well-practiced dexterity plays only one among other roles staged in this drama.

What we see on these pages results equally from visual judgment, movements of a hand synchronized with those of eyes. Just because we have separate sense organs doesn't mean they operate independently. Sketching is a judicious skill. And there is still another actor in this performance: eyes and hands coordinated with interests, the personal and professional concerns that guide his focus on some places and themes, not others. And there is still more: emotions, ranging from the delight of discovery, to the pain of a dead end, and the sweet melancholy of a slow, aimless wander.

These pages remind us of the fact that word drawing is more or less equivalent to the term trace. Trace is cognate with track, its visible sign, probably because the two result equally from the action of pulling or drawing (*trahere*). The result: a scratch, ditch, furrow, or path on a sheet or in the soil. When the mark is graphic an intention (maybe the highest) is apparent (designation), but traces or tracks also result from unintended drawing.

So while the surface may shift variously, the action too, the result is always a mark, indication, or evidence that not only suggests sense but sometimes gives rise to hope, as with Aristippus, for whom traces of the shores of Rhodes promised a civilized alternative to the shipwreck he had just suffered. The pages of this book show that Morabito vividly recalls the several shipwrecks suffered by we moderns. His forms are often broken, but he remembers more.

For the philosopher there seem to be two basic questions about memory: of what? and whose? For the architect and landscape architect a third line of questioning is also important: where? The fact that places sometimes prompt memories suggests that spatial situations have some measure of agency in the workings of recollection, precisely to the extent that they do the reminding, that they not only accommodate practical affairs but activate recollection. This is hardly surprising, for every trace always resides somewhere.

A trace is the impression that appears once some remote force comes to rest; or, put differently, it is the rest of the movement, its remainder or remnant. The partial and inadequate nature of the remnant—inadequate to the reality of the impression-making force—also indicates the ambiguous nature of the memory image, absent presence, whatever its place, as well as the interpretive task it invites. The reality of the past is inseparable from the marks its movements have left behind, even if they are partial and require deciphering.

Why deciphering? Because traces provide incomplete testimony. They are the means by which the past remains present, but always only partly so, minus its lively movements. On the plus side, every trace is factual. But its fragmentary character means that it is always inadequate to the whole story. Surface impressions are communicative nonetheless, for every remnant invites interpretation, a wondering kind of apprehension.

This means their survival is self-evident but their sense is not, or not fully. Because it preserves what is perishable, the trace can be said to compensate for time's passing. Melancholy often qualifies its perception, but also gratitude verging on delight.

One way to identify a bad building or landscape is to observe the work's inability to register traces of life, its insouciant neglect for the exigencies and pleasures of inhabitation, perhaps because of an overridding concern for attractive form. A good place, by contrast, has the ability to both suffer and withstand impressions (strength in passivity), absorbing the traces of human life and taking on a specific richness and depth of expression. Evidences such as this give objects a particular kind of beauty, another of Morabito's concerns in this book. Any town, upon first sighting, is already somehow remembered—though never exactly or fully—seen anew but known from the past, vital in many respects, but in others decaying. In New York or Palermo people and things express themselves in a characteristic way. But they intimate even more. Each is a segment of a larger reality whose origins are no less remote than its end.

Empty streets especially accommodate the town's no longer and not yet. Morabito's drawings suggest that a city's particular qualities are most apparent in moments of stillness, for then a spectral force and hidden violence give rise to an eruption of images. The city's emptiness, its meager and incomplete signs, draw memories out. Towns allow this author to establish links between our shared present (the common world) and his private past. He shows that time's passing leads to a renewal of life. Life is not found in what it has accomplished, but in the coming to life, which is sensed most poignantly when an individual discovers his or her solitude, thanks to countless iterations of neglect, of which one's life is neither more nor less than a constituent part.

AFTERWORD
THE CITY OF IMAGINATION

David Leatherbarrow

THE REVEALED CITY OF NEW YORK

The revealed City of New York is a combination of drawings sketched over several years. Collected in one drawing, they form a unique imaginary representation of New York. Even if Manhattan's morphology is quite flat, the drawing represents a city that goes up and down, always in movement. As with all the others in this book, this drawing is a tool to go around with for sniffing traces. Morphologies, buildings, parks, and public spaces are no longer real elements to be represented, but weightless matter to be transformed into ideas. Italo Calvino wanted to subtract weight in his narrative to give lightness to the stories he wrote. In the same way, the aim of this book is to subtract weight from cities, giving them the lightness of an imaginative landscape narrative.